Becoming A Wise Counselor

현명한 상담자 되기

Anyoung No

BWC

HAKJISA
www.hakjisa.co.kr

Becoming A Wise Counselor
-현명한 상담자 되기-

Published by Hakjisa Publisher
5F Mind World Bldg, 352-29 Seogyo-dong,
Mapo-gu, Seoul, 121-837, Republic of Korea

World Wide Web: www.hakjisa.co.kr
Community: cafe.naver.com/hakjisa
First Published March, 2011

Preface

I wish every counselor become a wise counselor. Socrates said, "The unexamined life is not worth living." As life itself is a process of learning, we are students until we die. As a student of counseling psychology, I have been seeking for an answer to my hwadu (話頭; head of speech), 'How can I be an effective counselor?', since I began my journey of specialty. This text mainly came from an exploration of that hwadu. Just twenty years ago, I did interview seven professors who taught me in order to find an answer of that hwadu. From in-depth interviews with those professors, I got seven invaluable descriptions which I could not learn in classes. Since I got those transcripts, I have been expecting a chance that I will share those invaluable data with other counselors. Now I feel excited because I finally publish this text, 'Becoming a Wise Counselor', which includes those transcripts.

The specialty of counseling psychology emphasizes the scientist-practitioner model as a training model of counselors. The assumption of scientist-practitioner model implies that counselors need to have not only knowledge but also experience of counseling for them to help clients effectively. The Chinese word for wisdom consists of two pictorial characters (智慧). The first character 智 means knowledge and something (experience). The second character can be divided into two parts. The first part 彗 means a comet. The second part 心 means heart (mind). Literally and figuratively, wisdom means that a comet hits the heart (mind) of a person who has knowledge and experience. Therefore, we can interpret wisdom (智慧) as understanding or insight based on knowledge and experience. In this perspective, I believe that counselors need to become wisdom-seekers because a counselor's wisdom comes from his knowledge and experience of counseling.

This text consists of three parts and fifteen chapters. The first part, 'Wisdom in Counseling', has two chapters; Introduction and Overview of wisdom in counseling. The second part, 'Wisdom and Counselor's Perspective', has nine chapters which mainly include seven professors' perspectives related to wisdom in counseling. The third part, 'Wisdom of the Counselor', has four chapters; Wisdom defined by experienced counselors, Relationship between wisdom and counseling, Counselor's wisdom emphasized by potential clients, and Becoming a wise counselor.

I believe that counselors as readers will learn wisdom emphasized by seven experienced counseling psychologists. And I wish this text be contributed for counselors to become wiser in performing their roles as helpers. Based on the findings about wisdom of the counseling psychologist, several important characteristics necessary for becoming a wise counselor I suggest are as follows:

- A wise counselor is a good listener.
- A wise counselor has and displays ethical responsibility and is particularly someone who keeps confidentiality.
- A wise counselor displays empathy or empathic understanding.
- A wise counselor has or displays trustworthiness, credibility, and honesty.
- A wise counselor is a good observer and particularly a good observer of human relationships.
- A wise counselor has and displays communication skills.

- A wise counselor has and displays self-understanding, particularly an understanding his/her limitations, and an understanding of human uniqueness.
- A wise counselor has and displays a positive attitude toward life.

I thank my professors, Dr. Kyungja Hong and Dr. Jangho Lee, for guiding and teaching me to become a counseling psychologist. I deeply appreciate the teachings and wisdom of seven professors who were also my interviewees, Dr. Gordon Liddle, Dr. James Barclay, Dr. Raymond Wilkie, Dr. William Stilwell, Dr. Rory Remer, Dr. Pam Remer, and Dr. Ralph Crystal, University of Kentucky. They deserve my respectful bows for their kind caring and consistent encouragement. I also thank Dr. Emanuel Mason, Northeastern University and Dr. Beth Goldstein, University of Kentucky, for their invaluable suggestions and contributions. I am indebted to Dr. Youngshin Kang for her comments and editing assistance. My American friend, Gary Lovan, continually encouraged me to deal with this difficult topic by suggesting a critical view based on his philosophical background. My wife, Jinmyung, deserves to be recognized for her priceless caring and enormous support as my faithful friend and lover in a journey of life. My daughter and son,

Dahyee and Byungwoo, also provided me with power to endure in many difficult times by showing their dreams and smiles. Finally I appreciate the careful work that Yeonjae Kim made an effort for editing this book. I also thank my student, Seungchul Jung and the president of Hakjisa, Jinhwan Kim for their caring and support in publishing this book in English.

February, 2011

Looking at the Moodeung Mt.

Anyoung No

Contents

PART 2
WISDOM AND COUNSELOR'S PERSPECTIVE

PART 1

WISDOM IN COUNSELING

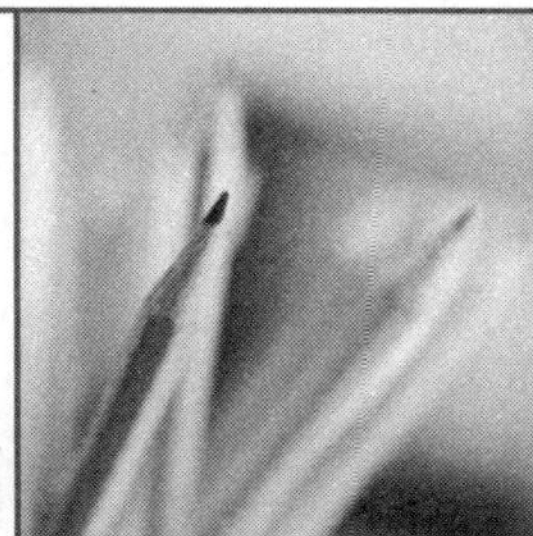

Chapter 1
INTRODUCTION

In a rapidly changing world, we want to live in a wise way. We often regret about what we've done and also wish we had been wiser. Life itself is a process of learning. As it is suggested in the Oriental adage, "We are the students who are continually involving in learning to survive and improve our lives until we die." Counseling psychologists continually seek ways to become better and more effective helpers, just as everyone seeks a way to be an expert in his/her own area. Counseling psychology is generally defined as an applied psychology, because it is based on psychological or behavioral principles derived from theoretical or experimental psychology. Counseling techniques and practice are based on those theories and research findings. In a similar way, counseling specialty as an applied psychology emphasizes a scientist–practitioner model as the training model of counselors.

Many counseling theories and techniques are founded or developed based on psychological or behavioral principles. Counseling psychologists import their knowledge not only from general psychologies but also the other human sciences. A good example is F. S. Perls, who said, "I have often been called the founder of Gestalt therapy. That's crap. If you call me the finder or refinder of Gestalt Therapy, okay. Gestalt is as ancient and old as the world itself" (Perls, 1971, pp. 15-16).

Even though it has been one decade since positive psychology launched, many people say that this society is becoming a therapeutic society. From the humanistic point of view, the 'therapeutic' is not appropriate because it implies a kind of one–way relationship between the therapist and the client, or the decrease of individual potentiality or power to overcome and solve one's own difficulties as a human being. Erickson was fond of saying that life's difficulties were merely necessary roughage (Havens, 1989). "By taking over the conceptions of others as our own, we lose contact with the potential wisdom of our own functioning, and we lose confidence in ourselves" (Rogers, 1971, p. 12). An uncompromising aim of counseling is to help clients act independently. Therefore, counseling psychologists should raise serious questions about any contemporarily "therapeutic" advertisement which emphasizes human dependence even in clients' trivial problems.

Beginning counseling psychologists can be especially confused and flummoxed by many counseling theories and techniques that their mentors, other counseling psychologists, and professors emphasize. What is the best way to train students in counseling area to become good or effective counselors? How can the collected knowledge and theory of the various counseling approaches and techniques be integrated into an effective paradigm for counseling? I believe those questions are very meaningful to both educators and students in the counseling specialty.

The scholarly ambiance which emphasizes specific techniques or observable evidence sometimes obstructs a comprehensive view that integrates the many approaches. Indeed, the classic function of all philosophies is to offer a comprehensive view of the many things that make up our own world and thereby assist and guide a person in the search for meaning and order in life (J. T. Fraser, 1990).

It is necessary for a beginning counseling psychologist to

consider the spectrum of counseling approaches. His/her own unique counseling approach and techniques are developed through considering many different counseling approaches. Therefore, to be effective counseling psychologists, beginning counselors need to seek wise and comprehensive guidance from senior counseling psychologists' different points of view and experiences. A counseling psychologist's experience makes his/her horizon of understanding broader.

> Experience stands in an ineluctable opposition to knowledge and to the kind of instruction that follows from general theoretical or technical knowledge. The truth of experience always implies an orientation toward new experiences. That is why a person who is called experienced has become so not only through experiences but is also open to new experiences. The consummation of his experience, the perfection that we call 'being experienced', does not consist in the fact that someone already knows better than anyone else. Rather, the experienced person proves to be, on the contrary, someone who is radically undogmatic; who, because of the many experiences he has had and the knowledge he has drawn from them, is particularly well equipped to have new experiences

> and to learn from them. The dialectic of experience has its proper fulfillment not in definite knowledge but in the openness to experience that is made possible by experience itself (Gadamer, 1989, p. 355).

In practical counseling situation, three sets of categorical variables, that is, counselor variables, client variables and intervening variables may be considered in any analysis of counseling. These three categorical variables of course dynamically interact with one another to help clients change. Counselor variables are especially important when we consider why a client is helped by one counselor and not by another.

Many techniques and skills have been developed for helping a client change. Unfortunately, these techniques are not panaceas for helping clients change because of the uniqueness and potential complexity of each human being. Even though we have good techniques which are established by various practice and research, we get different outputs according to a client's characteristics and a counseling psychologist's philosophy and theoretical approach. Perls, the founder of Gestalt Therapy, said that "One of the objections I have against anyone calling himself a Gestalt therapist is that he uses techniques. A technique is gimmick.

A gimmick should be used only in the extreme case" (Perls, 1971, p. 1). The wisdom of the organism was emphasized as organismic self–regulation by Perls (1971) and organismic valuing process by Rogers (1971). Frankl, one of the great psychotherapists as the founder of logotherapy, said that "Our scientists need to have more than knowledge: they need to have wisdom as well. And wisdom I define as knowledge plus the awareness of its limitations" (Frankl, 1985, p. 70).

Strickland (1971) proposed tentative definitions or descriptions of the terms: "philosophy," "theory," and "practice," particularly from the viewpoint of the counseling psychologist. Philosophy can be considered as the counseling psychologist's frame of reference: his/her attitudes, values and feelings concerning himself/herself and others. Theory consists of behavioral guidelines which emerge from, and are consistent with, philosophy. Practice consists of the operational approaches, methods, and techniques which achieve the goals of the philosophy through the design guidelines of theory.

One's philosophy represents an approach to life that determines how one lives. This way of life postulates and requires certain knowledge. In its worldly sense, philosophy is the science of the relationship between all knowledge and the essential goals of human reason (Marias, 1967, pp. 1-6). In the same way, a counseling psychologist's perspective based on his/her philosophical position is applied for his/her client's change in the counseling relationship. A person needs self-understanding to define his/her way of life. If counseling psychologists seek their self-understanding and help clients find their self-understanding, they become wisdom-seekers in the more practical and philosophical sense.

Csikzentmihalyi and Rathunde (1990) explained that wisdom has three major dimensions of meaning based on past thinkers: First, wisdom as a cognitive process, or a peculiar way of obtaining and processing information; second, as a virtue, or socially valued pattern of behavior; and third, as a good, or personally desirable state or condition. More directly, Pascual-Leone (1990) explained the three aspects of wisdom: wisdom-as-will within vital reason, wisdom as valid existential counseling, wisdom's ability for empathic intuitive experiencing of the problems and issues of the other or of nature. Wisdom for Pascual-Leone can be seen in the act of giving others counseling in such a way as to impart autonomy, and in the ability to feel for another person's concerns.

Recently, many psychologists have become interested in studying and understanding wisdom. Regarding to this trend we could think of two reasons. The first main reason is because wisdom is an important concept of positive psychology. The second reason is partly because the increase in the number of aging people stimulates interest in wisdom since older people are assumed to have wisdom. However, wisdom, would seem to have an inseparable relationship with counseling, or finding a person's desirable way of life. This leads naturally to the following questions: How can we define a wise counseling psychologist? What are the components of wisdom of the counseling psychologist? Anyway, the concept of wisdom is both elusive and inclusive, to be sure, but not will–o'–the–wisp. It would seem that wisdom is a high level and broad ranging concept related to all counseling approaches and methods.

Searching for the Counselor's Wisdom

It has been stated that counseling psychology is a scientist–practitioner specialty. This implies that the training in a counseling program emphasizes both knowledge as a scientist and experience as a practitioner. Similarly, knowledge and experience precedes wisdom. That is, a wise counseling psychologist needs knowledge and experience.

On the one hand, many psychologists or doctoral students think that it is important to study or carry out research about wisdom and self-understanding of the counseling psychologist. On the other hand, they, who have been accustomed to make quantitative researches, recognize the difficulty of doing research on this subject and try to avoid this area, asking, "How do you measure wisdom?" or "How do you make a wisdom scale?"

Therefore, by a qualitative research we need to explore or investigate the counselor's wisdom, the wise counselor's characteristics, the relationship between and wisdom and counseling, and so on. The finding results should be useful not only to beginning counseling psychologists, but also to senior counseling psychologists in order to help them understand some largely unexplored aspects of counseling. How can we achieve the purpose of searching for the counselor's wisdom? I believe that I can achieve that. I also believe that the best way of searing for the counselor's wisdom is just from listening about the counselor's wisdom emphasized by senior experienced counseling psychologists who are assumed as the best experts in counseling specialty.

For an exciting journey for exploring an intriguing issue, the counselor's wisdom, I confidently believe that an in-depth interview as one method of qualitative researches can be used. So the counselor's wisdom was found by in–depth interviews with thoughtfully constructing questions with senior experienced counseling psychologists.

In–depth Interview Questions for Exploring the Counselor's Wisdom

Counseling psychologists and trainees often emphasize various techniques or skills rather than their understandings of philosophies and theoretical approaches. Many people in the counseling area emphasize and seek effective methods which produce imminent changes. "Even if one did opt for an analysis, it would be far from irrational to consider the personality and wisdom of the analyst no less important than his theories" (Kaufman, 1980, p. 470).

This in–depth interview addresses and includes thoughtfully planned questions related to a counseling psychologist's wisdom. In order to explore wisdom and several delicate or subtle issues in counseling, twenty main in–depth interview questions were designed. These questions were prepared to guide the present author in interviews with senior professors of counseling psychology and experienced counselors. These questions mainly intended to get diverse ideas related to wisdom in counseling. Intended ideas were definitions of wisdom from counseling experience, difference between the wise person and the good counselor, the counselor's characteristics and wisdom, wisdom versus counseling techniques, change of behavior versus change of ends (telos) of behavior, determinism versus free will, the counselor's attitudes about him/herself, origins and development of wisdom, counseling training and wisdom, the counselor's attitudes about different theoretical approaches, self-understanding and wisdom, values and moral issues in counseling, the relationship between social influence and wisdom, and so on.

Twenty-two in-depth interview questions for exploring the counselor's wisdom are as follows:

- Questions about personal background are as follows:
  - How old are you?
  - Why did you choose counseling as your job? What was your motivation when you decided to study counseling?
  - What is your main philosophical or theoretical orientation?
  - When did you start studying counseling areas? How long have you been working as a counselor?
- What is wisdom? Would you define and describe what

wisdom is according to your personal and counseling experiences?

- What is not wisdom? Would you define and describe what wisdom is not according to your personal and counseling experiences?
- What is the difference between a wise man and a good counselor?
- What kinds of wisdom do you think the counselor needs or has to have?
- If you need help to solve your problems, what do you think the most important characteristics of the counselor are?
- Which counselor would choose for solving your problems?
  - the counselor who tries to teach (or emphasize) wisdom for problem-solving
  - the counselor who tries to teach techniques or skills for problem-solving
- Do you believe that the counselor is basically a behavioral manager (or technician)? Or is the counselor more concerned with the 'ends' (telos) of human behavior?
- Do you believe that there are general laws which regulate human behavior, such that one can scientifically

predict the probable success of counseling techniques?

- If you were a client, would you get counseling from a counselor like you? (Answer: Yes or no.) If the answer is yes, what kinds of advantage would you get from counseling? Which of your strong points do you think help your clients change?
- Where does wisdom come from? How have you been developing your wisdom? Then how do you think about the relationship between the counseling experience and wisdom?
- What is the best way to teach students in counseling psychology areas to make good counseling psychologists?
- If your counselor or psychotherapist were Freud (or Skinner, Rogers, Perls, Ellis), would you get counseling or psychotherapy? (Answer: yes or no.) Why? (The interviewer will suggest the different great counseling psychologists or psychotherapists from his or her philosophical or theoretical orientation as a counseling psychologist).
- What do you think the relationship between your level of self–understanding and understanding and helping with the client's problems?
- What do you think about the issue of the counselor's

value neutral position?

- Do you believe that it is appropriate for the counselor to engage in moral issue or to debate it in counseling situation? (i.e. about what is right or wrong?)
- Would you explain what is your position about the issue of a prenuptial agreement? If you had a client who needed help about a prenuptial agreement, how would you help your client?
- When you have value conflicts between yourself and client, how do you solve that problem? Would you explain about that?
- Could you explain what is the relationship between wisdom and counseling techniques or skills?
- According to the social influence theory in counseling, there are three important counselor characteristics, that is, expertness, attractiveness, and trustfulness as perceived by the client. Which do you think is the most important variable among those three variables? Why? What is the second important characteristic? Why?
- How do you think about the relationship between a counseling psychologist's power in terms of social influence and his/her wisdom?
- Would you give any comment and feedback about this interview?

Chapter 2

OVERVIEW OF WISDOM IN COUNSELING

Relevant literature on wisdom in counseling will be reviewed in this chapter under six sections: First, General definition of wisdom; Second, Characteristics and function of wisdom; Third, Relationship between wisdom and characteristics of the counseling psychologist; Fourth, Wisdom and value in counseling; Fifth, Wisdom and technique in counseling; and Sixth, Qualitative research versus quantitative research.

General Definition of Wisdom

Wisdom has been defined from various points of view. Many famous scholars in both Western and Eastern societies have been defining and studying wisdom from their points of view. Most of them focused on an investigation of the definition of wisdom and a relationship between wisdom and knowledge by using a metaphysical or qualitative approach. For example, wisdom in Christian teaching is different from wisdom in Greek literature. Wisdom in Western thought is different from an Eastern concept of wisdom. Wisdom is a concept influenced by the intellectual, moral, and cultural climate of each era (zeitgeist).

First, in defining clearly the essence of wisdom, it seems to be desirable to follow the linguistic approach. In the Western tradition, wisdom was defined during the Greek period in which the word sophia represents wisdom as the aim of the philosopher. "To be a philosopher means, etymologically, to be a lover of wisdom" (Sallis, 1986, p. 380). There is also wisdom in the form of phronesis, or "practical wisdom," a reasoned and true capacity to act with regard to human good. Aristotle (1984) distinguished practical wisdom (phronesis), scientific knowledge (episteme), developed in those who know the nature of things and the principles governing their behavior, and technique (techne). Practical wisdom is concerned with not only human beings and things about which it is possible to deliberate but also action.

In the Eastern tradition of thought, wisdom can be defined by an analysis of Chinese characters of wisdom. The Chinese word for wisdom consists of two pictorial characters (智慧). This word is used at least in China, Japan, and Korea. The first character 智 means knowledge and something (experience). The second character can be divided into two parts. The first part 彗 means a comet. The second part 心 means heart (mind). Literally and figuratively, wisdom means that a comet hits the heart (mind) of a person who has knowledge. Therefore, we can interpret wisdom (智慧) as understanding or insight based on knowledge and experience. Analogically, this word means and suggests the way by which Buddha reached enlightenment through his struggle.

In another approach, wisdom can be defined as a category of virtue in both Western and Eastern classical traditions. Plato's (1987) 'The Republic' explained that the ideal city contains three classes. First, the rulers have the virtue of wisdom. Second, the soldiers have the virtue of courage. Third, the workers and the artisans have the virtue of moderation. Similarly the individual's psyche has three aspects: the rational, the spirited, the appetitive. The virtue of reason is wisdom. The virtue of spirit is courage. The virtue of appetite is moderation. Aristotle (1984) defined practical wisdom in 'Nicomachean Ethics'. He emphasized that practical wisdom must be a reasoned and true state of capacity to act with regard to human goods. Furthermore, in 'On Virtues and Vices', Aristotle explained that wisdom is an excellence of the rational part, capable of procuring all that tends to happiness. "To wisdom belongs right deliberation, right judgment as to what is good and bad in all life that is to be chosen and avoided, noble use of all the goods that belong to us, correctness in social intercourse, the grasping of the right movement, the sagacious use of word and deed, the possession of experience of all that is useful" (Aristotle, 1984, p. 1983).

In the Eastern thought, the best example of wisdom as virtue is the Lao–Tzu's explanation. The Oriental classic, Lao–'Tzu Te–Tao Ching' (Henricks, 1989) mainly shows that the wise man keeps virtue (Te) based on the way or the universal principle of Yin and Yang (Tao). To understand others is to be knowledgeable, to understand yourself is to be wise (Te–Tao Ching, chap. 33). To know that you do not know is best. Not to know that you do not know is a flaw.

Therefore, the Sage's not being flawed stems from his recognizing a flaw as a flaw. Therefore, he is flawless (Te-Tao Ching, chap. 71). Wisdom and virtue are like the two wheels of a cart (Japanese proverb).

In summary, general definition of wisdom shows that the concept of wisdom basically includes something more than both knowledge or technique and virtue. Therefore, these two main characteristics of wisdom will be discussed in relation to values and techniques in counseling

Characteristics and Function of Wisdom

Wisdom remains an elusive word because it encompasses an attitude, a disposition toward life, past, present, future, only occasionally recognized in a wisdom-seeker. Many scholars try to find what wisdom is or what kinds of characteristics the wise person has by both explicit and implicit methods. Wisdom should be considered comprehensively in relation to age, experience, intelligence, knowledge, intuition, common sense, personality, human limitation, motivation, education and other relevant aspects.

Clayton and Birren's (1980) data indicated three distinct clusters of attributes that defined for them the cognitive, affective, and reflective dimensions of wisdom. Brent and Watson (1980) identified four clusters of attributes that they labeled person-cognitive, practical experiential, interpersonal, and moral-ethical. Baltes and Smith (1990) described the prototheory of wisdom as an expert knowledge system about the fundamental pragmatics of life. They suggested five wisdom-related criteria: rich factual knowledge, rich procedural knowledge, life span contextualism, relativism, and uncertainty. Sternberg (1985) investigated the relations among intelligence, wisdom, and creativity and emphasized the implicit theory of psychological constructs by people in defining wisdom. He found that the correlations between ratings of the three variables were .94 for wisdom and intelligence, .62 for wisdom and creativity, and .69 for intelligence and creativity. He suggested six components of wisdom: reasoning ability, sagacity, learning from ideas and environment, judgment, expeditious use of information, perspicacity. Holliday and Chandler (1986) asked three age cohorts (young adults, middle-aged adults, and senior citizens) to generate lists of attributes or characteristics judged by them to be especially descriptive of persons who are wise, intelligent, perceptive, shrewd, and spiritual. They reported five distinct factors: exceptional understanding, judgment and communication skills, general competence, interpersonal skills and social unobtrusiveness.

Kitchner and Brenner (1990) explained four aspects of wisdom related to the development of reflective judgment. The first aspect is that wisdom operates in the face of difficult, real life problems–often ones that involve pragmatic decisions. The second important aspect of wisdom is breadth and depth of knowledge. The third characteristic ascribed to wisdom is the understanding that human knowing is characterized by uncertainty. The fourth aspect of wisdom is the capacity to make sound judgments and decisions about life's problems in the face of uncertainty.

J. M. Erikson (1991) emphasized wisdom as an all–pervasive goal of every stage of life, because wisdom is the strength which reaches full fruition only with old age. The ten attributes of wisdom which she explained are independence and interrelatedness, acceptance of the cycle of life from integration to disintegration, resilience, empathy, humor, humility, a sense of the complexity of living, recognition of the complexity of sustained relationships, caring, and existential identity.

Arlin (1990) explained wisdom as the art of problem finding. He suggested six features shared by problem finding and by wisdom: the search for complementary, the direction of asymmetry, openness to change, pushing the limits, a sense of taste for problems that are of fundamental importance, and the preference for certain conceptual moves.

Kramer (1990) explained wisdom in terms of the context and relationship between affect and cognition, and wisdom. Cognition and affect are interdependent and attain their meaning in the praxis, or activity, of the organism. He emphasized five functions of wisdom in adult life. The first function of wisdom is the role it plays in enabling the individual to resolve dilemmas and make decisions in his/her life. The second function of wisdom is that of advising others, which would be particularly useful for the generative tasks of middle-aged adults, according to Erikson's theory. The third function of wisdom is the management and guidance of society. The fourth function of wisdom is life review. The fifth function of wisdom is questioning the meaning of life.

As Socrates emphasized, "Know yourself", the wise man understands his own ability. Therefore, as Perls (1978) indicated, the ability to resign, to let go of obsolete response, of exhausted relationships, and of tasks beyond one's potential, is an essential part of the wisdom of living (p. 79).

In summary, as many scholars indicated, wisdom has very diverse characteristics and function. Such characteristics and functions of wisdom are important components for improving our ways of life, well-being, quality of life, and so on. Therefore, it can be asserted that the characteristics and function of wisdom are necessary for a counseling psychologist who serves for helping clients change for improving their lives.

Relationship between Wisdom and Characteristics of the Counseling Psychologist

What are the most important characteristics of a wise counseling psychologist? In Havens' (1989) broad review of Milton Erikson's works, he concluded that Erikson's objective observation yields his wisdom. Havens summarized six different kinds of observations; observations regarding the influence of breathing patterns, observations regarding learning about one's body, observations regarding the meaning of words, observations regarding nonverbal communication, observations regarding physiological and behavioral patterns, and observations regarding cultural differences. It implies that a wise counseling psychologist must be a good observer of a client's range of behavior.

More theoretically, Strong (1968) characterized counseling as an interpersonal influence process, and suggested a two stage model of counseling. In the first stage, counseling psychologists enhance their perceived expertness, attractiveness, and trustworthiness, which serves to increase their clients' involvement in counseling. In the second stage, counseling psychologists make maximum use of their influence to precipitate attitude and behavior changes in clients.

Strong and Matross (1973) suggested that a therapist power base (P) is a function of correspondence of a client need (N) and a counseling psychologist resource (R): $P = f(R, N)$. They emphasized a counseling psychologist's five power bases: expert, referent, legitimate, informational, and ecological. In Strong's (1968) and Strong and Matross' (1973) research, the social influence theory in counseling means that counseling psychologists build their power resources in terms of social influence by pointing out their unique control of test data, confidentiality, objectivity, patience, and relationship skills.

Barak and LaCross (1975) developed the Counselor Rating Form and investigated Strong's prediction of the existence of three dimensions of perceived counselor behavior–expertness, attractiveness, and trustworthiness. In their research, 202 volunteer college students watched films of interviews given by Rogers, Ellis and Perls and rated each counselor on the Counselor Rating Form scale. LaCrosse (1980) examined the predictive validity of the Counselor Rating Form and tested Strong's model of the impact of counselor social influence on counseling outcomes. They found that there was a positive relationship between final client perceptions and counseling outcomes.

Heppner and Heesacker (1983) suggested that perceptions of counselor source characteristics, namely expertness, attractiveness, and trustworthiness, are related to client satisfaction with real–life counseling. Heppner and Heesacker (1982) found that actual counselor experience level was not related to perceived counselor expertness, attractiveness, or trustworthiness. Heppner and Heesacker (1983) replicated this study with similar results and concluded that actual counselor experience did not deferentially affect the Counseling Evaluation Inventory and Counseling Rating Form scores. These results are not consistent with the conclusion that more experienced counselors establish "better relationships" (e. g., communicate more effectively, have higher levels of positive regard) with clients than unexperienced counselors (Auerbach & Johnson, 1977).

These inconsistent results suggest that a further investigation is needed. The present author finds that there is confusion in defining actual counseling experience level. One would assume that a counseling psychologist with ten years experience and active involvement in counseling activities is different from a counseling psychologist who has not had much experience in counseling.

Fassinger (1987) indicated problems in social influence theory by broadly reviewing related research. The problems he suggested include (a) validation of the tripartite structure of counseling psychologist characteristics; (b) the possibility of a legitimacy effect in which attributions of expertness, attractiveness, and trustworthiness may be based on the socially sanctioned counseling psychologist role, rather than on specific cues displayed by a particular counseling psychologist; (c) specification of the power bases (expert, referent, and legitimate) in which counseling psychologist characteristics are rooted; (d) failure to distinguish between actual and perceived counseling psychologist characteristics; (e) focus on client and counseling psychologist perceptions of change rather than actual behavior change; (f) little attention to the influence attempt and level of client disclosure in client attributions and change.

Most researches in social influence theory investigated and focused on a counseling psychologist's characteristics; that is, on expertness, attractiveness, and trustworthiness according to the perceptions of clients. As Fassinger (1987) indicated several problems in research on social influence theory, the present author raises the questions related to the relationship between a counseling psychologist's characteristics and his/her wisdom.

What really are a counseling psychologist's power bases? How can a counseling psychologist's power bases be specified? What are the most important characteristics of a counseling psychologist which he/she actually perceives? These questions can be investigated by considering the diverse components of wisdom of a counseling psychologist. The present author finds much similarity between a counseling psychologist's power and his/her wisdom even though those terms have largely different nuances. Therefore, an investigation of wisdom in which counseling psychologists define and the development of a scale of wisdom in the counseling psychology may explain and expand the concept of the counseling psychologist's power which Strong (1968), and Strong and Matross (1973) suggested in his social influence theory in counseling.

Implicitly, the present author believes that there are some dimensions of wisdom that counseling psychologists emphasize as Sternberg (1985) investigated. The dimensions of wisdom of a counseling psychologist that the present author (No, 1993) found from 202 counseling psychologists were personality, ethical responsibility, attitude, cognitive knowledge and intellectual skills, knowledge based on experience, training, relationship styles, understanding of human differences, and understanding of human nature. No (1993) also indicated that those nine dimensions of wisdom which counseling psychologists emphasized are necessary categories to be a wise counseling psychologist.

Wisdom and Value in Counseling

Gadamer (1989) emphasized the rehabilitation of authority and tradition which have become ambiguous and have been misunderstood by the fundamental presupposition of Enlightenment, namely that methodologically disciplined use of reason can be a safeguard from all error.

> The authority of persons is ultimately based not on the subjection and abdication of reason but on an act of acknowledgement and knowledge–the knowledge, namely, that the other is superior to oneself in judgment and insight, and that for this reason his judgment takes precedence–i.e., it has priority over one's own..... Acknowledging authority is always connected with the idea that what the authority says is not

> irrational and arbitrary but can, in principle, be discovered to be true. This is the essence of the authority claimed by the teacher, the superior, the expert (Gadamer, 1989, pp. 279-280).

In accordance with this meaning of authority, the present author believes that Freud, Skinner, and Rogers are the authorities in counseling and psychotherapy. Freud opened new horizons in understanding human beings by discovering the unconscious. Skinner tried to build the Utopian society (Walden Two) based on the principle of behavioral reinforcement. Rogers encouraged self-actualization in terms of human autonomy and the wisdom of the organism by focusing upon and accepting the person as a whole. They are three main protagonists of psychoanalysis, behaviorism, and humanism. They were tenacious in their beliefs and showed how to effect change in clients. This section focuses on the issues concerning values and wisdom which the protagonists of these three main forces of psychology have influenced.

Counseling is a process of deep human involvement between subjective valuing beings. Even at the outset of a counseling relationship, certain values are presupposed. Counseling psychologists, who are involved with individuals in the process of healing and making choices, by the very nature of their work, cannot afford to neglect the realm of values. As we explained its basic definition, wisdom is closely related to virtue or ethical responsibility. Therefore, a wise counseling psychologist should be aware of not only a client's behavioral change itself but also his/her values and happiness.

"Knowledge is certainly not wisdom nor is the more knowledgeable by any reckoning the more wise. ... wisdom is the knowing that combines the interpretative and the technical aspects into a way of life, for the greater fulfillment of living" (MacIver, 1955, p. 118). In studying and understanding a certain counseling theory, a counseling psychologist has to consider its axiological aspects as well as its ontological and epistemological aspects. Axiology refers to the study of beliefs about values. It raises the question about what is 'good' and consists of the investigation of the nature of the 'good', its criteria, and its ontological status.

"What we have learned is that ultimately, the best way for a person to discover what he ought to do is to find out who and what he is, because the path to ethical and value decisions, to wiser choices, to oughtness, via 'isness', via the discovery of facts, truth, the nature of the particular person" (Maslow, 1976, pp. 106-107). A. H. Maslow defined therapy as a search for values because ultimately the search for identity is, in essence, the search for one's intrinsic, authentic values. It is imperative for a counseling psychologist to consider and understand the philosophy of values and recognize the perplexing methodological questions in dealing with values that arise within the counseling relationship. It is also very important for each counseling psychologist to look honestly at himself and to be aware of his presuppositions in order to avoid subtly imposing values upon clients. Therefore, counseling psychologists need to continually examine and be aware of what values they serve and why they emphasize those values.

There have been three main philosophical doctrines regarding moral development: 'original sin' (Saint Augustine), 'tabula rasa' (John Locke), and 'innate purity' (J. J. Rousseau). Each of these views finds expression in the three major contemporary psychological approaches to moral development; psychoanalytic theory, cognitive learning theory, and cognitive developmental theory (Vander Zanden, 1985, pp. 302-311). Three philosophical doctrines are more or less parallel with Freud's psychoanalytic, Skinner's behavioral, and Rogers' humanistic approach. Like three protagonists in psychology, counseling psychologists have different points of view to understand their clients in moral and value aspects based on their counseling approaches. Therefore, the counseling psychologist must make explicit the values he/she serves in order to understand the direction of his/her influence. For example, if a counseling psychologist believes that man is inherently evil and that his tendency is toward evil, he/she is likely to be more active in assisting the client to control the evil impulses and to serve the right values. If a counseling psychologist views man as neither good nor evil, but neutral, he/she is likely to view the learning of positive values as an important part of the counseling process. If a counseling psychologist views man as inherently good with basic tendency in a positive direction, he/she will tend to allow the client to express his/her positive nature and will seek to help to eliminate hindrances to its expression.

Wallwork (1991) explained that in Freud's naturalistic theory, value is accounted for in terms of human pleasures and interests. Practical reason is directed toward certain values, as ends of action. He emphasized the credibility of Freudian theory on ethical and moral aspects. "No other contemporary school of psychology such as behaviorism, cognitive psychology, or even the developmental psychology of morals formulated by Piaget and substantially revised by Kohlberg and Gilligan is as preoccupied with the whole set of morals that underlie moral behavior" (Wallwork, 1991, p. 293).

The controversial debate concerning the control of human behavior between Skinner and Rogers was intriguing and arresting to many scholars' minds (Rogers and Skinner, 1972). Its main issue seems to focus upon human values. To Skinner, good things are positive reinforcements. "To make a value judgment by calling something good or bad is to classify it in terms of its reinforcing effects" (Skinner, 1971, p. 99). Skinner (1971) thought that freedom, dignity, and values were sources of trouble as the power of technology of behavior became more nearly commensurate with the problems to be solved.

On the contrary, Rogers strongly believed in the value of the person. "When the therapeutic relationship is most effective, it seems to me, it is marked by one primary value: namely, that this person, this client, has worth. He as a person is valued in his separateness and uniqueness" (Rogers, 1971, p. 12). He explained that evidence from therapy indicated that both personal and social values emerge as natural, and experienced, when the individual was close to his own organismic valuing process.

Although Skinner was competent to build a Utopian society based on the technology of shaping of behavior, he seemed to struggle and be haunted with questions concerning values as follows:

> Freedom and dignity illustrate the difficulty. They are the possessions of the autonomous man of traditional theory, and they are essential to practices in which a person is held responsible for his conduct and given credit for his environments. A scientific analysis shifts both the responsibility and achievement to the environment. It also raises questions concerning "values." Who will use a technology and to what ends? Until these issues are resolved, a technology of behavior will continue to be rejected, and with it possibly the only way to solve our problems (Skinner, 1971, pp. 22-23).

Thoreau's Walden experiment was the result of his belief and experience as a wisdom–seeker, "To be a philosopher is not merely to have subtle thoughts, nor even to found a school, but so to love wisdom as to live, according to its dictates, a life of simplicity, independence, magnanimity, and trust. It is to solve some of the problems of life, not only theoretically, but also practically" (Thoreau, 1968, p. 14). Similarly, Skinner's novel, 'Walden Two', was the result of his belief and ideal of a Utopian society based on the technology of behaviorism. Kinkade and her associates founded Twin Oaks, in rural Virginia, in 1967 based on the model of Walden Two. Kinkade (1973) published the story of the first five years of Twin Oaks Community as a Walden Two Experiment with the Skinner's foreword. Skinner's explanation and emphasis of wisdom is meaningful.

> The life portrayed in Walden Two was the goal of Twin Oaks, but it was not approached through the application of scientific principles. ... One great source of wisdom is now about to be tapped: Twin Oaks is ready to raise children. If the lives of those children are properly managed, lessons will be learned of extraordinary value to the community and to us all (Kinkade, 1973, p. x).

This statement of Skinner would not be acceptable to humanistic counseling psychologists. Rogers might ask again, "Where is the autonomy and uniqueness of a child?" Skinner's puzzling dilemma about "Who will use a technology and to what ends?" seems similar to Plato's quest, "Who will be the best leader?" Two classic novels (or films), Baum's 'The Wizard of Oz' (1976) and Burgess's 'A

Clockwork Orange' (1962), might represent well the basic philosophical beliefs of Rogers and Skinner. In 'The Wizard of Oz', Scarecrow, Tin Man, and Lion discovered brain, heart, and courage which they thought they did not have. In 'A Clockwork Orange', the young hoodlum, Alex, was conditioned and unconditioned to change his violent behavior with Ludovico's Technique. The arresting issue raised by these two novels is an ethical value of human being rather than change itself.

Doctors, psychotherapists, and counseling psychologists are in positions of special responsibility because they are often asked to help the immature, the weak, and the sick people who are in a vulnerable state. Doctors have been taking the Hippocratic oath and have their own disciplinary body. Psychologists also belong to professions governed by ethics and discipline. Ethical codes are least important when the counseling psychologist respects the client, but become most important when he/she does not.

Many famous psychologists such as Freud, Skinner, and Rogers had wisdom and authority in that their ideas have influenced many people. Counseling psychologists often refer to and unconsciously accept conventional wisdom because it has survived with authority and tradition.

Helpers are responsible for clients' happiness. Lang,

Molen, Trower, and Look (1990) explained four roles of the helpers: the confidant, the communicative detective, the teacher, and the coach. In that respect, the comments of Whitehead (1974) in an address to the boys in England seems appropriate to cite.

> I must remind you of the fine story of an Eastern king, who, in a vision, chose wisdom, because for its own sake he preferred it to all the treasures of Oriental magnificence. Power follows wisdom, because nature unlocks its secrets to the wise and dowers the temperate with zest and energy. Wisdom should be more than intellectual acuteness. It includes reverence and sympathy, and recognition of those limitations which bound all human endeavors (Whitehead, 1974, p. 177).

Wisdom and Technique in Counseling

Herink (1980) introduced 255 different psychotherapeutic approaches selected from a list of over 350 psychotherapeutic systems and techniques. Since each counseling and psychotherapeutic approach has several specific techniques, it is easy to see that many techniques are developed and used in therapeutic situations. Various psychotherapies are developed for diverse individual needs. Psychoanalytically oriented therapies use their techniques to understand mind in an interpretative way. Behaviorally oriented therapists use their techniques to change behaviors in a direct and problem–solving way. On the other hand, humanistically oriented therapists use their techniques to facilitate a client on exploring his/her problem in an indirect way.

As techniques are important to becoming an expert in one's specialty area, counseling techniques are essential to becoming an effective counseling psychologist. It is not only important to learn many techniques but also to understand how and when a counseling psychologist uses those techniques. Perls said that "One of the objections I have against anyone calling a Gestalt Therapist is that he uses technique. A technique is gimmick. A gimmick should be used only in the extreme case" (Perls, 1971, p. 1). Counseling techniques are means or tools that can be learned. In that aspect, genuineness, empathy, and the unconditional positive regard which Carl Rogers emphasized, can be considered to be attitudes rather than techniques. "It is important to recognize that empathy is not a technique, but an attitude. ..... Teaching a technique is probably not the best way to make a therapist empathic" (Kahn, 1991, p. 152).

A counseling psychologist's belief and scientific knowledge is closely related to his/her chosen approach and techniques. In terms of "curing" a client or causing a client to adjust in a desirable way, a counseling psychologist applies the preferred counseling approach and techniques. Counseling psychology is a process of studying principles of mental state through understanding and interpreting dialogues between a therapist and client. Any counseling approach is related to a value system in that a counseling psychologist encourages a client to live in a happier and more realistic way.

In becoming a wise and effective counseling psychologist, scientific knowledge and techniques are necessary but are not sufficient conditions. Wisdom is neither a science, theory, nor technique. This is because wisdom always implies value and virtue. Therefore, to be an effective counseling psychologist needs not only counseling theories and techniques but also wisdom.

Socrates explained that professional experts, like skilled craftsmen, have impressive knowledge and technical proficiency. Their knowledge and techniques are not wisdom (Plato, 1987, Apology, pp. 8-9). Aristotle (1984) showed that practical wisdom is neither knowledge (epiteme) nor technique (techne) as follows:

> Practical wisdom cannot be knowledge nor technique; not knowledge because that which can be done is capable of being otherwise, not technique because action and making are different kinds of thing. It remains, then, that it is a true and reasoned state of capacity to act with regard to the things that are good or bad for man (Aristotle, 1984, Nicomachean Ethics, p. 1800).

Furthermore, Aristotle (1984) specifically distinguished the difference between practical wisdom and technique as follows:

> Practical wisdom must be a reasoned and true state of capacity to act with regard to human goods. But further, while there is such a thing as excellence in technique, there is no such thing as excellence in practical wisdom; and in technique he who errs willingly is preferable, but in practical wisdom, as in the excellence he is the reverse. Plainly, then, practical wisdom is an excellence and not a technique (Aristotle, 1984, Nicomachean ethics, p. 1800).

The hermeneutical approach in human science can be

applied to understanding psychotherapy or counseling psychology in analysis of dialogues between a counseling psychologist and a client. Gadamer (1989) used a hermeneutical approach to show that Aristotle's understanding of practical wisdom/moral knowledge (phronesis), scientific/ theoretical knowledge (epiteme), and technique (techne) can parallel a counseling psychologist's wisdom, counseling theory or approach, and counseling techniques.

> The distinction that Aristotle makes between practical wisdom (pronesis) and theoretical knowledge (episteme) is a simple one, especially when we remember that science, for the Greeks, is represented by the model of mathematics, a knowledge of what is unchangeable, a knowledge that depends on proof and that can therefore be learned by anybody. A hermeneutics of human sciences certainly has nothing to learn from mathematical as distinguished from moral knowledge. The human sciences stand closer to moral knowledge than to that kind of "theoretical knowledge. They are "moral sciences." Their object is man and what he knows of himself. But he knows himself as an acting being, and this kind of knowledge of himself does not seek to establish what is. An acting

> being, rather, is concerned with what is not always the same but can also be different. In it, he can discover the point at which he has to act. The purpose of his knowledge is to govern his action. — We find action governed by knowledge in an exemplary form where the Greeks speak of technique (techne). This is the skill, the knowledge of the craftsman who knows how to make some specific thing. The question is whether practical wisdom is technique (Gadamer, 1989, p. 314).

For Gadamer, the contrast between practical wisdom as ethical know–how (phronesis) and technique as technical know–how (techne) is more important than the distinction between practical wisdom and scientific knowledge (episteme) (Bernstein, 1988). Gadamer stressed the contrasts between practical wisdom and technique as follows:

First, technique is learned and can be forgotten: we can lose a skill. But we can not learn practical wisdom, nor can we forget it. We do not stand over against it, as if it were something that we can acquire, as we can choose to acquire an object skill, a techne. Man always finds himself in an "acting situation" and he is always obliged to use practical wisdom and apply it according to the exigencies of his concrete situation (Gadamer, 1989, pp. 317-320).

Second, we see a fundamental modification of the conceptual relation between means and ends in technique and practical wisdom. The end of practical wisdom unlike that of a technique is not merely a particular thing but pertains to right living in general, whereas all technical knowledge is particular and severs particular ends. Practical wisdom can never be knowable in advance like technique. The relation between means and ends here is not such that one can know the right means in advance, and that is because the right end is not the mere object of knowledge. Where there is a technique, we must learn it and then we are able to find the right means. We see that practical wisdom, however, always requires this kind of self-deliberation. Practical wisdom is really knowledge of special kind. In a curious way it embraces both means and end, and hence differs from technical knowledge (Gadamer, 1989, pp. 320-322).

Third, practical wisdom, unlike technique, requires an understanding of other human beings. Beside practical wisdom, the virtue of thoughtful reflection, stands sympathetic understanding (synesis). "Being understanding" is introduced as a modification of the virtue of practical wisdom since in this case it is not I who must act. Someone's sympathetic understanding is praised, of course, when in order to judge he transposes himself fully into the concrete situation of the person who has to act. The question is not of a general kind of knowledge, but of its specification at a particular moment. This knowledge also is not in any sense technical knowledge or the application of such. The person with understanding does not know and judge as one who stands apart and unaffected; but rather, as one united by a specific bond with the other, he thinks with the other and undergoes the situations with him (Bernstein, 1988, p. 147; Gadamer, 1989, pp. 322-324).

Beginning counseling psychologists might learn the general procedures of counseling techniques in a short period. "A technique is a standard method that can be taught. It is a recipe that can be fully conveyed from one person to another" (Barrett, 1979, p. 22). But any technique in counseling and psychotherapy cannot apply to a client as a standard method. The effectiveness of a counseling technique totally depends on both the counseling psychologist who uses it and its appropriateness for the client. Furthermore, a counseling psychologist can be critical about B. F. Skinner's technology of behavior according to his/her counseling approach. Barrett (1979) suggested an illusion of technique as a criticism of B. F. Skinner's book, 'Beyond Freedom and Dignity.' "The ideal of the free and self-governing (autonomous) personality is a traditional part of our thinking in law and political philosophy. For Professor Skinner this idea is not only an illusion, but also a pernicious relic of the past that stands as a barrier to our future progress" (Barrett, 1979, p. xiii). He concluded that "Every technique is put to use for some end, and this end is decided in the light of some philosophic outlook or other" (Barrett, 1979, p. 177).

In philosophy, pragmatism, and in psychology, behaviorism has been popular historically in America. "American psychology even today, in its theoretical state, is still largely dominated by the trilogy of behaviorism, operationalism, and logical positivism" (Deese, 1972, pp. 16-17). "The technique of shaping behavior are the preoccupation also of our own American psychologist, B. F. Skinner" (Barrett, 1979, p. xii). Even though many changes in applications of behavioral techniques have occurred such as Meichenbaum's Cognitive–Behavior Modification during the last two decades, the essence of B. F. Skinner as idea of the centrality of reinforcement is still popular in American psychology.

In summary, counseling techniques are important to effectiveness of counseling. However, techniques have limitations in terms of individual difference and uniqueness when they are applied to clients. Technical strength involves weakness in application because the counseling process always includes both a counseling psychologist and a client with a problem. Therefore, a wise and effective counseling psychologist should never forget that, as Bernstein (1989) indicated, "Technique without practical wisdom is blind, while practical wisdom without technique is empty".

Qualitative Research versus Quantitative Research

Recently studies by qualitative research in psychology are getting popular. But 20 years ago very few studies were conducted by qualitative research. Anyway, to find the counselor's wisdom I used in-depth interview, one method of qualitative research 20 years ago. Therefore, I briefly want to explain strong and weak points of both qualitative and quantitative research in performing psychological researches depending on the philosophical tradition of psychology.

Catania and Harnad (1988) extensively demonstrated the influence of the operant behaviorism of B. F. Skinner in the book, 'The Selection of Behavior: The Operant Behaviorism of B. F. Skinner'. This book consisted of commentary from

142 scholars on Skinner's canonical papers and his responses to them. Skinner and his followers believed that methods and theories in the experimental analysis of behavior should follow laboratory research. Skinner criticized the flight from the laboratory, the flight to laymanship (Catania and Harnad, 1988, pp. 77-87). He also asserted that the statistical pattern is incompatible with some major features of laboratory. Observable behavior is, as in physics, his primary task. The statistical research based on observable behavior that Skinner advocates is different from the statistical research based on unobservable behavior or data collected by survey and questionnaire, which is popular in the counseling field. Therefore, in terms of Skinner's explanation, quantitative research based on statistical analysis may be less satisfactory than qualitative research.

Even though many psychologists think that wisdom and self-understanding of counselors is important, they are reluctant to study this subject because of the difficulties in measuring wisdom. Furthermore, much our thinking about research still seems demonstrated by the quantitative orientation.

Joseph Kockelmans(1973) identified three main possibilities in the human sciences: the empirical, the descriptive and the hermeneutic. Empirical approach is represented by the deductive and pragmatic systems of inquiry. Knowledge obtained through empirical approach is quantitative in that the formalization is categorized and described in numerical relationships.

The basic philosophy of positivism led to the notions of logical positivism, operationalism, and reductionism. "Positivism is the attempt to apply to the affairs of man the methods and principles of the natural science" (Heather, 1976, p. 13). Psychology, another victim of the winner of positivism, has cultivated qualitative methods more routinely for clinical purposes than research ones. This field is also beginning to show a new interest in qualitative methods, and diverse theoretical orientations as well, including ethnography, narrative psychology, and phenomenology (McCracken, 1988).

We cannot deny that many research methodologies derived from logical positivism and behaviorism have contributed to finding and explaining human behaviors and phenomena. Quantitative research has also contributed to understanding human behavior. But its limits are not recognized by quantitatively oriented researchers, compared to current criticism of logical positivism and behaviorism.

Consequently, other approaches which compensate for the limitations of the empirical approach are needed. The phenomenological (descriptive) and hermeneutic (interpretive) systems provide two other contexts of knowledge in qualitative research. The phenomenological approach focuses on the structures of experience, the organizing principles that give form and meaning to the life world. The hermeneutic approach concentrates on the historical meaning of experience and its development and cumulative effects at both the individual and social levels (Polkinghorne, 1983).

There has been the historically parallel approach between philosophy and psychology. The hermeneutic and post-modern approaches, recently popular trends in philosophy, also have been beginning to be seen in psychotherapy and counseling, in which language and its interpretation and the constructivist's point of view are very important. For example, through the historical review of psychoanalytic paradigms, Cooper (1987) indicated that a question seriously debated today is whether psychoanalysis is by its nature a purely psychological and linguistic effort at understanding meanings, or whether it is a scientific discipline with biological roots.

Twenty years ago, in 1990 when I performed this research by an in-depth interview, when I examined a number of qualitative articles published in reputable journals and dissertations in counseling or clinical psychology, they were "as scare as hen's teeth". Currently, qualitative studies are getting popular. Anyway, it is very important not only to recognize the limitations of quantitative research but also to try to go beyond those limitations.

"In the human sciences we cannot speak of an object of research in the same sense as in the natural sciences, where research penetrates more and more deeply into nature. Rather, in the human sciences the particular research questions concerning tradition that we are interested in pursuing are motivated in a special way by the present and its interests. The theme and object of research are actually constituted by the motivation of the inquiry" (Gadamer, 1989, p. 284). It is important for the researcher to choose a quantitative or qualitative approach according to the topic research. Further, to avoid the limitations inherent in either approach, it is desirable to appropriately combine both approaches. Therefore, the present author combined qualitative and quantitative approaches for exploring the counselor's wisdom.

Sternberg (1985) emphasized the necessity of implicit theories of intelligence, creativity and wisdom, because implicit theories can be useful for providing a conceptual framework for the development of explicit theories. He defined implicit theories as constructions by people (whether psychologists or laypersons) that reside in the minds of these individuals. Explicit theories are constructions of psychologists or other scientists that are based on, or at least tested with, data collected from people performing tasks presumed to measure psychological functioning.

In this research, an in-depth interview and a survey by open-ended questions were designed to explore the conception of wisdom of a counseling psychologist, and the variables related to wisdom. The qualitative approach was used to determine how an effective counseling psychologist perceives wisdom in accordance with Cronbach's (1955) and Sternberg's (1985) conceptions of implicit theories of wisdom in counseling psychology.

The quantitative approach used in this research tested the reliability of the Counseling Psychologist's Wisdom Scales which was developed from the results of the qualitative researches. In addition, research hypotheses about relationships with wisdom and the other independent variables were tested. Therefore, the quantitative approach was used to study relationships between variables which are operationally defined for the purpose of this research.

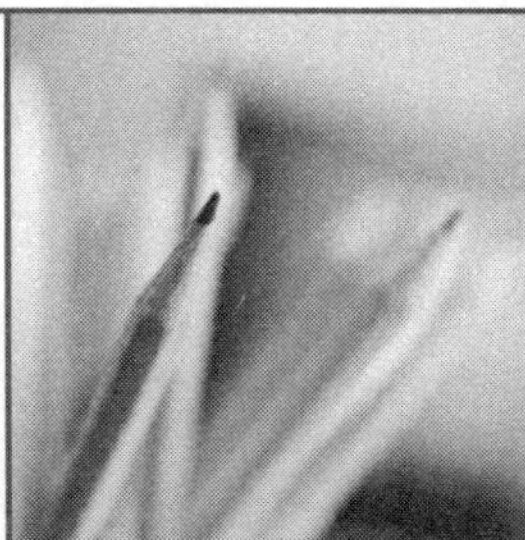

PART 2

WISDOM AND COUNSELOR'S PERSPECTIVE

Chapter 3

OVERVIEW OF IN-DEPTH INTERVIEW

The present author interviewed seven professors in counseling psychology who agreed to participate in this study for exploring the counselor's wisdom. The main method of this study was an individual in-depth interview. The present author also described and interpreted the in-depth interview data by using the descriptive and hermeneutic approaches.

Purpose

The main purpose was to find how experienced counseling psychologists define wisdom and explain the relationship between wisdom and counseling. Respondents were interviewed about their views on wisdom. They were to respond from their personal background and counseling experiences. In order to find general and meaningful content pattern from the in-depth interviews, the present author used the following several presumptive research hypotheses:

1. Dialogues will show the strong relationship between wisdom and counseling.
2. Desirable approaches to teaching beginning counseling psychologists will be implied in the relationship between wisdom and counseling.
3. Professors in counseling psychology will define wisdom based on their personal experiences and their theoretical or philosophical approaches to counseling.
4. Professors in counseling psychology will define wisdom in differently than in other specialties.
5. Dialogues will reveal the counseling psychologist's value position in counseling.

6. Dialogues will reveal views about the characteristics of counseling psychologists that are seen as important.

Method and Procedure

The present author served as an interviewer. He interviewed seven professors in counseling psychology. The interview included twenty main questions about wisdom or self-understanding, values, and several main issues in counseling areas. Each interview required about ninety minutes to two hours. Interviews were conducted in a quiet place of mutual convenience in which distractions were minimal.

Interviewees

Subjects were seven professors at the Department of Educational and Counseling Psychology, University of Kentucky. They had a low of twenty years and a high of forty-two years of experience. Six of seven were male. They ranged in age forty-two to sixty-four years.

Development of Interview Questions

The present author who came from South Korea was

interested to the topic of wisdom in counseling as a result of his reading about the diversity of counseling approaches and philosophy literature in his attempt to understand Western thought. As a result of this reading, a feeling that self–understanding is closely related to wisdom as Socrates advised: "Know yourself". The book, 'Wisdom' (Edited by Sternberg, 1990) especially reinforced the present author's determination to carry out this research.

The present author's statistical background and his experience of serving as a quantitative analysis consultant to graduate students and faculty at the Center for Professional Development, University of Kentucky, combined with his experience in a course in field study stimulated a plan to combine quantitative and qualitative methods in a study of the mean of wisdom. The instructor of the field study class helped the present author to develop a series of interview questions. The book, 'The Long Interview' (McCracken, 1988), provided guidance.

Interview questions were mainly intended to explore how a counseling psychologist defined wisdom based on his/her theoretical and philosophical orientation. The present author verified that these interview questions were valid and reasonable for obtaining a desirable purpose by going over them carefully with a graduate student in the Ph.D. program in Philosophy at the University of Kentucky and several colleagues in psychological studies.

All in-depth interview questions were directly and indirectly related to wisdom or self-understanding. The questions were related to the origins and development of wisdom, the relationship between counseling techniques and wisdom, a counseling psychologist's values, social influence theory in counseling, and a counseling psychologist's characteristics. Each interview question was intended to explore aspects of wisdom that a counseling psychologist might emphasize.

Interview Procedure and Data Analysis

Permission to interview and tape the session was obtained from each respondent. The present author briefly explained this interview when he called or visited each interviewee. Interviews mainly were done in the interviewees' (professors) offices and were tape-recorded. The present author let all interviewees review the interview questions for two or three minutes before starting the interview to stimulate thought and understanding of the general intent of the interview. It was also requested that the interviewee answer or explain each question during a period of approximately four to six minutes before starting the main interview.

Approximately 200 pages of transcripts were produced from seven interviewees' recorded tapes. The present author then went through five steps to interpret and organize the data, in a procedure summarized by Giorge (1974) as follows.

First step, the researcher reads the entire description... straight through to get a sense of the whole.

Second step, the researcher reads the same description more slowly and delineates each time that a transition in meaning is perceived with respect to the intentional discovering of the experience.

Third step, the researcher then eliminates redundancies and clarifies or elaborates to himself the meaning of the units just constituted by relating them to each other and to the sense of the whole.

Forth step, the researcher reflects on the given units, still expressed essentially in the concrete language of the subject, and comes up with the essence of that situation for the subject with respect to the phenomena under consideration. Each unit is systematically interrogated for what it reveals about the phenomena for that subject. The researcher transforms each unit, when relevant, into the language of psychological science.

Fifth step, the researcher synthesizes and integrates the

insights achieved into a consistent description of the structure of the phenomena (Polkinghorne, 1983, p. 211).

The present author also continually considered the four steps method of inquiry in understanding and interpreting interview data which McCracken (1988) suggested as follows.

Step 1: Review of analytic categories.
Step 2: Review of cultural categories.
Step 3: Discovery of cultural categories.
Step 4: Discovery of analytic categories.

The present author's cultural experience and study of counseling in America probably contributed to the analysis. People are imbued with their own cultures and unconsciously live with their cultural habits.

Chapter 4

WISDOM IN AN ADLERIAN PERSPECTIVE

Introduction of Transcript 1: This interview was done on October 1, 1990. When the Professor 1 was interviewed, he was the professor of counseling psychology and his age was 64 years old. On that time his career experience of studying of counseling psychology was forty-two years. Currently he lives a happy life in Kentucky after retirement and he is 84 years old. He indicated that his theoretical orientation of counseling were a client-centered, existential, and Adlerian.

Author: First I want to know your personal backgrounds. How old are you?

Professor 1: Ok. I will be 65 next month, I am 64 right now.

Author: How did you choose counseling as your job?

Professor 1: Well, I think probably there are a couple of things. One is that I admired my father. My father was involved with counseling although that was not his primary job. He taught in high schools and talked with kids about problems they were having and so on. He worked for the Young Men's Christian Association. He was more an executive and administrative person, was responsible for the YMCA in the states of West Virginia, Indiana, and so on. So I think counseling was related to what my father did for a living. And I admired him. And then I was in the navy in World War II and I admired some people, particularly a young man, named, Pat Smid who was an officer with me on the ship. I was on. And he was very good working with people. And I thought that I would like to learn to do that. I would like to be effective and comfortable with other things. Those were sort of background kind of things. Then I found myself at the University of Chicago and I met a number of people who were interested in counseling, Tom Gordon, and Carl Rogers.

Author: Personally you met them at the University of Chicago?

Professor 1: Yea, I mean, I was a student and I started taking courses with them. That got me interested in counseling specifically.

Author: Specially also you mean, your father as a teacher influenced you to decide your career for taking care of....

Professor 1: Well, my father wasn't the teacher. And he didn't make his living as a counselor, but he was the YMCA secretary. At that time, he ran summer camps, for example, and he started clubs for people who was in high schools, and talked about values. He was interested in international students. The kind of things. So counseling was sort of related to the kind of person he was, and the kind of things he did. He was active in church work, for example. I am not active in church work, but it was related to the kind of person he was and some of things that he did. So you know, it fits better, than for me to go into business with my family background.

Author: There are a lot of different theoretical or philosophical counseling approaches. I am wondering what your main theoretical orientation of counseling is.

Professor 1: Well, I suppose I started from a client–centered point of view because that was what I began. And it was because it suited me and generally worked well for me. I like psychodrama very much. I suppose if I had to choose one individual, as I understand him, if I had to choose, I might choose Adler in the field of counseling. Then I would say he would be kind of a grandfather to my views. I would be fitted well with Adler. In philosophy, I see myself pretty much as an existentialist. I don't know very much about Rollo May, an existential psychologist. I have read a little existential writers' works and so on. But I am in tune with a kind of existential view of world. Adler would be one. I like something that I see from Gestalt therapy, the focus on here and now, the focus on how you are and what's going on inside yourself, and so on. I could say better what I am not, you know, I think I am not a behaviorist by and large. That doesn't mean I might not give clients some homework, or that I would not say "Well if you are trying to give up smoking, let's see, how many cigarettes do you smoke? And what time of a day do you smoke? Do you smoke with or without somebody else? What's going on to your mind when you find yourself smoking cigarettes and so on." I am not opposed to that. It's just that wouldn't be natural for me. It's something I have no objection to. But I wouldn't call myself a behaviorist.

Author: My understanding is that if you choose one approach among Carl Rogers' person-centered therapy, Freudian psychoanalysis and behavioral approach, maybe you like the person-centered approach.

Professor 1: Right sure. I am not psychoanalytic and I am not behavioral. I am not cognitive-behavioral.

Author: I also want to know how long you have been working as a counselor.

Professor 1: I started taking coursework about 1948, so 42 years. I was in the graduate school program in psychology at Chicago in 1948. So I started taking courses with Rogers and Gordon '48, '49. I worked at the counseling center at 1950 in Chicago. So, it's a little over 40 years.

Author: Thank you. Now I think we are ready for the main questions of this interview. First of all, what is wisdom? Would you define and describe what wisdom is according to your personal and counseling experience?

Professor 1: Ok. I probably don't use the term very often. But I do think about wisdom. That is, wisdom as being clear about what is important and what is preferable. I think, in terms of wisdom. What are you really aiming toward? Or what do you really want? What is going to be important as the whole? So I hope, I would expect counselors to be trying to wise, to be aware of what is vitally important or what is not so important for the client, for himself or herself, and for the counselor in terms of what is good for persons, what is good for people that are going to be involved with clients. They are spouses, children, employers, and so on. So I think that counselors ought to have a broad view of life.

Author: In the same way, what is not wisdom? Please define and describe what wisdom is not from your personal and counseling experience.

Professor 1: I think we are trying to help somebody make decisions about thinking through the implications of their choices, so I think it's not wise to be too much in a hurry, too push prematurely for closure. That is, "You either are going to go to New York or not, that's decided." Some would say, "There's no point in taking a lot of time talking about it. I mean, that's not at all vital. Let's make a decision in the next five minutes whether you are gonna go to New York or not." My view is "Let's take it slow. There's more to going to New York than just a decision." In an immediate situation, why do you want to go? What does New York mean to you? So on and on. I think that is wise to try to think about many different possibilities, not to make a decision rapidly. And I think people need to make good choices. I guess wisdom is making good choices. Choices about a relatively wide group of people, and about a relatively long-time plan.

Author: According to your explanation, somebody who has wisdom doesn't have a lot of problems and can solve problems and prevent problems because he or she makes good choices.

Professor 1: We still have problems because every choice that we make means not making other choices. That is, to make a choice to buy a new car instead of using the old car we have means maybe that the old car is going to be thrown away in a junk yard and that creates a problem or what we do with the old car may make a problem for the next generation if they may not have iron or so and so. Every decision that we make has positive and negative valencies. And we still have to move. We can sit here think and think about it forever. That's a view, I think, I would like people to try to think about as many of the consequences as possible in the time they have.

Author: You have been working over 40 years as a counselor. Also I believe you have been thinking about what life is. What is the difference between a wise person and a good counselor?

Professor 1: Yes. One thing you bring in here is that a wise person needs to think in broad terms, think in terms of consequences and a good counselor does that too. Being relatively wise, being relatively a good chooser oneself, and being self–aware. At least being self–aware is a prerequisite for being a good counselor. Some wise people are not particularly interested in helping other people make good decisions. They're interested in helping composing music or inventing the better carburetor or car or something else. I think that people who choose to try to help other people learn how to make good choices, need to think clearly about themselves and people whom they are in significant relationship with. For those people who decide to go into counseling, I would want them to be wise and therefore I want them to be well read. I would want them to have some understanding of history, economics and ethnicity. I don't see a person being a good counselor and narrowly educated. I think that the narrowly educated person who doesn't read, who isn't aware, who's very ethnocentric, could not be a good counselor. I think that's my objection what I see going on in psychology, more and more emphasis on a narrowing education.

Author: What kinds of wisdom do you think the counselor should have?

Professor 1: The counselor has to be rather self–aware and aware of his/her relation with other people and be a good observer of interrelationship among people and human interaction patterns. That's his/her special area. But as I indicated, I think he also ought to be aware of history, economics, and so on. The fact that we live in a very complex world and which religion, philosophy, physiology and so on, all have an impact on who we are, how we think and feel, how we interact with each other. So I would want the counselor to be curious about lots of things. The person, who is not curious, in my opinion, can't be a good counselor. He may have some techniques and be able to help a few people who are at the particular place and time and so on. As a general rule, I don't think those people are very effective. If you are curious about each individual, you see. However, if I say, "I know I have lots of people just like you and you are in the category 1A and so on, what you need to is...." Now I have you got in a little box. Now I know what to do about you. I will get you out of the box you are in. I don't think that counselor is going to be very effective.

Author: If you need help to solve your problems, what do you think the most important characteristics of the counselor are?

Professor 1: I surely would want a person to be someone who cares about me. You know, if the person wasn't interested in helping me, I wouldn't want to explore myself with a very judgmental person. I wouldn't open up to a person I regard as highly judgmental. If I should, I think maybe that person might give me some advice, but probably I would not open up to that person. I don't like people who can see through me and don't like me. That's threatening to me. Huh, I would like somebody who would be curious about me. How did you try? How have you been doing? What have you been doing? What was your work about? Have you thought about anything different? If that person had ideas about alternatives, I'd be interested in, I would not want to avoid that, and I might think about that. I might say, well, that might work for me. I also would want the person to be able to let go, if he had an idea. I wouldn't want them to keep coming back and hammering and insisting that I see it their way. But I would be interested in their views. Confidentiality is very important to me. Confidentiality and willingness to help me explore what is bothering me. I don't think they would have to be super–persons, you know, who have no problems. I don't see that as important. They might be having some difficulties in some areas they are unsure of themselves. I don't see that as hindering in helping me.

Author: This is a special question. Not kind of either way but you can say both. Please explain which counselor you choose to help with your problems: (a) the counselor who tries to teach wisdom for problem–solving, (b) the counselor who tries to teach techniques or skills for problem–solving.

Professor 1: I think sometimes a person can make suggestions. For example, I might be thinking about maybe changing occupations. You would say "Well, what occupations have you thought about? And what have you done so far to explore those occupations? Where do you think you could get some further information about them?" Or a person would like to say "Well, I know a good book that will tell more about that." That will be fine. So a person might try to be helpful in that way. You might say, "Well, one technique that might work for you, since you are thinking about accounting, and also thinking about being an academic economist. Those two jobs you are thinking about. What would you think about the idea of following an accountant around two or three days and following an economist around two or three days?" So that might be a technique. I don't see any harm in suggesting that. That might be helpful. But whom I am looking for, would be looking for, is somebody who understands that choosing an occupation is a very important choice and has a lot of implications. I would be giving up a lot when I chose the occupation so on and so on. I want somebody to be wise. That would be important? Somebody who understand the ramifications, the difficulty I would experience in establishing a new identity and some of the joy I would experience in establishing a new identity. So I would want s person who had listened to himself/herself inside and who had talked to a lot of people, who had made changes of an occupation. Helpful counselors would be curious about people who had made changes and tried to understand what happened to them and how they talked about them, and what problems arose in their experiences. Then, I would not want somebody who would say "Oh, at your age you should not consider changing an occupation. I have seen that too many people have big problems about it. So don't do it."

Author: You mean kind of a fixed idea.

Professor 1: Yes, that fixed idea would be not very useful. And even a person who would say "Oh, if you're thinking about changing occupations, we have a book here. In chapter four it lists things you ought to do." Ah, I mean, that might be OK. We might consider that. But I wouldn't do that and I wouldn't praise that value.

Author: Do you believe that the counselor is basically a behavioral manager or technician? Or is the counselor more concerned with the 'ends' of human behavior?

Professor 1: I am not interested in a behavioral manager. And I think that people need to give thought to the long range of implication of how they spend time, whom they spend time with, how they spend money, and so on. An examined life isn't worth living, I think. Far too many people do not spend much time thinking broadly and end up life bitter and end up life feeling that they wasted their life. And my view is that life is much too short, anyway. I am having a little trouble to the original question. I am surely not interested in a behavioral manager as a counselor.

Author: Or is the counselor more concerned with the 'ends' of human behavior?

Professor 1: Sure, I think the counselor is concerned with helping people face the end of life with satisfaction about what they did and who they are. Say well, I made mistakes and I hurt some people, but I've gotten better at not doing that. I haven't hurt people intentionally in recent years, and I am trying to make good choices and I think, by and large, I have made good choices. I would say that's life–long satisfaction.

Author: Do you believe that there are general laws which regulate human behavior, such that one can scientifically predict the probable success of counseling techniques?

Professor 1: I think that the counselor is a person who's making choices all the time, who's letting something go by or calling attention to something the client has said. The counselor is sometimes making suggestions about things clients might want to look at or try. That's based on one's experience with other people. So, yea, the counselor is constantly making decisions and about what techniques to used, he is, deciding whether or not to interrupt the client, or let the client continue to talk, whether to suggest to the client that we make some specific plan or something that you will ask the client to do prior to next week, or something like that. How many, how specific that plan ought to be and all that sort of thing. The counselor is making those decisions in part based on her/his past experience with this type of client, with a person with this much anxiety, with these kind of resources and so and so. I think we're playing scientists.

Author: Do you believe that there are general laws....

Professor 1: Yea. I don't think they are always operative. I mean, you know, just because 95% of the people like you enjoy something or not. That doesn't necessarily mean you're in 95%. You might be in 5%. I think it's OK to tell you that 95% of people like you will not like this movie. If you go and see the movie, you might be in 5%.

So I'm telling you something that is factually correct in my opinion. But choice is up to you and I wouldn't want to dictate a solution for you. I might say Korean Christians generally don't have very good marriages with Pakistani Muslims. That wouldn't necessarily mean that if you decided, fell in love with a Pakistani Muslim, that I'd say, "You shouldn't marry that person. I know that's not going to work. You have to make that decision." And always, there are times we choose a way that doesn't look wise, that doesn't lead directly to the goal and so on. And people make those decisions for themselves. I think the counselor just raises the flag and says "Hey, have you thought about this? Are you sure what you want to do?" If the person says, "Yea, I've thought about it. That's the direction I want to go." Or "Let's go that way. We'll look and see how it works out." So we can make a course correction if we're heading for rocks. The counselor leaves the choice to the client.

Author: If you were a client, would you get counseling from a counselor like you?

Professor 1: I think a lot of people would be helpful. You know, I mean it's helpful spending some time with somebody like me. And maybe some people that would find that very distracting would not want that. But I think I could be helpful to most people.

Author: If you think it's helpful, what kinds of benefits would you get from counseling?

Professor 1: I think that persons would have a lot of freedom to go into their own directions. They wouldn't likely be, eh, forced to or pressed into going to one direction rather than another because I don't feel that's my role. They may choose to marry, choose to get divorce or something. I don't have any prejudice that they're getting a divorce, that it is either a good thing or a bad thing. That's something they're working on and deciding after looking at their own situation. I don't feel like I have an agenda. I think that's something they'll get from counseling. At that time they need somebody who cares about them. I think that'll be done. I think I am pretty relaxed about that. If you choose to drop out of the doctoral program, I don't say "Hey, you got invested three years of your life, that would be a stupid thing to say," because I don't know.

Author: Where does wisdom come from?

Professor 1: I think that wisdom comes from being curious

about self and others and interpersonal relationships, and being curious, and well informed, about the broad world. In other words, somebody, who reads, probably knows what's going on in the world, and who sees patterns and can see similarity and dissimilarity between the Hindu and Muslim conflicts in India, Black and White conflicts so on. They are taking time to become well informed and taking time with other people around themselves to find what's going on with them and how they feel about the choices they've made, in the intellectually broad sense, reading all those books and listening to others and also being curious, and asking about and trying to understand the interpersonal dynamics of the people that you know best, those people around you.

Author: Then, how have you been developing your wisdom?

Professor 1: Well, I do a lot of reading and I watch MacNeil and Lechrer news where you get both sides of issues on TV from seven to eight in the evenings and I read the newspaper and I read lots of magazines and read some books. And I try to some time to get to know another people at least around me, some students and faculty that I care about. And I see a different side of life in my other occupation which is being a farmer. So I see people who are not educated and work with them, and talk about a somewhat a different agenda.

Author: You have been working as a professor in a university for many years. What is the best way to teach students in counseling areas to make good counselors?

Professor 1: I think people learn best by doing, I think they have to do some reading, but they have to learn by doing. So I would want people to be doing counseling almost from beginning of reading about counseling. And I want them to talk to other beginning and experienced counselors about what they are doing. I would want them to have as wide a variety of cases as possible. Unless they feel that the variety is too great at present. That is, some people say, "Well, I want to concentrate only right now, by working primarily with adults or only adolescents and so on. I would go along with them. I would accept that for the time being. But I would not keep people from dealing with people who are severely disturbed or who are suicidal and so on." I wouldn't have restrictions on people. I in general would not say, "Well, this person is too sick for you to work with." I think people need a wide variety of people who are, or either have some transitory problem or some major life–crises. I don't think you can learn unless you deal with a broad range. I just think we can't restrict the clientele. I would like people to work at a prison, to work at a mental hospital, work at a home care, work in the school, etc. I would like them to work a lot of different places. The more places they experience as students the better. I would like it. That's why I think, it's wise that we only take people with master's degrees and experience into the doctoral program. Rather than trying to find the brightest young 22 year olds who are bright but who haven't lived very long and haven't had experience with a variety of people, and therefore cannot help their follow students from that experience, they just wouldn't have it. I think our students can learn more from other students than they can from the professors. Partly, just because there are more other students than there are professors. And in our situation at least the students have often had more counseling experience than the professors have, so I would want students to learn from other students as well as professors.

Author: You told me your counseling approach is Carl Rogers' Client–Centered approach. If your counselor or psychotherapist were Freud, or Skinner rather than Rogers, would you get counseling or psychotherapy?

Professor 1: I don't know very much about either of them. I know far less about than I do about Freud. But I think that I could, and would be interested in working with Freud if he tries to be helpful. I think Freud was a person of his time, and not very aware of people who were significantly different from upper middle class Jewish Viennese people. But I think Freud, as you indicated earlier, was a life-long learner. And I would be willing to working with Freud. I don't know much about Skinner. I wouldn't expect to get any help from Skinner.

Author: Mainly, why would you get counseling from Freud and not Skinner?

Professor 1: I guess I wouldn't choose Freud. Freud wouldn't be my first, second, or third choice as a counselor. But Freud was looking in depth at people, mostly trying to understand them, and (to help them) find greater life satisfaction. He surely would not be very judgmental. You know, I like that. I just don't know about Skinner. But it seems to me that Skinner maybe had a kind of simplistic view of that I would be looking at rewards and punishments in a rather narrow way and

.... It seems to me that the problems that we face in life very complex. The issues that we face, the choices we have to make that are significant, are not between a Wendy's hamburger and a McDonald's hamburger. They are more complex than that. I don't know.... I don't think that it's a simple reward/punishment kind of situation.

Author: How do you think the relationship between your level of self-understanding and understanding the client's problem?

Professor 1: Well, if I don't understand myself very well, I probably put some pretty severe limits on what clients can explore and what they can be. I think if I am afraid of an area, then I suspect I am gonna keep them from exploring that area very thoroughly. If I have a very strong vested-interest in the direction I have gone choices I have made and I feel insecure at a deep level about those choices, then I probably will, want other people to make the same choice I did. So I can feel comfortable. So I think I need to have a fair amount of self-understanding to be helpful to people. And if I am uncomfortable..., I probably would make clients be uncomfortable in exploring that. I want to be effective with all kinds of people, I would like to be. If I am not, I would hope that a person would go to somebody else. And hopefully I would be aware that I wasn't being helpful and I would say, "Well, I am sorry. But I, for whatever reason, I don't think I could be of help to you." And I would suggest you go find somebody else.

Author: The beginning young counselors sometimes are afraid of giving counseling because they don't have a lot of experience. What's your opinion about the relationship between your counseling experience and self-understanding?

Professor 1: I don't see having lived a long time being highly correlated with being wise. I think a 24 year old can be wise. And a 64 year old person can be ineffective because they're not wise. I don't think you have to have lived all of the choices or considered all of the alternatives and so on that the client is living with or choosing in order to helpful. I think it's more attitudinal. I stress curiosity more than knowledge; if I had to choose between curiosity and knowledge, I would take curiosity. Openness to another person's experience, openness to the fact that another person may see a different way, may hear a different drummer.

Author: What do you think about the issue of the counselor's value neutral position?

Professor 1: I don't think any of us is value neutral. Really, we try to be more value neutral than most other people. We try to be aware of our lack neutrality and not be insistent that the other persons have the same values that we have. I think that's difficult to do. But I think a striving toward and for that is very helpful. Being very value–neutral is pretty impossible. The view of world we have makes a difference. We know pain and enjoyment; values make difference.

Author: Do you believe that it is appropriate for the counselor to engage in a moral issue in a counseling situation?

Professor 1: I think that a counselor needs to be open about what his/her values are and so that they are not trying to sell values sub rosa, under the table. I think if value differences seem important, I think the counselor ought to say what his or her values are, and try to let go of that, and try to focus on what the client sees as valuable. If the value differences are very great, then the best thing to do is to terminate the client–counselor relationship. The counselor would say, "I am sorry, we are on very different tracks and I find myself uncomfortable with the directions that you are going. I am uncomfortable with decisions you're making relative to other people as well as yourself. And I just don't choose to continue." I don't think I would likely do that very often. I don't think I would be saying, "Well, I think you should spend more time with your child or less money on stereo equipment something like that." I think I'd go easy, very easy on those kinds of things. But I think if I saw a person manipulating other people, hurting other people and not being interested in whether the other person is hurt or not, if that continued for very long, I think I probably would terminate them.

Author: Even though you mean, you don't say directly what is right or wrong, but you suggest kind of indirectly that client should do something.

Professor: I guess it would depend on whether or not I thought the person was interested in, involved in finding the better way, in being more helpful and less hurtful to other people. If they were using the experience with me as a way of becoming a better manipulator, then I would want to dissociate myself with that process.

Author: Would you explain what your position about the

issue of a prenuptial agreement is?

Professor 1: Well, I suppose that if two people came to me and they said, "Well, we would like to, we are thinking about getting married and we're planning to get married and we want to set up a prenuptial agreement." Well, I'm quite willing to talk to you about that. I guess, my thought is that if you are not very trusting of each other, then maybe you ought to wait and not get married until you're more trusting. I am willing to talk about that. Then I would try to help them see why they want a prenuptial agreement, what values they are trying to protect. I suppose that everybody and every relationship have some reservations. There is whether we admit it or not. There are limits to how far we would go with our children, with our spouse or somebody else. I guess my general thought is, if you have to have a prenuptial agreement, you aren't ready to get married.

Author: You mean, your position is "No" to the prenuptial agreement?

Professor 1: No, if they wanted a prenuptial agreement, I would work with them in trying to set that up. But I would say, "I take it that you have a feeling that either you cannot trust this person in the present or you think that in the future this person may no longer value you." If two people want to get married and want to leave money to someone other than the spouse, there are ways of doing that through your will and so on. I think people ought to talk about those things. I would want to know, I would want to focus on a lot on "Why do you feel a need for a prenuptial agreement?" Do you have a reservation about the trustworthiness of...? I don't have a strong objection to a prenuptial agreement but it does seem a little peculiar. I would probably say that.

Author: If you had a client who needed help with a prenuptial agreement, how would you help your client?

Professor 1: I think that if they wanted a prenuptial agreement, I would want to know, "Do you both want that? Or does one of you want that? Why do you want it? What are you trying to preserve? Is it that you are not sure about whether you want to go into this marriage? If you aren't sure about whether you want to go into this marriage, that probably ought to be the main issue." If it is that, suppose, you and your wife were getting married again and you had three young children and she didn't have any young children. You might want to say, "In the event, this doesn't work out, my children by a previous marriage need enough money to be taken care of, therefore...."

Author: When you have value conflicts between yourself and a client, how do you solve that problem? Would you explain about that?

Professor 1: If you had, just as I have said, it's the major value conflicts you think that a person is abusing other people and that they are not trying to be less that way through time, terminate the relationship. There are always gonna be some differences of opinion about what is good or bad for a country or a society, or the economy or something or other. If I had a very strong value, for example, I felt that divorce is never ok, and people who get married should never get a divorce. Then somebody comes to me and says, "We are considering a divorce," then I would say, "I am sorry, I don't think I can work with you. I have got a strong value here on marriage. And you're not in agreement with that. I don't think I hold with you. Or if I felt that I could only work with Christians or I think that women are always taking advantage of men and I think that women are scheming gold-diggers and so on." Then I shouldn't counsel women. And I also should be looking at myself and I am saying, "Why is it that I can only deal with Christians or only with men?" I need to understand myself.

Author: Could you explain what the relationship between wisdom and counseling techniques or skills is?

Professor 1: I just think that there are choices all the time, good choices as to what techniques ought to be effective or not effective here. I guess I could say the counselor is wise when they make relatively good choices about techniques, and if they can give up those temporary choices, if they are ineffective. I don't know if that answered your question.

Author: What is the relationship between wisdom and counseling techniques? I mean, what is similarity or superiority of each other?

Professor 1: Well, you know, wisdom means letting go of things that don't work, and also having a notion as to something which might be helpful. But I guess I don't see wisdom and techniques as being very closely related. And I do think that some techniques work for everyone. Some techniques, A, or B, or C work for some people and not other people, work for one kind of client or not another. So it's choosing what technique might be effective here and if it's not effective, then dropping that and going to something else. I couldn't put a whole lot of emphasis on technique. I think it's much more important who a person is, what kind of person they are rather than what technique they are. Some clients choose to go to a counselor on the basis of whether they were or were not a Gestalist, were or were not an Adlerian, that is probably unimportant.

Author: If you emphasize either wisdom or technique to your student, which would you choose?

Professor 1: I would always come down on the rule of wisdom than technique. Technique can be a little helpful and can give some feeling of security to a beginning counselor that I have some techniques that I can try. But I don't think it's very important.

Author: According to the social influence theory in counseling, there are three important counselor characteristics, that is, expertness, attractiveness, and trustfulness as perceived by the client. Which do you think is the most important variable among those three variables?

Professor 1: I surely think that trustfulness is number one. Attractiveness, I don't see that as related to much of anything. Being expert is probably is the middle position. One hopes one's lifetime to become relatively expert about oneself, but to be expert about other people is much more different, you know, it's an impossible goal. You do come to have some notion that this might work, that might work or something like that. But a person could become expert about himself. Attractiveness, I don't know what that is really something except that we like people who like us or who we think can be helpful to us.

Author: Especially a lot of scholars who are interested in the counselor's power in terms of social influence try to understand what the power of counselor to influence clients is.

Professor 1: I realize there are some counselors that rely on some attractiveness or something to get the client to follow their advice. That is, I have a big, thick rug on the floor. You have to go two or three locked doors and I have a couple secretaries out there. I t makes it hard for you to see me. Then there will be people that think that what I have to say is very important and they will follow my advice. That's not the way to go in counseling. A good counselor would not play that game. Adler would not play that game.

Author: I asked all questions. I learned a lot from this interview. Do you have any comment or feedback about this interview?

Professor 1: I think we learn most by examining our experience. I think that's where we learn most. And I suppose that those people who are able to be really empathetic, who can listen carefully, who can understand carefully what other people around them are experiencing, can grow more rapidly as counselors themselves, because they can learn from the experience of other individuals as well as their own primary experience. And they're some people that just don't learn very much at all. They have one year's counseling experience for 25 years. They don't learn anything in the second, third, fourth years. I feel sorry about that. They can do a lot of damage to the client.

Author: You mean, to be a good counselor, one needs to be self–understanding and continually practice and change ideas and....

Professor 1: I think they have to. And I think that a good counselor can learn from things that their colleagues did, or try, will listen with some care and understanding to what other people have done and I have done. Then look and examine. Say to yourself, "I wonder if I tried that, would I do it in the same way or would I do it differently." Examining one's own experience in light of what someone else has tried and perceived similarity with that counselor, or with that client. I think wisdom is what we all are looking for, trying to increase our wisdom, our understanding of our world and of people helping people find their way in the world. And world keeps changing and we all experience it somewhat differently and we experience it differently than each other. We also experience differently because of where we are in the world, that is, what our social position is in the world, because of our age, because of our health. And the person who is self-aware would more likely to be able to put that aside or see that I am biased in this because of where I am. And the person, who doesn't see that, in my opinion, is not wise and is not likely to be a good helper. That's my summation of what I think.

Chapter 5

WISDOM IN A COGNITIVE BEHAVIOR PERSPECTIVE

Introduction of Transcript 2: This interview was done on October 5, 1990. When the Professor 2 was interviewed, he was the professor of counseling psychology and his age was fifty–four years old. On that time his career experience of studying of counseling psychology was twenty–eight years. He still works in the University of Kentucky and right now he is seventy–four years old. He indicated that his theoretical orientation of counseling was a cognitive behavioral therapy.

Author: First, I would like to ask several questions about your personal backgrounds. How old are you?

Professor 2: I am 54.

Author: What was your motivation when you decided to study counseling?

Professor 2: Ah, the decision to become a counselor was based upon least three major experiences. And in the first case, I did not have adequate counseling when I was growing up in high school and in social settings. Guidance was simply guidance and there was nothing else. So when I was in college I tried to learn a little bit more about myself and visited, for a semester or so the counseling center. That experience was more of a game than a process that resulted in any substantial outcome. However, near the end of my junior year in college I was invited to visit in California after I spent a summer in British Columbia working in the fields, when I got to California I was able to worked on by my aunt who happened to be a therapist. And that was some awfully good experiences for me; good in the sense that it clarified a lot things that happened as I was growing up. And when I graduated from college I returned to California where I worked and continued to be worked upon. The benefit of receiving good things in a counseling or therapeutic relationship was an important influence for me to become one of these things. The second influence was that when I was in Navy, I managed to defend in a court marshal a young man who had also not received particularly good counseling leading up to the time I got hold of him. And I decided that the combined effect of discovering that there are a whole lot of people who had the characteristic of being in need and that I seem to myself get a lot out of receiving that kind of help; those two things added together for me to say, "Hey, this is what I want to be when I grow up." Ok. I didn't know until I started to apply to doctoral programs that my family has had a long tradition of teaching like five generations of teaching.

Author: Your father also was a teacher?

Professor 2: No, but my aunts were. I have both sides of my family, either parents, siblings or grandparents, siblings or grandparents and their parents who were various kinds of teachers. So in another sense, one that I did not know until I'd already made the decision to become. My family has had a long tradition of teaching. So I was sort of stuck. I became what my history suggested that I would become, plus I became what I am.

Author: Right now, what is your main philosophical or theoretical orientation of counseling?

Professor 2: The main theoretical orientation of counseling could be one of at least two answers. One, I am the latter day what I am, that is, I do what is comfortable with me and the theory is derived from my background. That is a flip answer. If you want a label for what I am, I am probably close to a cognitive behavioral counselor.

Author: When did you start studying counseling areas?

Professor 2: I began to prepare for a counselor in the spring of 1962.

Author: How long have you been working as a counselor?

Professor 2: Well, I know, in 1962 and I think in 1963, I was taking undergraduate psychological courses because I was not a psychology major. And I began to work on master's degree in January of 1964. I was admitted to the doctoral program in the fall of 1964. I graduated in the spring of 1969. Your arithmetic on how long I have been working as a counselor might be right if you start in 1962.

Author: Then, let's go to the main questions of this interview.

What is wisdom? Would you define and describe what wisdom is according to your personal and counseling experience?

Professor 2: Wisdom is a thing that young people do not have, which middle age do not have, which old people do have. Wisdom is a way that logic is expressed to young people. And the way is important because the way is a style, a method of transmitting logic and the experience from one generation to another. That's the behavioral way of looking at wisdom because it has to do with how those ideas are transmitted. It has nothing to do with the philosophical basis of wisdom. It has to do with the behavioral questions of wisdom. How do you get it? Through two kinds of experiences; reading about it and doing it.

Author: According to your explanation, wisdom is related to age. Is that right?

Professor 2: Right.

Author: In the same way, what is not wisdom? Would you define and describe what wisdom is not from your personal and counseling experiences?

Professor 2: Wisdom is probably not common knowledge.

Wisdom is something to which not everyone has access. If everybody knows about what it is, that's not wisdom. Wisdom is something special.

Author: Would you explain further about that?

Professor 2: OK. If every knows about it, that's not wisdom. But if somebody doesn't know about it, and has to ask about it, remember that stuff, that's asked about it, that's beginning of wisdom. Once everybody knows it, it's no longer wisdom. Common knowledge is not wisdom. Somebody answered what is wisdom question. Common knowledge does not know why, common knowledge does not why not. Wisdom struggles with why and why not.

Author: What is the difference between a wise man and a good counselor?

Professor 2: All right, a good counselor has that judgment made about them when they perform ways which people call good. So good might be being effective. Good might be having a good relationship with somebody, but not necessarily being effective, but might be because they went to some fancy training place. Good really depends upon somebody else's judgment of this performance. A good counselor may not know anything about wisdom. A good counselor may be extremely effective with techniques. A good counselor can use a cookbook and solve all the problems of the world. A wise person can observe many of the variables which influence a person's behavior, and that wise person can ask many, 'what if' questions about those variables, "What if we try this, what will happen?" A wise person can ask questions that can't be answered. A wise person cannot have an effect on changing behavior at the client. So it is possible to have a counselor who is a wise person who cannot help a client change. It is possible to have a very good counselor who can change behavior but does not have a system of values related to any wisdom. You are going to look for a very long time to find that person, who can both ask and answer questions, who can both think about and transmit whatever they think about words or actions which will help a client change behavior. So if you want a very simple way to answer your question, a wise person can think, a good counselor can do, it is unusual to find a thinker and doer in one person. I've been through that sequence before. I know that one.

Author: Then, what kinds of wisdom do you think the counselor should have?

Professor 2: Oh, wow! That's toughy. I fall back on Freud for that. I don't go back any earlier. Three things are important: work, love, and play. A counselor, a therapist or whatever you want to call that person, needs to know much about the things, the stuff, that make up work, love and play both in general and for the individual. Those three things are what people do in either balance or imbalance. That's what makes a client or clients because they don't have one of those things figured out. A therapist needs to know as much about each of those as they can learn — book learning, maybe experience — so that they can translate those knowledge which, if they put together, uniquely become wisdom into client terms. That way of thinking is probably a logical positive way of thinking and not a very cognitive behavioral. But that's all right. That is a mechanistic way of thinking but it's an useful way of thinking. Not going back much further than Freud.

Author: Still I didn't get an exact picture about a good counselor's characteristics related with wisdom. Would you explain what kinds of wisdom the counselor should have?

Professor 2: They should have knowledge about how to understand the relationships between the things that make up work, love, and play. Wisdom is being able to observe the elements, the stuffs that make something up. In this case I am saying work, love, and play. How to carry out. Work, love and play is career, family and leisure, depends upon what the client wants to talk about, work, love and play apply and how to take that stuff and turn it into client language. You can do that if you are mechanical, if you know only how to be a good counselor.

Author: If you need help to solve your problems, what do you think the most important characteristics of the counselor are?

Professor 2: If I want to find a counselor, what kind of counselor do I want? Oh, my goodness, gracious. All right, let's think about that for a while. The kind of counselor that I want has wisdom. The kind of counselor I don't want is one that has a bag of tricks. So what I don't want is a good counselor, but what I do want is a wise counselor who has wisdom. As far as I believe, a bag of tricks will not have a permanent solution because

I believe that the wisdom which is seeing relationships might have a permanent effect. So what I want is a wise counselor: one who is probably older than I (and at this stage that' s becoming hard to find); one who has had experience with whatever I am working on; one who in my opinion is better than I–better, more experience, effective. All that stuff that makes up a good counselor but they better be wise. If they give me a cookbook answer, they waste their energy. I don't want to put up with it.

Author: Would you explain which counselor you would choose to help your problems? (a) the counselor who tries to emphasize wisdom for problem–solving; (b) the counselor who tries to teach techniques or skills for problem–solving.

Professor 2: What I prefer is a wisdom counselor.

Author: Why?

Professor 2: Because once that kind of person begins to work on me, I will be able to ask questions that will make me develop techniques. The guess that I have is what the wisdom counselor would be able to increase my own personal breath of wisdom. My guess further is that the bag of tricks counselor would not do anything to my wisdom. So given a choice, I want a wise counselor, I would. All right, there are million people in the world who wouldn't want a wise counselor. They don't want that stuff. They want to know how to fix it right now. That's the place for the technique-oriented people.

Author: Do you believe that the counselor is basically a behavioral manager or technician? Or is the counselor more concerned with the 'ends' of human behavior?

Professor 2: I don't like your question because I do not see your use of the word or as correct. I do not see a behavioral manager or technician to be the same thing. I do not see a behavioral technician to be the same thing as a behavioral manager because management implies for me a far broader frame of reference than behavioral technician.

Author: OK. Then, a behavioral technician.

Professor 2: All right. Now you want to ask me the question again with behavioral technician then. I don't like that one either because both are asking the same thing. One's means and one is ends. A technician is the means that ends.

Author: I raised this question because I recognized that a lot of counselors emphasize techniques too much whenever I read books.

Professor 2: I guess the answer that I will feel comfortable with is that whether you want a technician or a person who is interested in the ends, depends upon what the client wants. If the client wants something fixed right now, probably the technician is the one who can fix it right now. There are lots of clients who want things fixed right now. And the problem becomes for those people, is that maybe something else will come up that needs also to be fixed. So it's like repairing a car that's going old. You keep on fixing this, fixing that and fixing something else. And it might be, it's choice that people can make. You want to fix the little parts or you want to work on something else, something bigger. The problem becomes if you spend all your time working on the little things. There is a good chance that the joy, the satisfaction that's derived from the process of working on the little things. It's like being hypochondriac. You keep on coming back for more for whatever eats thing of whatever happen. All right, when that happens, you can get taken all over the briar patch looking for something. Incredibly a wise counselor would say, after the second or third time, "Don't go all over this briar patch. I don't think we are doing it quite right. Let's spend some more time becoming wiser about what we are doing. Maybe what you want is not what you really need. So I am going to impose my values on you and I am going to do some sorting and I am going to choose what I view." What a wise man views. What my wisdom suggests is the right way to go. I think you don't know that's going to happen until the second or third symptom is worked upon. There are some agencies that put out flyers that deal with symptoms. And it's not really helping the person alone.

Author: I think you still didn't answer my question. Mainly you explained from the client's intention. My question is "Do you believe that the counselor is basically a behavioral technician? Or is the counselor more concerned with the 'ends' of human behavior?"

Professor 2: I don't think that has an answer. I don't think that one is an either/or kind of thing because each of those techniques solve problems which are a part of a larger end. So I don't think it's fair. It's not fair to pin down me or to pin down a counselor who is wise to make them choose between the technique and the end.

A wise counselor, one who has had experience, knowledge and some other things will say, "Hey, each of those techniques is a part of a larger picture. So don't pin me down." A young one will say, "Oh, I can give you technique number 32 and it will work." It's fine as long as it works. When the 32 doesn't work, either there is panic, which is the beginning of wisdom, or they give up, which is another beginning of wisdom, or they leave their profession, which is great wisdom. I think you got to be able to juggle things that work with things that don't work in helping people. So don't pin me down. It's not an either/or.

Author: Do you believe that there are general laws which regulate human behavior, such that one scientifically predicts the probable success of counseling techniques?
Professor 2: Yes.

Author: Would you explain further?
Professor 2: I believe when you describe in detail your intervention so that a person can imitate, repeat or duplicate the intervention, your strategy or whatever for the same kind of client with the same kind of problem under the same kind of settings, then, you can begin to

assign probability values to counseling strategies. I believe that can be done. I believe that is not being done because people are afraid to depart from what they believe to be wisdom. Therapy is a mystery. I am not gonna tell you what really happens. People are afraid to share the secrets and to teach other people what works. What works is an expression of the philosophical underpinning, the wisdom of the counseling. In other words, all those little skills a counselor has, a wise counselor has, are expressions of those various assumptions, values of the counselor. I believe it is possible to analyze a counselor's behavior and to convert it into reproducible behavior. My evidence for that belief is found in two experts by the analysis of Rogers' Client–Centered Therapy in the Journal of Abnormal & Social Psychology, 1966, Volume, pages, whatever it was. It was true. It was demonstrated that Rogers manipulated human behavior. And second, Neuro–Linguistic Programming is a mathematical model of a counseling process by a man named Milton Erikson. So I think it works. It's not popular. It takes the out of it, makes it more like medicine. But I think there are such things as treatments of choice.

Author: If you were a client, would you get counseling from a counselor like you?

Professor 2: Probably not.

Author: Why?

Professor 2: Because it would be like being counseling by mirror. I would want something that complements me. I can't talk to my mirror all day long! I would rather deal with somebody who was wiser than I, who might have the same values who was different. I don't know the same thing.

Author: Then, what kind of characteristics would you seek for?

Professor 2: I go back to the characteristics of a wise counselor. Those characteristics for a wise counselor, wise person, wise whatever it was, will be the kind of person whom I would seek out. I would hope that once the relationship was established with this wise person, the discussion of techniques would reveal ways that I could improve or reduce the mistakes that I was making.

Author: According to your experience, where does wisdom from?

Professor 2: Wisdom comes from common experience of man, observed by somebody who is wise. Read the book — Lao Tzu's Te-Tao Ching — you gave me. Those are common experience but they are observed by somebody who is wise and that becomes wisdom. If somebody doesn't observe those common experience, knowledge, behavior, and try to make sense out of them, then he isn't very wise. So wisdom is derived from the human experience.

Author: Then, how have you developed your wisdom?

Professor 2: Oh, I am supposed to develop wisdom? Oh, I find that to be terribly interesting, I didn't know I was supposed to develop wisdom. I was not part of the agenda. All right, wisdom occurs or is developed by my trying to learn what I really need to know about what domains. I probably have a pretty good wisdom related to how to survive the graduate school experience at the University of Kentucky. For example, I probably have absolutely no wisdom on how to deal with substance abuse. Wisdom that I acquire is derived from experience and reading in given areas. It's not at all purposes kind of thing. And that really isn't wisdom. Maybe there is a higher wisdom than a specific wisdom which I am talking about. My wisdom is limited to certain domains.

Author: Would you explain more about certain domains?

Professor 2: Certain domains will be like the domain of how to survive the University of Kentucky graduate school experience. With lots of experience with young children, I would probably acquire wisdom in dealing with young children. With lots of experience in divorce or family mediation, I would probably develop lots of wisdom. In these areas I would develop lots of wisdom, because I would have a chance to observe, to ask questions about the relationships between the various elements of the stuff that makes up that domain. So wisdom is acquired through reading and doing.

Author: What is the best way to teach in counseling areas to make good counselors?

Professor 2: Oh, well, now wait just minute here. Do you want to train people to become good counselors? Or do you want to train to become wise counselors? If you want to train them to become good counselors, it's a matter of teaching them techniques, how to do it, how to evaluate it, when to do it for what kind of problem. That's over the area in that technique–oriented, highly behavioral logical positivist side of things.

Author: You still didn't answer my question. Would you explain how to teach students to make good counselors?

Professor 2: Is that your definition of good or my definition of good?

Author: Definitely, your definition.

Professor 2: My good counselor has a little bit of wisdom. OK, and a little bit of wisdom is like an infection it spreads and spreads and spreads. All right, how do I make somebody a good counselor is by having them focus upon both what they can do well and what they can badly, because I believe that what any person must see is both their successes and failures. And I believe that a good counselor can identify what they can do. A wise counselor can do something about what they can do. What I would do in teaching somebody to become a wise counselor is to have them tell me about their successes and tell me about what they can't do. I believe they can handle anything which I know they can't do.

Author: You mean you would emphasize some kind of wisdom?

Professor 2: I would be emphasizing a kind of wisdom to be able to say "I can do or I can't do." To make some decisions based on observation and to either act or not. That's the beginning of wisdom because they start to ask that question. They might be helping somebody, is their being changed. The fact that they even ask the question is the beginning of wisdom.

Author: You told me you are close to the cognitive behavioral counselor. Now, if your counselor or psychotherapist were Freud or Rogers, would you get counseling or psychotherapy?

Professor 2: If I had either one of those, I'd probably have, "Well, there two answers." One, well, I probably won't have anything to do with it. That's one answer. But there is another interesting part of that. They might be Rogerian and they might be Eriksonian. And there are values in their preference. But what they do might be very different because what Freud dictate by his description of a person's development, what the preferred treatment is and he doesn't tell you what it must be. Rogers says this is how you teach a client to develop one to one, talking about yourself. Freud doesn't have a treatment of choice. I do not know. Further a person's theoretical background will override my choice of therapist if I happen to like the therapist, that is, to say the personality of the therapist might override any other decision or any other criteria? Helping because not staying in the theory is important. I don't know. My first reaction is that I probably won't deal with a Freudian. Freudians are no longer true and blue. They are no longer what they used to be. They are all mixed up with other things. If that brand mixed-up was presented in a pleasant way, I might go with it, I might not. If I had somebody who had little gritty in black suit and white shirt and had me lie on a couch, I probably tell him to go fly a kite. If I had somebody who was pleasant and carry on a different kind of expression, that's fine. I think it's awfully hard to find today somebody who is a pure almost anything. That why I said one answer is I am, the latter day what I am. You don't think that anybody is that pure.

Author: You prefer a cognitive learning therapist rather than Freudian or Rogerian.

Professor 2: Oh, yeah, I probably prefer, know that there is more to behavior change that a limited way that either of those positions seems to go. They need to be more interaction. Interaction will have to do with the personality of the agent of change.

Author: You mean, you wouldn't get counseling or psychotherapy from Freud or Rogers?

Professor 2: On a desert or island if I had no other choices, I'd probably go with them. But we don't live on desert or island. So I could try to get somebody who had a little more possession, a little bit more excitement than either of those two people or two kinds of people.

Author: What do you think of the relationship between your level of self–understanding and understanding the client's problems?

Professor 2: A lot of my understanding of the clients' problem depends upon my ability to ask questions about the clients on the level of understanding about their problems. In other words, I have to ask a lot of questions in order to get to a level where I am comfortable about clients' problems. I cannot accept at face value a client's self reported problem. I need to probe, make sure that the client presents that valid or reliable problem. If the problem goes away in the course of the dialogue, then it probably isn't a problem. What I want to do is to find out just how big this problem is.

Author: My question is your level of understanding yourself about understanding the client's problem.

Professor 2: You mean my level of self-understanding either interferes or facilitates my understanding of the client's problem.

Author: Yes.

Professor 2: All right. I believe that my self-understanding or a therapist self-understanding does interfere with the clients' ability to express their problem. And that goes far enough to say a therapist or counselor, a wise person, needs to know what client's problem areas are okay or and what client's problems are not okay. A wise man will know that not all client's problems are okay, that the therapist, the good counselor, the agent of change cannot be all things to all men.

What you have to is find out what things you can't. Why do they help somebody else? I think if you come to a level of understanding or higher level of understanding — I am going to work on this and I am not gonna work on something else, that is one level on understanding. It's a good level of understanding. A bad level of understanding is, "Gee, I don't know what I am gonna do." I am overwhelmed by the whole thing. And the client doesn't benefit from the therapist not having a higher level of understanding about each of the various client problem areas. A counselor who cannot handle the client's problem is not going to help the client. So the counselor needs to learn to become wise, see the strengths and weaknesses to whether deal with it or not.

Author: What do you think about the issue of the counselor's value neutral position?

Professor 2: I think it's a full of bunk. I think a counselor has a valued position and I think that anybody who says that a counselor has a value free position is not wise, is technique–oriented person. I think that every counselor's value is to interact in the relationship that some of those values facilitate, some of those values interfere but they are acting. Anybody who says they are not has their heads in the sand.

Author: Do you believe that it is appropriate for the counselor to engage in moral issue in a counseling situation?

Professor 2: Sometimes the counselor has already worked those moral things through and can deal with them.

Other times a counselor should say "I can't deal with them." It's important to know your limits. I think it is important for a counselor to learn their limits, to be within yourselves.

Author: You mean you support the counselor's dealing moral issues in a counseling situation?

Professor 2: Yeah, if you have some thoughts on the topic or you've worked them through and you feel comfortable with them. That's ok. But for those things you don't feel comfortable, don't touch them.

Author: What is your opinion on the issue of prenuptial agreement?

Professor 2: That's easy for me. It is consistent with my previous statements. I hadn't thought about it. So I have nothing to say about it. However if you want me to think about it?

Author: Please think about that, right now.

Professor 2: All right. Now, what I do are two things. I have the value that says 'prenuptial agreements interfere with normal marital relationships.' I have that value. What I would do is take that value and try it out some people whose opinion I respect. I would some wise counselor on that topic, present my value, present the question, present my value and listen. I might not change it. I might change.

Author: Change?

Professor 2: I might change! But right now I don't like them.

Author: If you had a client who needed help with a pre-nuptial agreement, how would you help your client?

Professor 2: If I had a client who needed help with that, oh fine, I would say, "Hey, I don't know anything about these things." Now, is what you are talking about, the fact that you want a lawyer to help you write one up? Fine, I will get you a lawyer. If you're talking about is the fact that you don't like them either and you don't want to talk about it or you do want to talk about them. I can talk about them but don't know anything about them. I don't think that's very good. Or we can bring somebody else in, who knows something about them, then they can talk, "What do you want to do?" I really think it would be a mistake to have my ignorance added to the client's ignorance. What I would prefer is not to talk about it, to talk to a lawyer about it, that is, to have the client talk to the lawyer about it or me talk to the lawyer, or to seek wise counseling from somebody else.

Author: Then you don't give counseling?

Professor 2: I would try not to touch that one with a ten foot pole. I would try to stay away from that–simply because I haven't had any experience with it. Remember, experience precedes wisdom? Isn't that interesting? Experience precedes wisdom!

Author: When you have value conflicts between yourself and a client, how do you solve that problem?

Professor 2: Okay, Anybody will have value conflicts with anybody else not all the time but sometimes. Knowing about a value conflict is to know what your values are. So you talk about that stuff and try to figure out what your values are so that if there is a conflict you can say, "Hey, you and I are having a value conflict. I don't buy what you are talking about. Now either we can talk about my not buying your idea, or we can talk about what you're going to do to solve your particular problem." But I might not be a part of that solution. Maybe some of those value conflicts might be simply hypothesis testing by the client, maybe simply trying to get their own values clarified. There is real honesty, goodness, and well developed thought through values, and the client is therefore wise. On that area if there is a conflict, I don't buy it. Then I am gonna send the client somebody else, Or I am gonna get the client a choice — he can talk about it but I am not gonna listen. There will be value conflicts. Sometimes, they come up really quickly and mess up the whole relationship. Other times they come up after the relationship has developed and you can spend time exploring that value conflict. That's maybe fine. What you don't want to do is to go out and find a value conflict in the first week of therapy. You can have all these arguments and get it behind, build your credibility. So the client believes what you have to say. How do you do that?

Author: Mainly this value conflict problem could be what I asked you about the prenuptial agreement and what your position about it is. Whether you agree with it or not, I think that's a big value conflict.

Professor 2: On the issue of prenuptial agreement versus value conflict, all right. Prenuptial agreement for me is a very clear–cut value conflict. Your conflict might not be very clear, or your conflict might be a preference for peach ice-cream versus strawberry ice-cream. Then it's no big deal. I am not gonna worry about that one that much. The things that are beyond me outside of my limits, I am gonna try to find somebody who knows more about it than I do. I don't try to deal with those things that are beyond me. I am wise. OK, I am exhibiting wisdom! That answers you?, all right.

Author: Could you explain what the relationship between wisdom and counseling techniques or skills is?

Professor 2: Yes. Wisdom, as I've laid out several times, what it is. Counseling techniques or skills are those things which make up a good counselor — a bunch of techniques, a bunch of skills. It's a cookbook. You can pick it out of anywhere and say, "For this particular situation we do this, all right." Now those techniques or skills are easily taught, they are behavioral events that can be mastered, they are techniques which when a person does them well, they can do anywhere to solve a problem. A person, who does not have wisdom, does use those techniques anywhere. He performs those well-developed techniques all over the plays and fails to exhibit wisdom. Wisdom says, "Hey, I got all those techniques, now. I am gonna choose when to use those techniques." Wisdom occurs when you begin to know the relationships among the things, among the stuff that's surrounding the client, around the client's work, love and play. As you get more wisdom, you will be able to choose more wisely those techniques that are going to help the clients. If you are a wise counselor, you'll also have a lot of techniques. Of course, there are wise counselors that have absolutely no techniques.

Author: According to the social influence theory in counseling areas, there are three important counselor characteristics, that is, expertness, attractiveness, and trustfulness as perceived by the client. Which do you think is the most important variable among those variables?

Professor 2: The most important of the three? Oh, I think that trustfulness is the most important of the three. I think that attractiveness is least important of the three. Expertness, that's the middle.

Author: Would you explain about that?

Professor 2: OK. Why? All right, attractiveness occurs when the environment surrounding the client and therapist is pleasant. That is, all the diplomas are up there, the rug color is pleasant, the pictures are nice, the therapists has had warts removed from the top of his nose, looks nice. That's about how deep it is too. OK, skin deep. Expertness, that's techniques. I think you need to know at least Rogerian techniques. You probably need a few more other techniques on top of relationship skills. What you really need is that ability to make the client feel that they are in a safe environment. If a client feels that they are in a safe environment, he will produce or get a sense of trust.

Author: How do you think about the relationship between counselor's power in terms of social influence and counselor's wisdom?

Professor 2: All right. Earlier, I already said that a value–free counselor is bunk. I believe further that a counselor is not equal to the client, but the counselor is superior in social influence to the client. After all the client is paying money for this service. After all, the client seeks out this special kind of person–a therapist, a counselor, an agent of changes, and this client expects things to happen, unequal things to happen. So when you hear or some therapist says, "Oh, I need to work with my clients. I am not dealing with that. fine, I believe you. Now, will you give me your evidence?" Now when you say, "I believe you. That's not being very trustful. Okay? Let me see your evidence." The evidence that I look for on this uniqueness will be who leads the dialogue, who chooses the topics. By choosing and asking questions, you have signaled your own values to what things you encourage, to what things you discourage — it's back to Rogers, and his relationships. So don't tell me that the social influence is insignificant, that it is not important that the counselor does not have a leadership responsibility because they do all right now. When wisdom fits in with all that, wisdom occurs and fits into all that. When a counselor begins to believe that they have power over the client, it is important you have trust, expertise and even a tab of attractiveness. You can be a little ugly. But wisdom occurs when the stuff, and in this case we have defined the stuff, the stuff is social influence; trust, expertise, attractiveness and the stuff goes further because you can define each of those more. But wisdom occurs when you know and you can talk about the stuff that is influencing the client. So that's a relationship among those various things. You will notice I use the word 'thing' a lot, use the word 'stuff' a lot. Because I was told by logical positivists that the technical terms to describe, that makes up our philosophical environment.

Author: Why don't you use the word 'fact'?

Professor 2: because they are facts, some of them are not facts, some are not reproducible, some of them are opinions, attitudes, and values.

Author: OK, now I want to listen to your comment and feedback about this interview and questions.

Professor 2: OK, feedback and comment about questions. I didn't believe in talking for an hour and half. I feel sorry for you because you have to type it all up. Three; for me it was a good experience to wrestle with the therapeutic model which you are advocating. And as a result of that wrestling, I am probably wiser. Thanks.

Chapter 6

WISDOM IN A PHENOMENOLOGICAL PERSPECTIVE

Introduction of Transcript 3: This interview was done on November 19, 1990. When the Professor 3 was interviewed, he was the professor of counseling psychology and his age was 64 years old. On that time his career experience of studying of counseling psychology was forty-one years. Currently he lives in Charleston, South Carolina after his retirement and he is eighty-four years old. He indicated that his theoretical orientation of counseling was a phenomenological approach in a broad extension.

Author: First, I would like to ask several questions about

your personal backgrounds. How old are you?

Professor 3: I am 64.

Author: Why did you choose counseling as your career?

Professor 3: Why did I choose counseling? OK. I really didn't. I was interested in learning and in human behavior, and at the time I began looking at the field. Counseling didn't really exist as such except clinical psychology, because we are talking early fifties and I studied essentially para-clinical psychology. All right.

Author: OK. Then, what was your motivation in deciding to study counseling?

Professor 3: Motivation? Well, I think I kind of answered that. I got into counseling more by accident because during the 1950's I was in Idaho after I finished my dissertation and my degree at Idaho State, and I was the only person really in counseling and another person who had any kind of background and there was a national defense education grant which each state could apply for and I applied and got the institutes for training counselors for three years in a row in Idaho. I also was director of the University Counseling Center and the testing area. So, I had the background in really clinical school counseling and a lot of different things. So I can't say that I ever studied counseling as a course. I did have some of the courses you people have, but I had other kinds of courses, I mean, I just was not an APA program. Okay? Let's go on.

Author: I want to know what is your main theoretical orientation.

Professor 3: It's very difficult for me to answer. It's like saying what form of Buddhism are you in, what form of Confucianism do you believe in, what form of Christianity? The various approaches to counseling are all based in one way or the other on what an individual's human nature, on what the thinks human nature is, I am perhaps very much phenomenological. Phenomenology is the greatest extension of that word. It includes existentialism; it includes behavioral approaches; it also includes psychodynamics. I believe nobody should be a counselor without a good understanding in a pyschodynamic theory and I think that the reason why people do certain things in life is because of the existential fact that time is always limited. To go further than that I would say that behavioral techniques are very superficial; they work only as long as the reinforcement is continued but they do nothing about the internal representation or perception of the human mind and that's the most important.

Author: OK, then when did you start studying the counseling area?

Professor 3: Well, I think I have kind of answered that question. My courses were in clinical psychology where courses were not defined the way they are today. It was a psychologist curriculum, and counseling was considered part of it, but it was more like studying therapy. In terms of actual investigating of theoretical areas relative to counseling, I began that really with the preparation for my book in counseling theory which was all through the 1960's. I did my doctoral dissertation on Freud and the historical perspective and philosophical background that influenced him. How long have I been working as a counselor? Well, you know, I have been in this program for 21 years. I taught counseling courses at Idaho, at California and here. I certainly have been working every year doing counseling either as my job or a part of my teaching since 1959.

Author: Let's go to the main questions of this interview.

What is wisdom? Would you define and describe what wisdom is according to your personal and counseling experiences?

Professor 3: I believe that wisdom is something that was defined by Aristotle as the pursuit and application of virtue. I think Aquinas also refers it as a form of a higher skill what he calls synderesis–the application of principles of life to specific problems with a perspective. I think Maslow, from the counseling point of view, is perhaps the one who comes closest to understand the hierarchy of human needs that goes up, finally to the top of the hierarchy to identifying whether that which you need comes to terms with the world. I think that wisdom is essentially the habit of virtue and virtue is related to judgment — making appropriate judgment within the sequence and order of your own life and that of other people.

Author: In the same way, would you define and describe what wisdom is not from your personal and counseling experiences?

Professor 3: It is not a technical competence. It is a knowing how to do this or that or how to deal with applications because no two circumstances are ever alike. So I think by and large that a program which is technique–oriented misses the whole vision of what it is to be a good person, a rational person, a logical person, and above all to be a wise person. Wisdom is not a state that one can enter into and remain. It is a constant seeking for perfection. I think that for the most part people entering into counseling today are motivated essentially by entrepreneurial and financial needs. They wish to make money and set up a shop, and lots of times they really meddle in people's lives without knowing what to do. So I think if a person is wise, it in spite of counseling. Wisdom is something that is helpful if that is part of the character of a person. But if it is not part of the character, then counseling can be a very hollow and shallow experience both for the counselor and the client.

Author: What you are saying reminds me kind of Socrates versus Sophists. Sophists tried making money, selling knowledge.

Professor 3: It is the pursuit of wisdom. That's why they call it the pursuit of wisdom. It doesn't matter how old one is. One can always become wiser and one begins to understand more and more as years pass.

Author: Then, what is the difference between a wise person and a good counselor?

Professor 3: I think a person may be a good counselor but not necessarily wise. The two are not all–inclusive terms. A good counselor may be a person who is technically quite competent. Whether there is wisdom, there is a fact that is not easy to determine. I have always said this to students: "Do not take a person apart unless you know how to put them back together again." So I've always been very cautious in terms of counseling and in terms of what I do because I think that you can you can injure psychologically. I think that a good counselor ought to have elements of wisdom, ought to be concerned about other people. Probably, it's because this is a motive for entering this profession. Studying counseling does not necessarily make you wise, and more than studying philosophy makes you a philosopher, or studying religion makes you virtuous. It is something totally outside of that. I used to believe that the most and greatest insights in religion came through Christian tradition until I spent six months in Taiwan. And then I realized there are many wise people who were not Christians, who were maybe Buddhists, enlightened Buddhists and maybe Confucian. It would appear that responsibility and moral judgment is not the province of one religion specifically but rather of all religion. All religions are faces of God. God is imperceptible and untouchable and we only understand God through other people. And so as we grow older, we can meditate on any one of the great religions, the great religious traditions. There is a great deal of food for thought. There are ways and means that other religions like Buddhism have learned to access themselves to higher orders of consciousness. I think that is all important. I am not sure that the kinds of people who go into counseling have the kind of scholarly background in classics or an understanding of history and culture that might lead them to these kind of conclusions. I don't think that being a good counselor is necessarily identical with beginning on the path of wisdom. In fact, I have seen many people who have become very popular as counselors and who devote most of their time and energy to the running of seminars in order to tell them what is the right way to do things. They may consider that this is wisdom. But it is not in my view. I think the wise man is indeed like Socrates. The wise person knows how to ask the right questions. He may not know what a right answer is but he continues being a seeker of the truth.

Author: Then, what kinds of wisdom do you think the counselor should have?

Professor 3: Real practical wisdom. The practical knowledge to know when not to do something and to know when to do something and above all to know what is the difference the two; when it is possible to help and when it is only possible to be supportive. I see counseling as that kind of thing, you know. Counseling, like a lot of other things in life, is an imposition from outside. The only person that we can truly change the behavior is ourselves. Everyone else has to change his or her own behavior. Sometimes you can have considerate influence on people and sometimes we have a little influence. Very little things often make life-long changes. So I think that in so far as the counselor knows what he/she can do and what he/she cannot do, that this is a kind of practical wisdom.

Author: Everybody has a kind of problem. Now, if you need help to solve or cure your problems, what do you think the most important characteristics of the counselor are?

Professor 3: Well, I think in general, if I can answer that in general, probably the first important characteristic is the ability to listen and to be, non–judgmental, in the sense of foreclosing on ideas. I think many times people solve their own problems just hearing themselves talk. So I think that is one of the first important characteristics. After that I think a good counselor needs to be aware of individual differences. You have had my course, so you know that I believe in assessment. You can do assessment through an interview. You can look at strengths and weaknesses, and do some assessment through testing. All that has to be put into perspective of what the client wants to do, what the problem is, and how one can go about it. Some problems in counseling can be solved by listening, others by more detailed assessment and more diagnosis, and some need just learning skills and how to find out where the information is. None of these works at all if the counselor doesn't have knowledge. Knowledge in assessment and in diagnosis is important. In fact I am just telling you what is in my book and that's what I believe. In other words, I just don't believe that all questions of counseling and all problems can be solved just by listening and being non–directive. I think counselors must be pro–active.

Author: Would you explain which counselor you would choose to help your problems? First, the counselor who tries to emphasize wisdom for problem-solving, second, the counselor who tries to teach techniques or skills for problem-solving.

Professor 3: Well, That's a hard question for me to say. I have never thought of it exactly like this. I think usually people who come for counseling want some immediate help. So I think that one should focus on the techniques and the skills, and after that if counseling goes on for some time, then perhaps wisdom can be a part of the process. I think that it is very difficult to teach wisdom, techniques of wisdom. One learns more by models. I think throughout our entire lives we are constantly searching for models, individuals who can tell us show us how to do better. That's final stage of Maslow's hierarchy. Most people are not ready for that stage. Those who do acquire a certain percentage of wisdom are first of all wisdom seekers and they are people who have acquired a certain degree of meaningfulness in their own lives and that usually comes across in counseling.

Author: Do you believe that the counselor is basically a

behavioral manager or technician? Or is the counselor more concerned with the 'ends' of human behavior?

Professor 3: You always know my answer to that one. I do not believe a counselor, is just behavioral manager or technician. On the contrary, I think one has to look at the total picture of the individual–the individual aspirations and needs, and hopes, and who they are. I am not saying that at times techniques aren't helpful or that behavioral practices are not helpful. But to reduce counseling to the form of behavioral/technical management is not good logic. The computer can use such techniques much better and much more helpful than human beings.

Author: Do you believe that there are general laws which regulate human behavior, such that one can scientifically predict the probable success of counseling techniques?

Professor 3: Well. That gets us into the whole idea of causality in human relationship. And I believe that's a very difficult thing to try to judge. I think there are some causes. I think without anxiety no one makes change. There is no change possible at any time a group or organization unless a person is involved. If you don't have the person involved in their own change and they are not either hurting enough or desiring enough to make change, they ought to be susceptible to change, then there is no help. Then one corollary is that they must be involved in the change process. A second one is that positive results tend to be reinforced positively and negative ones reinforced negatively. Aside from those two kinds of things of involvements and the general positive and negative reinforcement that one would experience from this, the consequences of the interaction, I don't know that one can be very predictable. The studies which have been done would look at, for example, male counselors are better with male clients and female with female, do not seem to established this, nor does it seem that one has to have a black counselor for a black client or a Chinese counselor for a Chinese client. So I don't think that there are any scientific laws in the sense of Newton's laws or even the more recent laws of Einstein physics — that would be applicable to this kind of situation. There are so many points of contact. There are so many thousands of things going on in terms of perception that it's very very improbable that we will ever be able to get to the point where we can write an equation that will predict outcomes in counseling. And I think the reason for that is that much of human relationship is not similar to X to Y, or X, Y to Z. Many things that happen in human behavior that seem to be practical are very slight, not important things at all — a decision to go to a meeting, a decision to take a class, a casual meeting with someone. These kinds of things can affect one's whole life. So many times there is what you might call crisis theory — that a small event has very long-lasting consequences and that results in unpredictable outcomes. There is a new approach to physics which is called Chaos theory. I think Chaos theory has much to do with what happens here. Chaos theory would support very strongly the case for counseling because if Chaos theory is true, that it does not take efficient causes equal to the actual happenings to create that change, then it is entirely possible that very small events like counseling will make quite a difference. I remember that Williamson, the famous counselor out of Minnesota, interviewed many of the students in the graduating class maybe about 30 or 35 years ago, and 20 years after he did that, somebody did a follow-up, and every single person in that group of people that were interviewed, remembered in detail what happened in that hour 25 years ago. That's quite an interesting phenomenon. So, a little cause may be becoming a big effect in the lives of people.

Author: Now, I want to ask a little bit different and specific question. If you were a client, would you get counseling from a counselor like you?

Professor 3: I would try to.

Author: Then, what kinds of benefits or advantages would you get from counseling?

Professor 3: I would want to find somebody who is knowledgeable and has a wide range experience. I have at times in my life sought counseling and the people that I did seek it from were psychiatrists — people who had, I thought, a higher order of knowledge maybe than I have, and they didn't necessarily have that but they were really good at what they did. So I think, the more knowledge you have, the better you may be able to relate to other people. If you don't know where they are coming from, if you haven't any idea, and if you've never lived through that or similar situation yourself, how can you be of much help? It's like counseling in a cross-cultural setting. If you never had an idea of how people live in different cultures, then it's very difficult not to judge everything by your own culture. I don't know about some of these other things. You asked me "What kinds of advantages I would get from counseling?" and "Describe your strong points that you think your clients change." I really don't know what they are, but I believe that being supportive to others and providing them food for thought in order to consider new options are probably the strongest part of my own counseling. So I think possibly that my strengths are that I draw the key of where to go and directions from the actual or initial interview. I don't say this is what I need to do. I just keep reformulating the hypotheses, all the time on the basis of the information. In order to make good hypotheses one has to have knowledge and a wide range of knowledge. And so if you don't have a wide range of knowledge, if you don't know much about human behavior, you don't know anything about learning, and you don't know anything about history, culture, and other stuff, then you might as well as be a plumber putting pipes together.

Author: Would you describe where wisdom comes from?

Professor 5: Well, I think wisdom is like what we refer to in Christianity as grace. It's a gift of God. It isn't necessary to earn. It isn't merited. People just have it. One has to be a seeker of wisdom. I think we all seek to know how the world works together, to understand the nature of good and evil, to understand what is right and what is wrong, what is true, what is false. We learn some of these as a child and we formulate it. And I would not be so bold as to say I know where it comes from. I think I realize it when I see it. Although I am not sure that I have reached that wisdom, but I certainly see it as a goal in my own life. And I believe that it has been a goal of my teaching to teach students to think broadly and to recognize the complexity of human phenomena and how everything relates to everything else.

Author: Then, how have you been developing your wisdom?

Professor 3: I think mainly by studying, also by talking with people who are also wisdom-seekers. And I find that much of what is in the profession of psychology is like a soup, it's not substantial. People run off in all directions here, here, here. They seek to be entertaining, to learn some other gimmick, to learn some other trick, to do it faster and quicker, to make more money. And I think that's all a waste of time. It is as the Old Testament says "Vanity, vanity, all is vanity." And I think a lot of it is like that. I believe that one thinks about these things. I think that very many pursue wisdom in what is called meditation — to meditate, to withdraw from all the pressures and to sit back, to walk in the woods, to look at a beautiful painting, to listen to music, to be alone, and digest those things that are alive. If you open your ears, then God is at everywhere, Buddha is everywhere. Every great teacher has had to go out away from students, away from others and recharge batteries. Jesus used to go up on the mountain by himself or the desert, Moses did the same thing, Buddha did. I think that is important to do that, like I suppose I have had only a few students in my life who I thought were good counselors, maybe four or five; maybe one hundred were inclined in that direction, but only a few of them actually pursued wisdom.

Author: According to your explanation, you have been working around 30 years in the counseling area. I want to know, what do you think about the relationship between the counseling experience and wisdom?

Professor 3: Well, just as one doesn't acquire wisdom overnight, one doesn't acquire counseling skills overnight. It's a process of growing — growth! And when you finish a degree, about the only thing you can say is that you haven't made any big mistakes. After that you have to continue to work. The same thing with wisdom, you have to continue acquiring wisdom.

Author: What is the best way to teach students in counseling areas to make a good counselor?

Professor 3: Well, I think I've always felt that to give them the benefit of the knowledge that I have, to share my knowledge with them although I have never been able to do it completely because I always know so much more than I can put into courses. And I think that's a beginning, but I find that the real growth in a student, of course if they work with me for a period of time, if they are either my graduate assistants or they are my advisees and we spend time together, they learn much from me. I think that many of my students who are professors today call me, you know, and I talk to them or they come to see me or we meet when we go to conference and that relationship continues, it's doesn't just stop.

Author: Anyway I think you have been working and teaching as an instructor, I want to know your idea to make a good counselor.

Professor 3: Knowledge is power, uh? And all I can do is to

give them the opportunity to learn. That's what I do in the Assessment course. I mean, I lecture; and I explain; we have an assistant who helps them learn to be the best. They talk about tests, they write reports. There is a connection between the theory and practice back and forth. I don't think anybody can be a good counselor unless they are also interested in what is good and what is bad, what is true and what is false, I mean I'm not giving you any answer to those questions, bur if you are in counseling you should believe that those are ways by which one can live the good life, not the rich life, not the most luxurious life, but the good life. But meditation is very very important to all that. If there is any real problem I see today is that people don't take the time to think. They don't take the time to smell the roses; they don't take time to digest what they have learned, just to get some perspectives, to ask themselves. "What am I doing in this world? Why am I doing this? If I don't want to do this and I'm not going to hurt anybody if I stop, then why am I doing it?" That is where existentialism comes in, existentialism is very much concerned about death. and it is concerned about death because death is the only absolute which we really face, all of us and death limits the amount of time that we have to devote to this process.

Author: When you explained your theoretical or philosophical counseling approach, you told me you are near to the existential and humanistic approach. Now I want to ask if your counselor or psychotherapist were Freud, Skinner, Rogers, Perls or Ellis, would you get counseling or psychotherapy from them?

Professor 3: Not any of them.

Author: Why?

Professor 3: Because they are all technicians they all had knowledge and they all believed that they had arrived at wisdom. They all thought they had *the* answers, everyone of them. And I don't think any of them had the answer. I think these are portions of rainbow. But I would not like to be analyzed by Freud because I don't think Freud was a good listener. Skinner foreclosed on human behavior. He saw us only as an animal form. Rogers was naive. Perls and Ellis, both of them were arrogant, proud and believed that they had the answers. So I would not seek any help from any of them. You asked me who I would pick then. One of my good counseling friends who has probably a religious background like George Gazda in Georgia or several other people because I trust them and they are knowledgeable. I don't believe in eclecticism as such, but I don't believe that those great people are really that great. I think there is a certain amount of eclecticism. Eclecticism is not bad as long as it has some rationale. If you just throw all kinds of things together without knowing why, I have the rationale that are, which is kind of like what Maslow had, that you have a human side, the physical side, you have conscious will, and you have above all a certain amount of freedom of choice. Most of these people are determinists. I don't believe in determinism. I believe in indeterminism. I do not believe that just because the environment is bad, people will be bad or just because the heredity is flawed, there can be no progress.

Author: How do you think the relationship between your level of self–understanding and understanding the client's problems?

Professor 3: Well, I think if you have a certain amount of wisdom, you can gear yourself to the understanding of that person. You don't have to counsel just people who are intelligent. But you can, you know, counsel world people, people who haven't much education. A lot of counseling takes place in a very simple manner, just from people talking over a cup of coffee.

Author: What do you think about the issue of the counselor's value neutral position?

Professor 3: I think the counselor needs to be accepting and understanding, but I don't think he can ever be neutral of values. I think I don't have to judge you, but I have my own values. A person who is neutral of values, I don't think that's possible.

Author: Okay, then do you believe that is appropriate for the counselor to engage in moral issues in a counseling situation?

Professor 3: I don't think that the counselor should put his value system, tell the client what to do, but I do think that the counselor can say, "This is a moral problem and is one you need to address whatever way you can do it."

Author: Would you explain what your position about the issue of prenuptial agreement is? Specially, I am asking this question because recently a lot of sociologists and lawyers, they emphasize that you need a prenuptial agreement or something like that before you marry. So I want to know how counselors think.

Professor 3: I think that is essential kind of a legal question, but it all depends on the circumstances. If you have a rich old man marrying a street young woman, his second or third wife, and he wants to make sure that his children don't lose the real estate, well, they can have a prenuptial agreement. I don't think that it has much to do with counseling situation and I can't answer that any more than in vague terms because, as I told you earlier, I do everything on the basis of progressive information and so he would have to be specific, I would have to have a case and analyze it.

Author: When you have a value conflict between yourself and a client, how do you solve that problem?

Professor 3: Well, all right. I think that is a very real question. Suppose somebody comes to me and says, "I need some help from you in learning some skills," I say "Fine, what kind of skills?" "Well I want to learn how to work with locks so that I can open a lock," you say "Well, that's fine. Why did you want to learn that?" "So I can rob a bank, you know." Or something like that. Well, that's against my moral judgment. So I would not want to help that person, but I don't have to tell them how I feel. Likewise take promiscuity, sexual promiscuity — I don't believe in it. I think it's demeaning. I think it's very much like dogs' coupling and that's about it, and that there is no real love there. When the client comes up with a set of ethical judgments or principles of ethics which are counter to yours, you need to be very explicit that you don't agree with this. And let me correct that. If a person is about to tell you that they committed a crime, you are not like a priest in a confession room. You have responsibility to tell them, besides you become a party to that crime. So if a client asks you an ethical principle or judgment, if there is a real value difference and you cannot work this out, then I would suggest that you refer them to some other counselor.

Author: Okay, let's go again to wisdom question. Could you explain what the relationship between wisdom and the counseling techniques or skills is?

Professor 3: I think I've already discussed this much in length before, but briefly wisdom is a process of seeking and counseling is a kind of techniques, a kind of competency you develop. I see no intrinsic relationship between counseling techniques or skills and the development of wisdom. I see a possibility that people who engage in efforts to help other people in the process bring some wisdom into their own lives. But only if they are basically humble, have humility, have recognition of how little they know, that's what is the matter with these people.

Author: Stanley Strong published his paper on the interpersonal influence theory in 1968. After that there are a lot of researches done on social influence theory in the counseling area. Especially, he emphasized three important counselor's characteristics, that is, expertness, attractiveness, and trustfulness as perceived by the client. Now I want to ask the question. Which do you think is the most important variable among those three variables?

Professor 3: Well, my own judgment would be, the first thing that's important, the most important thing is trustfulness.

Author: Then, what is the second?

Professor 3: And the second would be expertness, and the third is attractiveness.

Author: Would you explain a little bit about that and give

examples? Why?

Professor 3: Well, I just think that of all the variables the people might value in a counselor is first of all that you are trustworthy. If you are not trustworthy, no matter how expert you are, then they won't want go any further. First of all you will have to be somebody they trust. And secondly, I think that they come to recognize that you have knowledge, that you are an expert, the way you talk, the way you're aware things with them. And I don't think attractiveness plays much of a role at all, I mean, because if attractiveness did, many people would be out of counseling because they are not very attractive. In fact I think attractiveness can be a hindrance. If you are being counseled by a very beautiful woman, you might think that the woman rather the counseling is the merit and the same is true with woman. So I think there are circumstances which relate to good counseling and like there should be quiet time, there should be comfortable chairs, all that. But I would place trustfulness first, expertness second, and attractiveness last.

Author: Then how do you think about the relationship between counselor's power in terms of social influence and counselor's wisdom?

Professor 3: Well, I don't... I tend to think that perhaps power and wisdom are at polar ends. The more power a person, the more they want to use it. I think that if a counselor is very powerful, he can influence policy. I have been virtue with administrators who are wise. The Dutch said some years ago that empty barrels always float to the top of water. Therefore, I tend to think that those people who are politically oriented or those who have power, they tend to seek office, they tend to get office, they tend to find themselves busy, busy, busy — always with things that keep them away from thinking but they make more money and they may influence more people. I don't know. It's very difficult, it seems to me, to be a socially powerful influence, at least as far as social relations go and also be wise. I do think through that wisdom, as it manifests itself presents a lot of power to the holder but indirectly. So there is influence and power in that way. But if you're talking about influence mainly, I think that, you know, whatever a person's heart is it tends to show, you know. It may, if they are really interested in social power, they will probably use counseling as a means to administration and to gaining some further design.

Author: I asked all questions. Right now, I want to listen to your comments and feedback about this interview.

Professor 3: Well, I think it's good for you to do this. You are asking some questions which I would be very interested in hearing what other people have to say and also think.

Chapter 7

WISDOM IN A HUMANISTIC EXISTENTIALISM PERSPECTIVE

Introduction of Transcript 4: This interview was done on October 2, 1990. When the Professor 4 was interviewed, he was the professor of counseling psychology and his age was sixty-three years old. On that time his career experience of studying of counseling psychology was thirty-six years. Currently he lives a happy life in Kentucky after retirement and he is eighty-three years old. He indicated that his theoretical orientation of counseling was a religiously oriented humanistic existentialism.

Author: First, I want to ask several questions about your

personal backgrounds. How old are you?

Professor 4: I am 63.

Author: What was your motivation when you decided to study counseling?

Professor 4: Well, I found psychology interesting in college as a subject matter, and I saw a relevance to understanding myself and my whole family, and to try to live a better life myself. So I think my original motivation was a sort of a personal motivation. And then later on I got a degree in anthropology and sociology, and an undergraduate degree in psychology. Then I guess, eventually, there was an opportunity for me to make a living as a psychologist. So, that was secondary, but it wasn't totally unimportant, you know, if I couldn't make a living at it I probably wouldn't have spent that much at it.

Author: How long have you been working as a counselor?

Professor 4: How long? Well, I started in 1954 in a training program at the V. A. hospital, so that's 36 years.

Author: What is your main philosophical or theoretical orientation?

Professor 4: Well, for a long time I would have said a Rogerian, but now I would say eclectic in a sense, but more specifically than that, it's humanistic, existential, and religious if you would understand religious the way I understand it. Most of what is called religious counseling is not what I think of as my orientation. But it certainly has an existential and humanistic element–religious existentialism.

Author: If you were to choose among a Freudian, a behavioristic, and maybe a social–behavioristic, and a Rogerian, which one would you choose?

Professor 4: If I had to take one or the other, I would take a Rogerian or a psychoanalytic. Rogers doesn't have much of a detailed theoretical analysis, his is more of a philosophical attitude of wisdom, if you like. The psychoanalytic gets more specific, into defense mechanisms and things like that. So, I don't see these as really alternatives to one another, you know. I guess I would see myself as neo–analytic like Karen Horney and Eric Fromm, neo–analytic with a Rogerian philosophy or attitude, but definitely not behaviorist. Cognitive–social learning theory is okay, but I see that as a sort of technique, and it's useful, but not as an overall orientation or philosophy. I think behaviorist approaches can be really destructive.

Author: Well, then, let's go on to the main interview questions. What is wisdom? Would you define and describe what wisdom is according to your personal and counseling experiences?

Professor 4: OK. Wisdom implies a certain amount of experience with the world and cognitive knowledge about it. I don't think you have wisdom if you are ignorant, but that's just the first level; much more important is, I think, an attitude toward life which I would call essentially a religious attitude of acceptance and trust, existential trust, and a notion of integration and balance and measure, realizing that the world has all kind of evil and good in it, and not demanding unrealistic expectations of the world or ideal solutions. But I think it goes beyond simply a cognitive perceptual knowledge to an affective sense of acceptance and trust — existential trust — in the sense that Martin Buber used.

Author: In the same way, what is not wisdom? Would you define and describe what wisdom is not from your personal and counseling experience?

Professor 4: What is not wisdom is the specific parts of wisdom taken as the whole thing. Certainly, cognitive knowledge by itself is not wisdom. I don't think that the sense of existential trust and acceptance of the world is wisdom if it is devoid of knowledge of the world. People that love everybody but are ignorant don't know what the hell is going on, that's not wisdom. Any one part of wisdom taken as the whole thing is not wisdom. Those are the types of things commonly thought of as wisdom. We often mistakenly think of wisdom as people who know a lot. All the various defense mechanisms that Freud talks about that are based on anxiety and fear — this is the antithesis of wisdom.

Author: You explained what is not wisdom related to knowledge. How do you define knowledge?

Professor 4: Well, I don't think you can define knowledge apart from the attitudes and the philosophy of the person that holds that knowledge. I don't think that knowledge exists out there in the dictionary–it's only when it is used by an individual or group that it becomes knowledge.

Author: What is the difference between a wise person and a good counselor?

Professor 4: First of all, it would be an intention. A person who calls himself a counselor intends, in this relationship, to counsel the other person. A wise person does not necessarily intend to do anything within that particular relationship and will sort of do what the relationship calls for. So, he is not limited by and doesn't have a specific intention. I think that a counselor who lacks wisdom is not a very good counselor. He is a technician, and there are a lot of technicians running around.

Author: Do you mean that a counselor has to have wisdom?

Professor 4: To be what I consider a good counselor. He can legally practice the trade of counseling, and I wouldn't say that he shouldn't be permitted to practice if he lacks, if he really lacks wisdom totally, then he shouldn't be counseling. I mean, to lack wisdom totally is to lack any sense of integration. Wisdom is not something you've got or you haven't got. I see it on a continuum, and maybe everybody has a little bit of wisdom, but a counselor—. A person who is wise is not necessarily a counselor. I think he can be a counselor; a lot of people can go to him for advice and for help and a lot of people's notion of a wise person is sort of like a guru who if you ask him a thing, he tells you. I don't think that's wisdom. It's certainly not a good counseling, I don't think, but I don't it's wisdom either. I think it's a mistaken notion of what wisdom is. I don't think a wise.... well, I'm not saying a wise person will never make a statement like that. It depends on what the situation calls for.

Author: Well, I still don't quite get what you emphasize to make a good counselor.

Professor 4: Well, a good counselor certainly has knowledges of certain techniques of counseling, of the literature of counseling, of theories of counseling, of what seems to work and what doesn't, of experience in actual counseling. Many wise people have never in any formal or official sense done any counseling, although I think that when other people come to them for help or advice, they are in a kind of counseling relationship. I think one of the crucial things about a counseling relationship is that it's a formal relationship recognized by both people as being a counseling relationship with a commitment: "I will pay you a certain amount of money for your help." and in return, the counselor will give me his time and will set regular appointments in that way, I mean.

Author: What kinds of wisdom do you think a counselor should have?

Professor 4: Well, what kinds do you have in mind? Do you have some categories of wisdom? I never thought of different kinds of wisdom. Could you give me an example of two kinds of wisdom? I am trying to understand your question.

Author: Basically, because you have been teaching many students in counseling area, I suppose you emphasized that a counselor should have something related to wisdom. "What kinds of wisdom" in my question depends on your definition of wisdom. What I mean is to listen to your opinion about wisdom.

Professor 4: I don't think of kinds of wisdom, I think of wisdom as being sort of a generalized way that people are integrated, that they have what I call a healthy personality, they are not neurotic, but by not being neurotic they have what I talked about a while ago — an existential trust in the world and an acceptance of the world as it really is. They don't have any need or motivation to misperceive the world and be delusional about it. So, I see wisdom as a generalized kind of thing. I haven't thought of it in terms of specific types like counseling wisdom, basketball wisdom, you know, mathematics wisdom, I haven't thought of it that way. If you have got categories of wisdom, I'll try to think in terms of those categories, but I don't think in terms of different kinds of wisdom. I don't think of counseling wisdom as opposed to psychotherapy wisdom, as opposed to mathematics, well mathematic wisdom, that would almost be mathematics is so much of a technical kind of thing. Wisdom, I think, does not involve cognitive knowledge about objects or about people considered as objects. Wisdom has to do with the way human being relate to one another or the world. I like Martin Buber's notion — 'I and Thou' relationships. I think that a person who has wisdom is a person who lives appropriately in I–Thou relationships with other people and with the universe.

Author: If you need help to solve your problems, what do you think the most important characteristics of the counselor are?

Professor 4: Well, it depends on what the nature of the problem is. Sometimes, I need information, period, or primarily information. I don't really think of that as counseling so much, but sometimes that's what people really do need. They come in and ask you, and if they can get the information, they can make their own decision. So, that's part of what a counselor should have, he should have some information, not only on his own, but also where people can go to get the information. He should be able to refer people to a physician, or to a lawyer, or to university, or the appropriate place, that informational kind of thing. It depends on what the nature of the problem is. Let's say, if the problem is you need some information, okay fine. Generally, that's not it. I think Carl Rogers' characteristics of a helping relationship, I would start with that: a counselor needs accurate empathy, unconditional positive regard, and congruence. I think those three things sum up pretty well what I think the basic characteristics of a counselor ought to be in terms of attitudes toward this client. I would also sum that up in terms of I and thou relationship attitude toward his client. Beyond that he certainly needs knowledge and experience of human psychodynamics and of social relationships. He needs knowledge and experience of those things. That's probably the most crucial because most people who come to counseling, that's where their problems are, are in the way that they are messed up in their own relationships with other people and the way that is internalized in their own psychodynamics, their own self-concept. So, a counselor surely needs cognitive knowledge and experience in dealing with those kinds of things, but that's not the same as this attitude I'm talking about. The wisdom is the attitude, but the attitude in the absence of the knowledge is kind of meaningless. You can't help anybody if you don't know anything about them.

Author: Please explain which type of a counselor you would choose to help to solve your problem: the one who tries to teach wisdom for problem-solving,

Professor 4: Wisdom for problem-solving? I don't think that generally wisdom is taught, but go ahead.

Author: Or the counselor who teaches skills and techniques for problem-solving?

Professor 4: Well, again it depends on the nature of what I think my problem is. I certainly would not want somebody who deals with techniques alone. But on the other hand, I don't think it's possible to work with wisdom alone. I guess I want somebody who can integrate the two. One without the other is pretty useless, I think. If you have wisdom, then you know the importance of techniques. You know that those are necessary in some cases. You know different techniques, and you know whether to apply them yourself or where to be sent the person for this. I don't see it as an either/or kind of thing. But I guess what I feel is that everybody knows about the existence of techniques. Very few people are aware of the existence and importance of wisdom. So, I'm glad to hear you emphasizing wisdom.

Author: Do you believe that the counselor is basically a behavioral manager or technician?

Professor 4: No, no, no.

Author: Or do you think the counselor is more concerned with the 'ends' of human behavior?

Professor 4: Well, I don't like that particular dichotomy you have drawn there, but certainly, I do not agree with the first one. He is not just a behavioral manager, but with much more than just the ends of human behavior. He has to be aware of the origins that the person to where is now. If I had to choose between the two, I guess I would choose the second one just because I don't like one at all. But I don't think, from my standpoint, it's an either/or kind of thing there, just like the wisdom versus techniques.

Author: Do you believe that there are general laws which

regulate human behavior, such that one can scientifically predict the probable success of counseling techniques?

Professor 4: Within very broad limits, yes. You can get empirical data the effectiveness of various kinds of techniques, but there are so many variables involved and most studies do not involve what you are interested in, and what I'm interested in wisdom. Human knowledge is always going to be limited and especially when it comes to dealing with human beings. There may be general laws, but our knowledge of those laws is always going to grossly inadequate. So, I believe there are, you might say, general laws, but within those general laws I guess I believe in the autonomy, which I will call the freedom of the will of the individual. The general laws are not opposed, in my viewpoint, to the notion that however the individual came to be what he is, that's what I am right now. I don't care whether I came from my genes, or my experience, or my parents or whatever. Here I am! And by God I am real, you know, and I exist! And if I think something or when I act well that's me doing, you know, and I don't care where I came from. Here I am now! And so I have in a sense, my will is just as free as I want it to be. I just can't imagine somebody saying, "Well, you're doing that because your mother treated you this way, or because your grandfather did those kinds of things." I really don't care about that. They may be true, but so what? Here I am now, okay. Well, I think there are general laws, yes, but the general laws start with that there's this kind of person who's like this, and given that, then we can predict certain things about what kind of techniques or counseling will be helpful.

Author: Now if you were a client, would you get counseling from a counselor like you?

Professor 4: Would I? Oh sure, I would! I have many times. I've been in counseling on and off every year of my adult life.

Author: What I mean, would you like a counselor like you?

Professor 4: I would like one that's better than me, but yeah, I'd be satisfied with one like me.

Author: Then, what kind of advantages would you get from a counselor like you?

Professor 4: Like me? Well, I think I have some of the characteristics that I've talked about. I certainly have these as an ideal, I mean, Rogers' three characteristics.

I'm not terribly high on these, maybe, but I strive and I think I have some degree of those. I think I have a fair degree of experience and background. I don't think I'm terribly neurotic — I don't think I'm neurotic. I think I can see things as the way they are. I think I have enough knowledge and experience, and I also have recognition of my own limitations. If a person comes in to me with kinds of problem that I can't handle, I think I can send him somewhere else. In fact, I do. If a person comes in with anything that looks like a physical problem, I never assume that it's psychological, and I always send him to a doctor for a physical diagnosis.

Author: Would you describe your own strong points?

Professor 4: My own strong points? My strong points are at the same time my weak points. I tend to be too talkative and too intellectual. I think I do listen to clients, but probably not as much as I ought to. I think I am empathic to a certain extent, but not as empathic as I ought to be. It depends on the kinds of clients. Some clients I am very effective with, and some I never get to first base with. I think I know which clients I work best with. I don't continue to work with clients that I think I am ineffective with, at least. I don't try to drag them on just to make money. I have had real–life experience with my life, my children. I've come to realize the limitations of counseling. I don't have unrealistic expectations, and I am as realistic as I want to be about what I can accomplish. But I have a positive faith and confidence. I think one of the things that a counselor offers more than anything else, is hope that things can be better, and I do have that for my clients, I think. Almost all of them, things could be better for them, and they are. So that's kind of strong point. I think I can be tolerant, for example, I do counseling with a fair number of people who have a strong religious orientation or they express their problems in religious terms. And I can talk with people whose theology is totally different from mine, and I don't try to hide it from them, but on the other hand it doesn't get in the way, you know. And I don't tell them about it unless they specifically ask me, and even then I will say, "Well, why is that important to you?" I am Catholic, you know, and most of clients that I counsel with are not Catholic, you know. Well, I don't tell them I am Catholic. Not only am I Catholic, I am a special kind of Catholic, you know, I have certain kinds of viewpoints, and I can talk their language.

Author: Would you explain where wisdom comes from?

Professor 4: Well, you have to have a certain level of intelligence. You have to be born an IQ of 100 or so, 90, at least. I mean, you can't be very wise if you just haven't got a brain for it. Wisdom implies some degree of intelligence. Well, I guess it comes from the grace of God, and being more specific than that, it comes from being around wise people. If you are never around people with wisdom, you are going to have a hard time having it just come out through your genes. I am not saying it's impossible, but it's going to be much more difficult. If you are around people who are wise and if they are significant others to you — your parents or your spouse or best friends — , they are wise people, and once you get started on that path and if wisdom is an important thing to you as a young person, then you will gravitate toward those people and those situations where there is wisdom. So it's like a tree reaching its roots out to get water and nutrients. For example, two people can be in apparently the same environment, like here in the College of Education, I am here in the College of Education, and somebody else might be in the same department in the same place, but we go out in different places; we associate with different people, and we have different kinds of experiences with our students. And so it's partly a self–directed kind of thing. It's not just wise people around you. There are wise people all over the place, but some people never see them, you know, and they never open themselves up to them. So, I'd say, at a very early age, people get from whatever sources a sort of a desire for wisdom. I don't think I am terribly wise, but I think I have a desire for wisdom.

Author: Then, how have you been developing your wisdom?

Professor 4: How have I been developing my wisdom? I intentionally seek out people and situations that I think are wise, like Thomas Merton, for example, to me is the wisest person I have known; and so I read his writings as a wise person, I go into seminars where we discuss his writings. I seek out wise people I consider to be wise in the College of Education and other places, and associate with them and talk with them. Wisdom is not just a matter of cognitive knowledge, you know, it's a matter of experience. So, I think my good deal of wisdom has come from my interaction with my wife. My wife is a counselor, and I've got a lot of wisdom from her, just the kind of person she is, not the cognitive knowledge she's got. She is a wise person in terms of relationship with people. So, I married her, I am around her, I talk with her, I observe her. And so I recognize wise people and try to associate myself with them and I say, "What are they doing, what can I do differently?" Clint Collins, is another person in this college that I think is very wise. You can get a certain amount from reading, but even more important, I think, dealing and associating with them.

Author: Especially, I would like to know also what you think about the relationship between counseling experience and wisdom.

Professor 4: Well, I would like to have a counseling training program that emphasizes what you're calling wisdom. I have never used the word wisdom a great deal in referring to counseling, but the terms I have been using are pretty equivalent to wisdom. Wisdom for a lot of people has more of a cognitive knowledge component than what I've been thinking. It's got that, but it's also got the existential attitude of acceptance and trust and looking at the world in a long range perspective in terms of how things really are rather than in terms of an illusion. I would like to see our counseling training program emphasize that. It did first four/five years that I was here. Then it changed, we had a new dean come in, most of the counseling faculty left that were here, then we got a new faculty, and the emphasis has been different ever since then. In spite of this APA accreditation, there is no emphasis on wisdom at all. I mean, we do give it a little lip service, but mainly, it's cognitive knowledge, behavioral management, and essentially power and control — how do we increase our status and income, and our control as professional psychologists.

Author: Would you explain what the best way to teach students in the counseling area to make a good counselor is?

Professor 4: You learn by doing — John Dewey. Counseling should be taught experientially as much as possible. Not only do you learn by doing it, by being a counselor, but you learn by being a client. To me a counselor who has never been a client himself, has never really benefitted from counseling, is like a doctor who is a Christian scientist who when other people are sick, he cures them, but when he's sick, he doesn't do anything; he doesn't go to other doctors; he doesn't even believe in it. So I think I learned about transactional analysis and

Gestalt therapy. I think I learned, I have read, and I have studied, but I have always gone to a therapist who used that orientation, you know. So I think you learn, well, it's not only learning the techniques, but also by self-examination, writing a journal. Self-examination — the unexamined life is not worth living. Well, I think that's especially true for a counselor.

Author: Now, if your counselor or psychotherapist were Freud or Skinner, would you get counseling or psychotherapy?

Professor 4: Would I be able to get something from them? Well yeah, depending what the nature of my problem was. I don't think I would get much from Skinner. Skinner was not a counselor or therapist himself. Well, he did experiments on pigeons, and he could make pigeons do this as opposed to that, but I am not a pigeon. One place I know of where he tried to help people. Some people set up a commune over in Virginia called Twin Oaks, and these people read his book, Walden Two. And so they went into the woods and set up this commune, they called it Walden Two and it didn't work. They did tried to use his methods, but it didn't work. So, they invited him to come down and show them what they were doing wrong. At first he refused to go down, but finally they persuaded him to go. And he went down and suggested all these different things — there is a movie made about this. They interviewed him and he said, "Well, do this," and they said, "Well, we have already tried that, and it didn't work." Then finally he said, "Well, I really don't think I can help." It didn't work. And I don't think behaviorism works except under very limited conditions. It's like a fly killer, you send off a dollar for and they send you two blocks of wood and the instructions say: "Put the fly on Block A and hit with Block B to kill it." Well that's like behaviorism. For behaviorism to work, you've got to be able totally control that person to make it work. Otherwise, well, you can mildly influence him, condition him, but generally, you cannot control a person's total environment.

Author: So you would choose Freud to get counseling or therapy. Why?

Professor 4: Well, it depends on, what you mean: Freud himself or just Freudian?

Author: Like Freud.

Professor 4: Well, there are some psychoanalytic therapists that I think are really excellent. I mean, psychoanalysts, there are a wide variety of different kinds of analysts. What I call a neo–Freudian, like Karen Horney, for example, she is one of the best ones. Have you seen any of Karen Honey's books? 'Neurosis in Human Growth', that's a great book. I don't know from experience what her counseling was like, but she is very knowledgeable, at least, about people. If you take her as an example, she's called a neo–Freudian because she has more of a social orientation than a biological. Yeah, I think I would have gotten a great deal from her. Graham Dimmick was my professor here. The Graham Dimmick Child Guidance Clinic is named after him, and he was a 200% Freudian, he was excellent, he was really excellent! So I think a lot of psychoanalysts are really excellent. They really understand psychodynamics, they understand people. The Freudian theory has some limitations to it, I think, but I think practicing psychoanalysts can be very good. Some are very terrible. I think some practicing psychoanalysts who are very rigid, they try to do it just like Freud did lt, they haven't changed in hundred years, they are probably pretty bad. My guess is Freud himself was, from what I've read about him, he was effective with some people.

I don't know if he would have been effective with me or not. I don't know if putting me on the couch and my free association would have solved my problems or not, I kind of doubt it. But I would take a Freudian over a behaviorist if I had that choice, because a Freudian sees the world in a much broader perspective. I mean Freud wrote 'Civilization and its Discontents', you know, and he looked at the whole, he looked at institutions of religion and so forth. And behaviorists, they look at pigeons and individuals, think, "How can we condition this individual?" At least in their professional lives, they don't look at the broader picture. I think they are as far from wisdom as you you can get. I am not saying that there aren't some wise behaviorists, I'm just saying their theory, you know, just rules out anything I would call wisdom.

Author: How do you think about the relationship between your level of self–understanding and understanding the client's problem?

Professor 4: I think there is a very high relationship, that's why I said a minute ago that in order to be a counselor, you ought to be in counseling yourself. You ought to have examined your own life. It ought to be a continuing process, not just something that happened when you were in graduate school, but a good counselor, whenever he has a client, he learns about himself, how he reacts to different people, and he changes constantly, and he thinks about this, and he examines himself. So I think there is a very strong relationship. But again the behaviorists wouldn't think so. To them it is the technique, it doesn't matter who is the person doing it, you know, the thing is we are all doing the same thing — we all agree with the law, the law of human behavior — and we all do exactly the same thing to that client over there.

Author: What do you think about the issue of the counselor's value-neutral position?

Professor 4: I don't think it's possible in any way for the counselor to be value neutral. I think he should know what his own values are and be able to put them into practice. And one of the values he ought to have is to permit the client express his values, to have his values, and not be put down by the counselor or have the counselor tell him, "You're wrong, my values are better than yours." But there is no way a human being can interact with anybody else in a value-free way. We are just not made that way. So I think the people who talk about value–free counseling are talking about an important thing, but they are talking about it with the wrong words. It isn't value–free at all, it isn't value–neutral.

Author: Do you believe that it is appropriate for the counselor to engage in moral issues in a counseling situation?

Professor 4: To engage in moral issues? He can't help it. There's no way that he can do counseling without being a moral act. I mean, as far as I am concerned all acts are moral acts, okay, because they all have a moral component. Whether an act is considered a moral act or not, does not depend on what the nature of an act is. It depends on whether your particular perspective and what you are interested in, what you focus on is moral or not. But everything that human beings do has a moral aspect to it — this is my orientation. I was talking yesterday to Clint Collins. Clint says there are three kinds of motives, they are moral, aesthetic, and instrumental. Well, I won't go into that, but I would say that aesthetic and instrumental acts or motives also have a moral component to them. Well, it's not appropriate, it's impossible for him not to, but he needs to engage in them in what I call a positive and moral way. He can do it in a positive or moral way or immoral way. And it's immoral for a counselor to use his authority to try to browbeat the client or push him in one direction or another. His whole purpose is to help the client understand himself, make his own decisions. Of course, this is a moral position on my part. This is a value position that I hold, other counselors don't hold that. But whatever they do hold is a moral position, whatever they say, even if they claim to be value neutral or non-moral, has a moral component.

Author: It's impossible?
Professor 4: Impossible!

Author: You mean you are aware of the moral issues but ...
Professor 4: Well, what I'm saying is you can do things that you shouldn't do, and if you do things that you should do but they are both moral, in the sense that you evaluate them as being high or low on moral dimension.

Author: Would you explain what your position the issue of a prenuptial agreement is?
Professor 4: A prenuptial agreement? Are you talking whether a husband and a wife, like that article you had in my paper? Well, it depends totally of the circumstances. Like my father who was 88 years old, he married this woman

that I told you about and had a prenuptial agreement. I think it was very good for them to have that. I don't think people over 80 years old should be permitted to marry if at least they should be allowed to marry, but there should not be economic laws applied as they do to younger people who marry and they have a common kind of thing because, you know, my father had a family. And here's this woman who uses marriage to try to get his money away from him, and tries to take money away from his family, but so you know it depends totally on the two individuals. I can see from that article that you gave me, there is a problem of distrust involved there. But I guess my viewpoint is that if there is a lot of money involved and two people come together, and one has money and the other doesn't, that's a separate issue to a certain extent than simply do they love each other. And it's good to take care of the business aspects of a marriage in a business-like way, because otherwise you get into all kinds of problem.

Author: I want to know what your main position about prenuptial agreements is.

Professor 4: From what I understand, prenuptial agreements are made or I always thought are made with older people who already had families or with younger people where one of them comes from an extremely wealthy family and the other comes from a family that doesn't have any money, and there is a fear that if they get married and things don't work out, half this man's money, I mean it may be a 100 million dollars, you know, will go to this woman. Well, presumably, they are not getting married in order to transfer money, but they are getting married because they have a relationship with each other. So, I don't think prenuptial agreements are necessary in most marriages, but it would depend on the individuals. I mean, if I was counseling somebody, I would probably say, "Why do you want a prenuptial agreement? What's the importance of it?" I would explore the meaning of it for these people. I am not against prenuptial agreements. I am not for or against any particular kind of act, it's a question of what does it mean to these people, and what are they.

Author: You just explained a little bit. Now, if you had a client who needed help with a prenuptial agreement, how would you help your client?

Professor 4: Well, I would help them explore in terms of helping, I would help both my clients, I would work with both of them, two people, about "Why do you want it? What are the issues being involved here?" and try to help them explore what those issues are. Then they might very well need to go see a lawyer who specializes in these things to get the information of what makes a good prenuptial agreement, and what things ought to be considered here, and so forth. But I think I would inquire "What does it mean about your relationship with each other? Does this mean you don't trust one another? Or what does it mean?"

Author: When you have value conflicts between yourself and a client, how do you solve that problem?

Professor 4: You always have differences, but don't necessarily have value conflicts. In fact, you should not have value conflicts, in the sense that if it comes to a conflict, you are not very helpful to the person as a counselor any longer. If he thinks that I am trying to think of example of.... Could you give me an example of a value conflict you have in mind?

Author: For example, a religious value conflict, what's right or what's wrong, — like homosexual?

Professor 4: Okay, I am working with a student right now,

and he's about 33 years old. He is a theology seminary student in Asbury College. He's a very fundamentalist in his religious beliefs, and at least he was when he first came in to me. I've worked with him for a little over a year now, and he's gotten much less rigid. So there is a very definite value difference. I mean, my religion, in terms of theology, was very different from his. You could say there was a conflict, but he never perceived it as a conflict, but I don't think I did either. I perceived it as a difference, and in fact, I didn't think it was, let me say, it was just his personality, he was a very rigid kind of person and he got angry very easily and this was just part of his religion in a way expressed his whole personality. So I have let him know from time to time that. Well I've tried to let him see that his being so rigid. Well, for example, he had this notion that when he came in that God had called him to go to some country in South America, Bolivia, I think, in order to be a missionary and to work with water quality control. That's being pretty specific, you know. And I tried to help him see that maybe he was called to some kind of religious thing, but how did he know that God wanted him to do that specific thing, you know, and there were other alternative for him that were much more realistic, and that wouldn't require him to be missionary. So, I don't see this as a conflict. It was a difference and my job was to help him become aware of what he was doing, and I guess if I differed from him, then I would ask him questions and not accept just everything he says in that area. In some other area, where we agree, I may never ask questions about that. So I think a counselor leads a client one direction or another by asking questions, by not accepting their value statement. But you don't say, "You are wrong about it, I disagree." That way you're not being very effective as a counselor, and he will walk out on you. Does that answer your question?

Author: Partly, but mainly for example, in some extreme cases like if you don't believe in homosexuality?

Professor 4: Well, homosexuality doesn't bother me. But a person who is violent, abusive, or sexually abusive to children or to women or to just people, I don't like that. And in the first place, the kinds of people I don't like generally don't like counseling. People who have values that are totally different than mine, not only probably wouldn't like me if they knew what I was like, but they don't like the process of counseling — everybody can't be helped by counseling. So that solves the problem to a certain extent, and they won't even appear in your office, you know. Well if they do, I think sometimes I try to see things from the client's perspective and try to let him know. I see it from his perspective. I don't necessarily agree with it, but the first thing for me is to be real sure that I understand it from his standpoint. And it may take a long time to try to understand it from his standpoint. So, in the meantime there may be conflicts or I might think that there are conflicts, but I don't know this for sure. I've got to find out what this person means by this. Like this boy I was talking about who thought God was sending him to Bolivia to be a missionary in a water control project, I didn't, it wasn't necessary of me to say, "Well, that's absurd, you have no proof for that." It took a long period of time, and we never attacked that particular thing directly, what we dis was find out what he really wanted, you know, and when he saw various alternatives, what I would say to him, "Well it seems to me that you can serve God in various ways, how do you know that this particular way is the way?" So in terms of a value, sometimes you don't have to say "I think this," you can ask him if he has a viewpoint. If it is totally different from yours, it's probably different from other people's as well, and he is aware of this. So you can help him discuss his difference between himself and society in general or other people, and keep yourself out of it. I don't know if that answers your question or not. But you try not to make if there is a difference here, and there always is a difference. I mean, your clients and you are always different in some remarkable ways. I mean, clients in general are neurotic, they've got problems! You are not a neurotic, you don't have the same problems they have. So these are differences, but you don't present it has a conflict. You just don't define it even to yourself as a conflict between you and them, between your values and their values. What you try to help them see are conflicts that they have within themselves or between themselves and significant others.

Author: Let's go back to a question related with wisdom. Could you explain what the relationship between wisdom and counseling techniques and skills is?

Professor 4: Well, I thought we hit this at the beginning. If the counselor has wisdom, then one of the things he wants to do is be wisely knowledgeable about techniques. You cannot know everything there is know about every kind of technique, but part of wisdom is accepting limitations on your own ability to know everything. So it's sort of good to choose one, not to choose, but to gradually come to one orientation as opposed to another. And every time a new kind of psychological fad comes out, I don't rush out to learn it. I did for a while, you know. After Rogers, Rogers was a big thing when I was in graduate school, but I knocked myself out to learn those things and I think I learned them fairly well and sort of integrated them into, then came along Neuro-Linguistic Programming. Well, I went into the Neuro-Linguistic Programming thing and it just seemed like wine in new bottles to me. I mean I couldn't see that they were saying anything better or additional, just different terms. So, I didn't spend any more time in learning that particular technique. So part of wisdom is learning to confine yourself and limit yourself to something that you can handle and you can do, and if the person seems to need something else, then you send him somewhere else. So wisdom always includes certain knowledge of techniques and knowledge of your limits of what you know. Techniques do not necessarily involve wisdom at all, but I would say that techniques, well used, require wisdom. That is if all you've got is a grab bag of techniques, you are going to pull this one out for this kind of client.

Author: You mean, when you give counseling to clients, you have to have wisdom?

Professor 4: Right! Right! I mean what's appropriate wisdom has to do with appropriateness, what goes with what and looking at the big picture. Wisdom implies a large broad perspective, and so techniques can fit into a broad perspective, but if they don't if they seem as here's one, here's one, here's one; I mean some people are going to use the same technique on everybody no matter what. Or maybe some people have two or three techniques and they are gonna take different kinds of clients and use different techniques with each one, but still it's well. I guess it involves some degree of wisdom although not necessarily where you can give them a test and they come up with a score and you use that technique and if they come up with another score you can use another technique. But techniques without wisdom I think is almost worse than useless. For one thing, techniques drive clients away. Clients do not like to be techniqued. I mean, when I was first learning a Rogerian style; "You felt strongly about that. Tell me about more." I tried that on my wife, boy, she picked up just like that, she said, "Don't use that technique on me!" and people don't like to be techniqued, even clients don't like to be techniqued. They like to feel that they are dealing with a real human being. Well in a sense, everything involves techniques. I mean, speaking a language is a technique. You're speaking English now, and well, you are aware that it's a technique because it doesn't come very naturally to you. But when you speak Korean it just seems like the most natural thing in the world! Any normal human being would speak Korean, right? It comes naturally, it doesn't seem like a technique, but it is. Any language is a technique. So we can't get away from techniques. But if you are limited to just techniques, if that's all, then you are in real trouble. I think a lot of students bring in a fair amount of wisdom with them. And I think we sort of take it for granted that they've got that. If a student comes and doesn't have any wisdom, any ability to integrate, to see the big picture, and uses this technique and that one and that one, which is what we teach, we think there is something wrong with that student. Well, there is something wrong with him, but the problem is we haven't emphasized the wisdom or the integration at all. The students, most students, happily bring this, some of this, in with them. But they don't bring it in, we are very aware that something is wrong.

Author: According to the social influence theory in counseling, there are three important counselor characteristics, that is, expertness, attractiveness, and trustfulness as perceived by the client. Which do you think is the most important variable among these variables?

Professor 4: Well, first of all, If the client won't stay with you, it doesn't matter. If any of these things is low that the client doesn't come back anymore than that doesn't do any good. So, I'll assume that the person is high enough on all three of them, so the client is not gonna go away, he is gonna stay there.

Author: If you give an order of importance among those three variables, How would you give it?

Professor 4: Well, I'd say the initial attractiveness doesn't matter because after the person gets to know you, if he likes you and thinks you are doing a good job, you will appear to become attractive over time, and if you are not doing a good, you won't seem attractive any more. So that leads us to expertness and trustfulness. Expertness sounds lot more like technique, and trustfulness sounds an awful lot like wisdom, but I wouldn't equate those. Expertness and trustfulness, well, again, if a person is really trustworthy, he will have become expert, he will not to try to do something he doesn't know how to do. And if a person really is expert, a part of expertness, I think he is being trustworthy, and I think I have a hard time separating expertness and trustworthiness, if you have one, you got the other.

Author: Oh no, you can separate them, for example, if somebody is honest but he doesn't have the skill, you know.

Professor 4: Okay, we can talk about this for an hour, I'll take expertness, but I can be argued out of that depending on what you mean by the term, expertness.

Author: The first is expertness, second?

Professor 4: Well, trustworthiness. As long as the client stays with you and doesn't leave because, as I say, I think attractiveness, but I could argue for any of those, I could argue for, I don't feel strongly about my answer.

Author: How do you think about the relationship the counselor's power in terms of social influence and counselor's wisdom?

Professor 4: Which has the greatest social influence, his power or his wisdom?

Author: No, what do you think is the relationship between two?

Professor 4: I really haven't thought in these terms before. By power, would you equate that with social influence?

Author: I mean, you as a counselor having the power to influence the other person, for example clients need your help because you learned a lot, you have the skills.

Professor 4: So, you are contrasting power then against wisdom. Okay, a part of my problems in answering these questions are that I tend to lump these categories and do not make, or at least to recognize that the distinctions are limited in their usefulness and they aren't absolute distinctions. So, I have a hard time absolutely distinguishing between what you call power and wisdom. It seems to me it's impossible to have wisdom without having a great deal of power, just as it's impossible to have power without wisdom. So, I have a hard time just making an absolute distinction between the two, and contrasting one with the other. So, your question is which one of these things is more important in counseling?

Author: My question is that, what's the relationship between the counselor's power in terms of social influence and his or her wisdom?

Professor 4: Okay. Well, I go back to Martin Buber again. Martin Buber distinguished between I–It relationships and I–Thou relationships. I've already told you that I think wisdom is essentially I–Thou relationship. Power is almost anonymous with I–It relationship when you treat things and people as objects to be influenced, to be manipulated, to be controlled. I–It relationship can exist, unfortunately, by itself without a I–Thou relationship. I think it's bad when it does. I think it's better if the world doesn't have power in that sense. The I–Thou cannot really exist by itself, I don't think. It always exists in alternation with or sort of Yin–Yang relationship with the I–It. So that's how I see the relationship between power and wisdom. Wisdom cannot exist all by itself. It always exists as a sort of integration of these things that we are calling power here, techniques and so forth. That's the ideal way that the two should be integrated. The power can exist by itself, unfortunately, as I said. I think the world would be worse off if people had power and not wisdom. It would be better for them not to be have power, period! And that includes counselors and everybody else. I don't think that wisdom can exist all by itself. So that's how I see the relationship between power and wisdom.

Author: Now, I asked all main questions. Would you give any comments and feedback about this interview?

Professor 4: I enjoyed it. It was great. I would say that from the nature of your questions it's sort of your own viewpoint. Anyway, I think wisdom is very important. I think I've tried to understand exactly what you mean by wisdom.

Chapter 8

WISDOM IN A PSYCHODRAMA PERSPECTIVE

Introduction of Transcript 5: This interview was done on November 15, 1990. When the Professor 5 was interviewed, he was the professor of counseling psychology and his age was forty–four years old. On that time his career experience of studying of counseling psychology was twenty–one years. He still works as the professor at the Department of Educational and Counseling Psychology, University of Kentucky and right now he is sixty–four years old. He indicated that his theoretical orientation of counseling was a psychodramatic and social learning approach.

Author: First, I want to ask several questions about your personal backgrounds. How old are you?

Professor 5: 44.

Author: Why did you choose counseling as your job? What was your motivation when you decided to study counseling?

Professor 5: I chose it because I went to a counselor and I liked what he did. That was my motivation. He was helpful to me. I went for some career counseling, I liked the way he interacted and I thought I could be helpful to people the way he was, I was looking for something to focus on, and that seemed to be what grabbed me at that moment. It may not have been the best reason, but it worked out well.

Author: What is your main philosophical or theoretical orientation?

Professor 5: It's a hard question to answer because philosophically I would believe I am psychodramatic, or what would really be more the theory of socio–metric. But that hardly doesn't speak well to most people, it has to do with a sense of existentialism. When comes to practicing, even though I use a lot of good techniques, I use a lot of family therapy technique, because I deal with a lot with troubled families. I would say that I'm probably a social-learning theorist at heart, particularly Bandura and the changes that he's made; so philosophical orientation and theoretical orientation are slightly different. I would see the psychodramatic perspective encompassing the other.

Author: My understanding of psychodramatic approach is that it mainly comes from the psychoanalytic.

Professor 5: It has to do with spontaneity and the ability to act flexibly in different situations — I think, would be the key — to what I could call the psychodramatic. It's true, it does have certain things in common with psychoanalytic in terms of emphasis on the use of the past. It also is a very existential theory in terms of acting in a here-and-now sense, but the key for me is the insistence on spontaneous action; the ability to make decision, enjoy life, feel creative.

Author: when did you start studying counseling areas?

Professor 5: From my perspective I would probably say Moreno. I have a great deal of affection for Bandura, partially because I know him, I see him as a good role model. Really emphasizing counseling was in 1969.

Author: What is wisdom? Would you define and describe what wisdom is according to your personal and counseling experience?

Professor 5: I think wisdom is a knowing what you know and what you don't know and being able to make a distinction between the two. I think the knowledge is at different levels. I don't just mean cognitive, but I mean by wisdom the ability to act appropriately, which sometimes includes not acting; the ability which incorporates knowledge of yourself and knowledge of context and anything else that you could possibly bring in to be able to act appropriately, to act in constructive way for the good of others, for the good of yourself. And in that the idea of knowing when you don't know implies to me flexibility, and I guess underpinning everything I think about is the ability to be flexible, and to realize that what you don't know can hurt you and that what you do know changes. It doesn't always apply the way it has in the past.

Author: Can you give me an example?

Professor 5: Take a relationship, my relationship with Pam. In that is a knowledge of what I know about her and what I know about myself and what I know about our interactions, and the wisdom in using that knowledge comes from; first, being able to balance–off those factors which I know about her, what her needs are, what my needs are, and to try to achieve some kind of balance, and then, maybe, the last piece is being able to step back and see that I not always going to be right that I can be wrong, that I should always take that into account. It's almost like always being able to take another step back and gain perspective.

Author: In the same way, would you define and describe what wisdom is not from your personal and counseling experiences?

Professor 5: Not having wisdom is thinking you have wisdom. I don't think wisdom is a thing, a quantity. I think it's process. And so, anytime... not being wise is assuming that what has been wisdom in the past is wisdom now, is applicable now. Yet, not discarding everything. It's that thing about knowing about what to keep and what not to keep, or knowing how much of a thing to use at a particular time, or knowing how to start the use of a particular skill, a particular interaction, and being able to be aware of it not being adequate in that particular context, and the knowing somehow, if not how to change it, at least how to admit that it's not right, and that can incorporate asking for help, or sometimes you can be appropriate giving–up and just crying in a corner. If you see somebody with a problem and you know how to solve it, that may be true if it were your problem, but a big part of wisdom is realizing that it may not be solution for the other person; or if it is, they may not want it, then. And I would guess that wisdom comes then from knowing how to ask the other person what they want at that point in time, which to me is the key in counseling. I can often give advice, but that may not be what the person wants. If I ask them if they want advice and they say "yes", then giving them the advice may be entirely appropriate, it might be very wise.

Author: You defined what wisdom is or not. Then, what is the difference between a wise person and a good counselor?

Professor 5: I think the difference between a wise person and a good counselor is that some wise people, on a Venn diagram basis, I think that they overlap. The best counselors are wise people and who know how to convey their wisdom and/or use it appropriately to help someone else. I suppose the ultimate wise person will know everything, which is of course impossible. But I think you can be a wise person in a lot of ways and not know how to help someone else. I think you can know how to help other people, and be pretty good at it within certain spheres and not know when not to be a good counselor, and when the two overlap, then you get an excellent counselor. The ones who know their clients and themselves, and not only use the process, but the meta-process that we were talking about before, about being able to step back. One other thing in here is the..., that's part of wisdom, is the willingness to go with your own confusion, and realize that sometimes there's not an answer or a closure, and be able to admit that to yourself, live with it.

Author: Can you give any example relating to your experience?

Professor 5: I think, for example, Albert Einstein, or Albert Schweitzer, or Mahatma Gandhi, or Jesus Christ, or Buddha, I would consider these people as wise people. I don't know if they would have made good counselor or not. For example, take Albert Einstein first. I think he was a wise person. He had a world perspective and flexibility and an ability to cope and a tolerance for even the mistakes he made. I think one of the things he said, was that the biggest mistake he ever made was collaborating on the atomic bomb. I think he regretted doing that. But I don't think he would have made a good counselor, in part because he didn't have some of the skills to convey that wisdom to others. Now it may be that he could have been a good model for some. I'm not certain he couldn't be part of a good counselor. I think being a good counselor also incorporates some skills at communicating your wisdom or lack of it, to other people. Like, for example, on the other end of things I think in many ways Albert Ellis is a good counselor for certain people and certain kinds of problems in particular. I don't think he's very wise. For one thing I think he's more than slightly inflexible. Another person who I'd say is probably a good counselor, but probably not my list of wise people, is Jay Haley, who is very perceptive and can be very helpful to families. Where I think he falls down is in a long term view of what he could be doing to help people. He goes only a short way. And maybe wise in that he knows that's as far as he can go, I don't know, but my sense is he also thinks that's as far as anybody can go, and that's not wise, knowing his own limitation is fine, but ascribing those limitations to other people.

Author: What kinds of wisdom do you think the counselor should have?

Professor 5: The main piece of wisdom would be to know your limitations. That doesn't mean that you can't try to. I would as a matter of fact think a good counselor would continue to try to expand, so that would be less limited. But I think there are just areas that everybody is limited in. And the first thing, sort of an addition of flexibility, is to know just how flexible you can be before you would snap. I think that counselors need to know their limitations, sort of corollary to that is they need to know their clients' limitations. I say that's it's a corollary rather than another axiom, mostly because I think that you don't see that if you don't know your own limitations. It would be useful to anyone, and certainly to a counselor, to be wise in any way that it's possible to be wise. And I would think that wisdom isn't just one category of action or knowledge. I think that if part of wisdom is knowledge, then the knowledge of certain skills that are applicable is a requisite; when to use those skills and when not to use them. In answer to one of your other questions about how you gain wisdom through experience, I think the only way is through a combination of knowledge and its application, so that simply knowing something — if I make a distinction between knowing and wisdom — isn't really wisdom. You have to have done it, tried it to understand how much of whatever it is that you think you know that you do know. And my example of that is from statistics. Any statistics book, when it comes to your doing your dissertation or a study or your helping someone else, or applying it in some way, there always comes a point where — for me at least — there is a question of "Do I really know what I'm doing?" And part of wisdom I think is asking that question, and then saying, "Well, this is how much I know, this is how much I don't know; how far from here to there can I go? How much should I try? Should I go find somebody else who knows more? How much is it worth to me to prove to myself that I know this?" It gets very complex.

Author: You have a lot of counseling experience. Would you explain what kinds of wisdom you acquire from your clients?

Professor 5: For example, a client who is resistant. Wisdom is a knowing the client will be resistant. It's a knowing different ways to deal with resistance. It's a knowing that some resistance is not bad; that there's a reason for resistance. It's a knowing that you can push, it's a knowing when to lay–off, and most important of all is being willing to, and knowing how to struggle with making the decision about when to do which thing. When to, like say, strongly encourage some moment even though it may be risky or scary; verses when it's time to let things just be for a while, and along with that knowing that in the process you're not going to know what's the right decision, why you're doing it, just sort of accept the wisdom in it. The last part of it is accepting that you can do the best you can do and try to do it in the safest way possible, so that you don't injury them. That, I think is very important for any therapist, counselor to know, and to struggle with. I think anytime you get stuck with a client that's probably just where you are. It's from that dilemma. I think sometimes you encourage people to struggle, sometimes encourage people to experience pain.

Author: If you need help to solve your problems, what do you think the most important characteristics of the counselor are?

Professor 5: For most, the willingness to be there with me, and to tolerate my struggle. There are limits when I think I could give you the answer, but in the long run that may not be the solution to your problem; as a matter of fact it might be your problem. I don't remember which book it was in, but it might have been. 'If You Meet the Buddha on the Road, Kill Him', by Sheldon Kopp, said something about what a therapist is is not a leader that takes someone down a path. He's more a follower, someone that's willing to be lost with you. To me, if I were going to be a client, what I did want is that sort of presence of someone, their tolerance of my struggles. How they can encourage, they can confront, they can say, "Well, it's your problem and you're going to have to struggle with it." But even in showing me to do that I want to feel a sense of worth and that's what I call kind of being there.

Author: Would you explain which counselor you would choose to help your problems? First, the counselor who tries to emphasize wisdom for problem-solving, second, the counselor who try to teach techniques or skills for problem-solving.

Professor 5: I would definitely choose the first, because the first would subsume the second. Being, if it seemed appropriate and the counselor checked it out and said, "Well, I could do it this way or I could do it that way. Which way do you want to go." And I said, "Well, what I want right now is some skills or techniques," the wise counselor could do that as well as more. And so, I wouldn't be giving up something to have the wise counselor. If I had somebody who only know has to teach skills and techniques, then, if the situation required more than that, I wouldn't get what I need. I would choose the counselor who had the most flexibility. Because if I were in a crisis, then that person would have some crisis-management skills and would know that now is the time to apply them. If I'm frantic and not where I needed to be taught problem-solving skills; what I needed to be told some skills to use here, that a counselor could be able to do that. From my own perspective, I am at the moment I would choose the one with wisdom/problem-solving skills, because that is where I would want to be extended, I don't find myself at the moment where I need a particular skill/technique. If I had time — this is part of the context — somebody knowing wisdom, problem-solving skills, I could go and get the other skills for myself, even though it meant going to somebody else and asking them temporarily to teach me problem–solving skills, or whatever.

Author: Do you believe that the counselor is basically a behavioral manager or technician? Or is the counselor more concerned with the 'ends' of human behavior?

Professor 5: It depends on what kind of counselor, which is begging the question. I think, to go back to the question only between wise people and a good counselor, I think you can be a good counselor and a good behavioral manager. I don't necessarily think that, that makes you a wise counselor. To answer the question: Is a counselor basically a behavioral manager? From my perspective, no. It's far broader than that. If I made a distinction between being a counselor and a therapist, a distinction between being a clinical psychologist and a counseling psychologist, I see a counselor as being more role–oriented, and providing not just a solution for the moment, although that may be part of what goes on, but providing a situation where the person can learn not only how to help himself now, but knowing how to learn how to help himself. So I'm not sure where that necessarily says something about the ends of human behavior, it's more like the process of human behavior is what I would say the kind of counselor that I'm talking about is concerned with.

Author: Do you believe that there are general laws which regulate human behavior, such that one can scientifically predict the probable success of counseling techniques?

Professor 5: Sure, it's parallel to the same kind of laws you'll find in physics. And that some laws that operate pretty well on a micro-level, like Newton mechanics, for example, and some laws that on a micro-level don't work very well, but on a macro-level work just fine. I think there are, well, I'm not sure I'd call them laws because they're more probabilistic — so they're laws again parallel to physics, not a law like if I take this mass and hit that mass, this one twice as big as that one and it hits the other mass, that mass will go twice as fast. I don't think there are any laws that deal with human behavior, that are simplistic, that work very well. As guidelines I'd say there as something, like the law of reinforcement, to go back to Skinner, that give you a generally good idea of how to operate. But if you count of operating deterministically, something will always come along and screw it up. I mean it just that human beings are too complex; you have so many more influences that... I do believe I am essentially a social–oriented theorist, behaviorist. I believe in the general applicability of those laws. They tend to be good guidelines for how to intervene in certain situation. Since I'm also into socio–metric theory/psychodrama, and believe in spontaneity, I believe there are also laws that have to do with spontaneity and how to engender it and teach people to be more spontaneous and thereby teach people to be more functional in life. They don't quite have the precision that behavioral laws do, but they still give you guidelines in a lot of ways. Help at — not at the macro–level, but at a level in between. I wish there were laws that operated on a macro–level and maybe there are if you start looking at this plant from outer space.

Author: If you were a client, would you get counseling from a counselor like you?

Professor 5: Yes.

Author: Then, what kinds of advantages or benefits would you get from counseling?

Professor 5: I would be forced to deal with the ambiguity of the world, therefore become more tolerant and flexible. At least that is the way I see myself. Sometimes I think

I'm blind, so I'm not as wise as I ought to be. But I fall into the trap of believing that I actually can do what I believe I can do. I think the overall biggest advantage is that in the long run I would like to be responsible for myself and my growth and to mesh that with my responsibility to others and their growth. So that's what I would see as the advantage. I probably believe that.

Author: Describe your strong points that you think help your clients change?

Professor 5: My strong point, and it's a strong point that's been hard to come to, is that I also struggle with the client, and I won't... that I'll be honest with the client, I will be genuine with the client a lot. What I am willing to do, what I can do with client, and I'll let the client make the choices, to some degree. That can get us into some moral kinds of things that you asked about. Then sometimes I'll draw a line and I'll have to make a choice about how my doing something with client is going to affect me in the long run and balance off what the client wants as against what I want. But I'm usually willing to lay that out with the client. I think that what that does is that models for the client. I also think it gives the client an opportunity to assume the responsibility. To me, and this is as much for me as it is for the client, it creates a bond with the client that I think a lot of clients need, in the sense of somebody being there with you, not abandoning you. Maybe the worst thing struggling with problems is often struggling alone. The least the counselor can do is be there while you struggle.

Author: Where does wisdom come from?

Professor 5: Everywhere. Isn't that broad answer? Primarily, I think from life experiences and being open to them, being willing to examine them, I mean, it can be reaching, it can be doing, it can be living through traumas, it can be a lot of things. It can be to some degree serious. I think you can gain wisdom in the sense of learning that there are some things that it would be just as well not to experience. I don't have to become paralyzed in order to have the real wisdom, now I may not have some wisdom that somebody who is paralyzed has, but I'm not willing to pay the price to gain that wisdom. I might approximate it in some way or other if I can do it, but I'm not going to go through that experience in order to gain that wisdom. A necessary but not sufficient condition to live life, to become wise, is — you have to live life, you have to experience things, you have to be open to the experience, as I said, to take them and incorporate them from a Piagetian sense, revive your schemata — but simply experiencing anything I don't think is going to make you wise. It has to be a process of being able to extract from the experience, extract but incorporate into what is already there, in order to perpetuate the process of gaining wisdom and expand it.

Author: How have you been developing your personal wisdom?

Professor 5: A lot of different experiences. Not only counseling experiences, just life experiences. Some of my either realizing where I need to work or the quantum leaps that have been the most painful things — that's where I thought I knew something and went ahead as if I dis and screwed it up — and then being able to tolerate the pain of those situations and go back and put myself in similar situations again, and take the risk, and be wrong again in different ways. And narrow, I don't know if I've narrowed at the answer, but I certainly narrowed it down now. Also being willing to go..., for a long time I stayed away from individual battlements for myself. I had a lot of rationales, excuses about not having the resources available, but still I think going and being a client was a big gain in wisdom. Look at it from both sides. To be willing to be a client at times, to be a counselor at times; to screw up at times to succeed. I think that screwing up all the time is highly overrated. It's useful. I think I have to have some successes from time to time, or also I wouldn't believe I was getting anywhere.

Author: Do you have any specific example?

Professor 5: The one specific example that comes to mind was a very painful one, a lot had to do with my training — it's been going on a very long time now, the last eight on ten years, very intensely — for psychodrama. And there's a guy I trained with, who I have a great deal of respect for. And I was very eager to please him, and to emulate him. When I was at a workshop at one point they asked for volunteers. I would see myself, well, if anybody will take a risk, I will take a risk. But there is always part of me that says, "That's not really much of a risk. You're a hot shot. So you can go on and do it." Well, I stepped into this thing and I did it sort of according to the rules. I missed the boat. It wasn't so much that I was wrong. It was that I could have been more on target. Maybe eventually I would have gotten around to what needed to be alone, but I went out there and I did this thing and then I just embarrassed myself horribly. But it was horrible in such a subtle way, because it wasn't wrong, it was wrong like in a very core, like how could I have missed that. And then I struggled with myself a lot about — what had happened is that I went and I did this piece of work and it was criticized, and in the critiquing, Carl went ahead and he did something that — what essentially he did is he picked up on what I missed, and I felt so embarrassed that I'd missed the thing, and I struggled for a long time with, this was in a group, so everybody could kind of see how masterful he was, and I felt so, like I'm never going to get there, and is there really any worth in trying anymore, and what's wrong with me anyway and am I just kidding myself, and I got angry with him in some ways and said, "Well, I wasn't really wrong, he was just different." A lot of the wisdom came from going through that whole struggle, and it's still not resolved. But where I am with it is that it's an OK struggle, and that the biggest flaw in there was trying to do something in a way to please me, and therefore to please him, and not going with what the client was giving off as clues, if I had just allowed myself to be more open to them. I think it could have been.

You can't go back and relive it, so. But the worth of that came in a number of ways. One was that I can go through it and I can benefit from it. There was wisdom in knowing that I have a lot more to do before I get to the level where Carl is. There's also a lot more to do in not trying to emulate him, and trying to see why it was so important, and still is so important to me. It's not easy to let go of. A wealth of material keeps coming back from it. I realize by the fact it's so varied for me and that still so painful to recall that particular incident, that I'm not finished with it. And so if I keep on looking at it, not compulsively, but as it comes back to mind from other things that I do, that it'll make much more sense to me, and that as the pieces form, then when I get to the point where I feel more comfortable with it, then I will have gained more wisdom from it, I'm still mining. I think those kind of incidents have to happen to people, if only to prove to them like it proved to me that I'm just as human as anybody else. So I'm going to watch my step.

Author: What is the best way to teach students in counseling areas to make good counselors?

Professor 5: Actually I've thought about this a whole lot, I believe that you have to start by giving students what they essentially want to begin with, which are some solid ways of doing the essential part of the counseling interaction; to give them some skills and techniques but primary skills. The two primary skills to start with are listening skills, which are the cornerstone, and confrontation skills, which mean to point out in a supportive way where people's blind spots are. I think, beyond that, where the real growth comes in and is sort of sneaky. What I do is I give them skills, then I have them go out and precipitate incidents from which they will learn, either from each other, or from significant others in their lives, or whatever. I want it to be safe. I don't want somebody to do harm to someone else or to themselves. But even so I put a great deal of value on personal knowledge. And so when I teach these skills I have people apply them to themselves. And what it has usually done, in the most gratifying cases, has started the process of opening up people's awareness to, call it the process of gaining wisdom. Because generally, people will do more things, riskier things, they will make some mistakes, be willing to make some mistakes, if they feel the proper climate is there for human beings to expand, develop, or benefit. I think there are some people who don't like it, because some of it is very ambiguous, like there's one assignment I give to people, that is to personally do something that is growth-producing, and some people just eat it up. They say, "I've always wanted to do such and such", and they go out and do it. For some people it's extremely difficult. They ask me, "What's growth-producing?" How am I supposed to tell you what's growth-producing for you? If people get very frustrated with me and shy at that point in frustration, I worry about them. The people who are at the point of frustration and then push to say, "Well, I guess I'm a person who needs structure and I guess that might not be so good in some instances. What I'm going to do about that?" That might be the kind of process which I think leads to producing a good counselor, because it gives you insight into yourself and your own process in coping with an unpredictable world. And in order to cope with unpredictable clients who have to cope with an unpredictable world, I think you need that ability like I said before, of being there with someone and so be able to convey support to learn this process themselves. It's sort of a passing along kind of thing. My ultimate goal with clients is that they will, not be a finished product by any means, but they will embark upon and accept the responsibility for living their own lives. To me, that here is the process of gaining wisdom. You live your life.

Author: If your counselor or psychotherapist were Freud or Skinner, Rogers, Perls, Ellis, would you get counseling or psychotherapy?

Professor 5: I would go to anybody, because I think I would much like experiencing that person in some way that would be beneficial. There are some people I would like more than others, but that doesn't necessarily mean I would grow more from them. The people I'd probably be least comfortable with would be Freud and Ellis. Perls, might be uncomfortable with, but I believe in what he's doing more than in the others, or at least in the way he's doing it. I might not be comfortable with Perls as a person. That would be another aspect of the growing. I have a real sense of what it would have been like to go to Skinner. He seemed like, from the way he wrote, he was such a technician. So I don't — unless I had specific problem that I wanted to go and work on, it doesn't seem to that he would be the person I'd approach. If he'd ask me "What is your problem?" I'd say "I really just want to grow." And he'd say "What does that mean in terms of behavior?" And I'd say "I'm not really sure because I like my behaviors a lot the way they are, but I'd like to tune them up." And he'd push and push and push to the point where I'd say "I can't be specific to the level of specificity you want, I want to grow in a different way for now." I would imagine I'd hit the same kind of thing in Ellis, although the growing in Ellis is that, Ellis comes from the same part of country that I come from, the part I've rejected. I don't like the brash, pushy New York that I read into his behavior. So perhaps working with Ellis, and perhaps learning the benefits of that behavior and to be more tolerant of it would be worthwhile. I'm not sure that there's going to be a lot from his technique that I'm going to learn, because I think I've got that down pretty well. I'd just like to be with Rogers. Of course, Rogers is gone too. He seems to me to be, as Aunt Gloria would say, a kind of grandfatherly person, and it would just be a very pleasant experience to be listened to in the way he would listen to someone. Freud of all of them would be the most interesting. I might just do that because I've so, well, let me put this in a way that has made it tolerable to me. I don't really know what it would be like to be with Freud. I have my idea of what it would be like to be with what they say Freud was. Because, what I have is his writings, and particularly is psycho-analytic interpretation of what he said. A hundred and some odd volumes, and generally he might not have been any more aware of those changes and his process of change than the people who read his volumes are. So there are some things that are very intriguing about Freud. He might, I don't really know what to make of transference. I do believe it exists but he seems to me to be missing something, and it might be interesting at least to have a blank wall. I don't believe in the psycho-analytic interpretation. I don't know if I've resolved my Oedipal Complex or not: I don't really care. The brilliance of Freud is in the general concepts of things like the defense mechanism. The specificity of his defense mechanisms, I tend to doubt the wisdom of those. The person who isn't here, who I might like to interact with most of all would have been Jung. I think I'm ready for Jung and archetypes. That to me would be fascinating, to explore say shadow-side. Also I like his mysticism, too. Inexplicable things that somehow seem to tie together that he just kind of accepts at that level, it's good enough to explain things that way. A lot of other people try hard to push for explanations, I think, because they can't tolerate the ambiguity of certain level of explanation.

Author: How do you think the relationship between your level of self-understanding and understanding your client's problems?

Professor 5: My level of understanding is essential to my understanding of the client's problem. I'll give a two-part answer on this. The first part is more obvious, which is without understanding myself, then I'm more likely to wander into my own blind spot, which I share with the client, and will not likely be useful to the client. So without some knowledge of myself, my limitation, my blind spot, my own difficulties in my life, I could do harm. You should minimize the chance of that happening. The more you know about yourself, the less likely it is to happen. It doesn't necessarily mean that just because I know everything about myself, that I'm going to be able to handle a particular client-problem. So I'm sure if it always directly converts into my being the best counselor for a particular person because my judgment of what a person needs may not match with what they think they need. And maybe at a particular point in time another counselor would be better for them. And if they — this is sort of getting into the issue of rules but, if someone else can help them better than I can, either because the other person knows what they need more, or because the other person is more willing to go along with it, what I mean by 'willing to go with it' is that. I know enough, probably because being on a university campus, all you do all the time is you look at this theoretical, you read this and you read that, you give this technique and that technique, all the time in the world to put together things. So somebody could come to me and say, "I have this particular problem. Could you help me this way?", the truth of the matter is that I probably could. And when I own up to my own biases, where I may hit is that down deep, I think there may be other people who need my kind of approach more. And so why not let this person go to somebody who would be able to and willing to help as much if not more than I could, and I'll take my resources and channel them somewhere else. I understand myself well enough that I can make those kinds of distinctions, I think. I don't know if I call it 'blind spot' but I go back to the wisdom of the decision-making, and when to push and when not to push, when to accept things and when not to accept things. In the short term or the specific instance that might mean that I'm not going to be very helpful to a client the way they want to me to be. In the long run, I guess what I'm saying is that I'll make those decisions as best I can, and I'm going to trust those decisions. And I'll be wrong sometimes. I guess what will be the most unfortunate part is that I won't know – it's just different kinds of hits and misses – I won't know if I sent a client away or did something for that client that might have been better than I did, because I'm not going to have any more interaction with them; whereas if I take one client as positive, and if I do something and then screw up, then I'll know whether I've made that kind of mistake.

Author: What do you think about the issue of the counselor's value neutral position?

Professor 5: I think it's impossible. I think any counselor who believes that is only kidding himself or herself at least on any value level. I think you can try to be value neutral — you can say to yourself I am going to be value neutral, but as long as you are aware of making that choice, you are already made a choice not to be value non–neutral in the other direction. The other way I can see of being value neutral is being unaware, but I also happen to think that counseling itself is a value system. So just from that as a basis, thinking its worthwhile for one person being involved in helping another person and thinking it's possible means that people who don't choose that mode of interacting, I think, are wrong. So I am not value neutral to begin with any way you look at it. I value those people who come in and ask for as opposed to people who don't. I think you can be values–honest. If I am aware of my values and can make them explicit to the client, the client can deal with my values just the way the client is going to have to deal with everybody's values he or she interacts with. That in and of itself would be very beneficial to a client, but I don't think it's value–neutral.

Author: Do you believe it is appropriate for the counselor to engage in a moral issue in the counseling situation?

Professor 5: It's harder to answer in a specific sense, because I am not sure what it means to be engaged in a moral issue, should I debate a moral issue with clients or should I say what my moral stance is. Since values and morals to me are very close, I don't think it's possible for me to be amoral. It might be possible for me to be immoral, not operate according to my own moral value structure.

Author: What I mean, you think some moral point — this is right; this is wrong. If you think the client's behavior morally wrong, how to engage in that kind of issue? That's my intention.

Professor 5: I think it is appropriate. I think it's essential, at least if I am going to be genuine, honest and true to myself and true to them. If I think a client is doing something wrong and I would go so far as to say that I am tolerant about examining what the client is doing and reasons behind it before ultimately saying, "I believe in what you're saying or I don't believe in what you're doing." If I believed that somebody was doing something wrong, for example, going out and committing a crime, then I would confront that and I think I would be necessary for me to confront it. Sometimes it's risky to confront that, particularly some of these homicidal ones, suicidal is one thing. I think that that's wrong from my perspective, but get the question becomes one of whom you're doing damage to. Homicidal — the person could turn on me, and I wouldn't want him to. But other less clear moral issues I..., on a behavioral basis you do take stands on one way another. For example, an abortion. If you choose to discuss abortion as an option with someone, then I think you are saying that you might not do it yourself, but it's a tolerable option for you, and that's moral stance. And if you don't believe that, then I think you ought to be up front about it. It's alright to argue with someone, and say, "I can't take that moral stance and I believe this way." And I keep counseling obviously. But if you are going to take stance, then you're going to have to find someone else to work with you. Or if you're going to work with me, then one of the things you ought to know is that I am going to do more harm than good to you and everybody else around you, If you want to work with me on that basis, I don't know how far we'll go but that's what you're buying into here.

Author: Would you explain your position on prenuptial agreement? Especially, I raise this question because a lot of sociologists or lawyers currently emphasize to consider it before marriage. I am interested in how counselors think about that.

Professor 5: I am in favor of it from, for a number of reasons, but I am for it in a counseling context from the idea of, forcing people to be honest and concrete. It's easy for me to say something to you about how I think I would act in a situation, but when it comes to acting in the situation you'll find out what I really do think. And in answer to a prenuptial agreement, there is something about stating it explicitly, putting it down on paper and signing it that will not just mean honesty to the other person, but it forces you to be honest with yourself. Could you live with what you've just said you're going to do? I'm in favor of a more general kind of prenuptial agreement. I think people ought to talk about what their expectations are in relationships, specifically the long–term, specific marital relationships right from the beginning. Because if they think although it might be painful. And if you're not going to buy into, what the relationship is made out to be now, I mean, certainly things change, you might want to revamp the agreement to or your expectations occasionally just to see if, allow for some change, sure. But if you're not willing to agree to be in relationship now, as the people in the relationship want it to be, by knowing the good and the bad and the give and the take of it, then you don't have much change when things change. And to believe that they're going to change just because you want to change is pure folly. So even in a more generic sense this idea of a prenuptial agreement is being "We agree that this is what we think we're getting into; this is how we're going to go about things." I think is a very good idea. Specific prenuptial agreement, well, for most people I would think it would be a good idea. Sometimes it just gets to be a big game, which I don't think is healthy, "Can I get you to sign this thing and then...?" I don't know if you watch 'L. A. LAW', but it's one of my favorite shows, and in it there are these lawyers, and one of them, when they're about to get married, draws up a prenuptial agreement and wants his wife-to-be to sign it. As soon as she signs it, he tears it up, because the thing that he wanted was her to show that she was willing to commit to the relationship. And her reaction to that was not she was not willing to commit to the relationship, but she didn't like to be manipulated that way, she was really severely angry with him for having put her through the process when all he wanted from it was not the agreement but the metaphor that the agreement stood for. He wanted her to say something about the relationship through the agreement. And she didn't think that that was a very honest way of going about doing it. In that sense, watch out what you mean by prenuptial agreement.

Author: If you had a client that needed help with a prenuptial agreement, how would you help your client?

Professor 5: First of all, I discuss what the agreement means and just like I just did about what I think it's good for, not good for, so that they can be honest about it. And then if they want it, if they want it in a legal sense I'll send them to a lawyer because I'm certainly not a person who can set up the agreement. If they want the more general kind of prenuptial agreement, then I have the little things I use in classes, where I'll point out different areas in relationships, in all kinds of relationships that have to do with family and money and problem areas, and I'll help people talk about those areas and what they expect in those areas and what their partner expects, and negotiate what they think for their going to be able to agree on, the way they are going to operate in the relationships, including some little like escape clauses like how often we're going to regulate these things: Are they willing to tolerate a certain amount of ambiguity for now, but like the classic one here is, well, "Do you want children?" "Yes." Well you're agreed in a real general sense, but how many do you want, when do you want to have them, and whose going to take care of them and about genders are you interested in having, if that's ever a thing that can be determined. And I think people could say, OK, we want children and we don't want to discuss it any further now, but at least part of that agreement is at least we ought to discuss it any further now, but at least part of that agreement is at least we ought to discuss it not someday, but let's set every year we're going to check in, or every six months we're going to check in, and see where you are in relation to making a more firm decision about this area. The reason I think that one is important is because there are a lot of areas, where things fall apart, the two people who were in the relationship, and it's, but it's tolerable. Relationships dissolve. But children are affected, there are other human beings involved, and they are not toys to be played with in relationships. So if you are going to make decisions about children, that's one area in which you would be, not only for your own sakes, but for the sake of children that you want to bring in to this world, to be pretty clear about what you at least think you want to do. That's my bias there.

Author: When you have value conflicts between yourself and your client, then how do you solve that problem?

Professor 5: When I become aware of them, that's the first thing. It usually starts as a general sense of discomfort. Optimally what I will do is I'll voice the discomfort and let the client move more and more into a direct discussion of our differences. I say optimally, because sometimes that harder to do. There's always a kind of hesitance of my part. Optimally what I like to do is to confront it (value conflict) head–on, but I know that like anyone else, particularly in counseling relationships. To confronting the value conflicts, and particularly confronting them in supportive ways, not just say "Hey, we differ, and were going to have to fight this out", but trying to understand, asking the client to explain, saying "You know, I am not sure I agree with you, I am not sure I even follow you, explain more about why you behave the way you believe." It's usually worked out pretty well. My, it's not that it works all the time, because usually the people who are in counseling share some value structure with me, otherwise they wouldn't be there. But that dealing on a one–to–one level usually allows us to work out and expand both our understanding, and so both our tolerances of other's values. There are certain values that I would imagine are not amenable. Some very strong culture I value kinds of things are: if somebody thought that his children were his to beat, because that's just the way kids are, and I have a very strong value against it, then I don't think there would be any chance..., you would have to agree to that, to agree to disagree and to find some other way to handle things. Fortunately that has not come up ever for me, that strong of a values–conflict. A lot of times if there's a strong value–conflict it comes out on an intake kind of thing, where I don't get into a situation in the first place, because I don't think there's much chance unless people seek why clients agree. My guess that if I did I would have been much more likely to have run into that situation by now.

Author: Could you explain the relationship between wisdom and counseling techniques or skills?

Professor 5: Well, probably someone who has wisdom could learn counseling skills. As far as wisdom particularly in regard to counseling, what I said before is important. I think part of the way to learn is that not that you will gain wisdom per se just learning skills, but in order to open yourself up to taking the risk that's essential to gaining wisdom you have to have some skills initially, and you have to have enough confidence in those skills to operate in a risky situation. Included in those skills are to know not get yourself so far out on a limb that when the limb gets cut off, you drop too far. I honestly think that skills are essential, and there are certainly useful. “Are they the be–all and end–all?” “No.” And the indiscriminate use of skills without gaining the wisdom of how to use them at best is going to be relatively ineffective, and at worst is going to be damaging.

Author: Since Stanley Strong published the interpersonal influence theory in 1968, a lot of researches have been done. According to the social influence theory in counseling, there are three important counselor characteristics, that is expertness, attractiveness, and trustfulness as perceived by client. Which do you think is the most important variable among those three variables?

Professor 5: I have, unequivocally, no doubt in my mind that trustworthiness is most important. Because I don’t think without trustworthiness the other two are going to amount to anything. You can be expert, but if somebody doesn’t trust you, and therefore trust your expertness, forget it. You can be attractive, and some people are attractive and aren’t trustworthy. Now I think the other two can enhance your trustworthiness, but the necessary — and if you believe in Rogers — the necessary and sufficient condition for change is trustworthiness. And that’s part of what I would call that ‘being there’ that talked about earlier.

Author: Then, what is the second important counselor characteristic?

Professor 5: The second most important variable from my own perspective, I think, is expertness. Again, I think that attractiveness can be..., like if you're unattractive person, maybe nobody will ever learn that you're trustworthy or expert or anything like that. But the chances are far better, that you can overcome lack of attractiveness, and have more control in some ways over it. You know that people's perceptions of your attractiveness change in regard to how to expert they perceive you. You may not initially be attractive, but if they get to know you and trust you, then you are more attractive. So of the three I would think that that's the least important. And being a systems' person I understand that there's some interactive aspects, too. Much like I said, maybe nobody will ever learn your trustworthiness if you're so unattractive that they don't ever want to interact with you. I will still say overall I think you have more chance of overcoming a lack of attractiveness than the other two.

Author: How do you think about the relationship between the counselor's power in terms of social influence and the counselor's wisdom?

Professor 5: Part of the counselor's wisdom is realizing that you have power. I don't think that you can appropriately employ the power that you have unless you have the wisdom to employ it. So wisdom is essential if power is going to be benign. For one thing I think part of wisdom is knowing to the extent and limitations of your power on both ends; not only powerless you can be in certain situations, but also how powerful you can be. When I first started out in counseling, John Krumboltz was one of my teachers. And something that I've always kept that he said was that, "The counselor's job is always to work himself out of a job." What I interpret that is to give your power away and to empower the client. And it goes back to the idea that overall ends..., if I do a good job of empowering the client and the client gains wisdom or whatever and then can carry on that process without me. And I think that's the way things ought to be going. For one thing, it's very enervating for me to have to carry–on clients' lives for them. They really should be carrying–on their own lives, and recognizing that — it's not that they can't do with some help now and again. We all can, but that they can struggle as well as anybody else can.

Author: What you are saying is reminding me of the book I read a very long time ago. According to that book, the counselor's best performance is that when the counseling session is finished, then the client thinks, "I've solved my problem for myself." If they think that way, then that's the best counseling sessions rather than they think, "I get help from counselor's idea, advice, something like that."

Professor 5: If a client can say, "What do I need you for, and feel happy about it", that may be a good sign that the client has grown and is ready to go out. This is always finding something else to work on. What I am with it at the moment is trying to say, "Well you have the skills yourself to work on it, and the step you need to take is to be able to hear that from yourself and not from me.

Author: I've asked all my questions. I appreciate your giving time to me, and I think I learned a lot. Now, I want to listen to your comments and feedback about this interview. Those questions are the issues I, as a counselor, have been wondering and being curious. What kinds of feedback do you want to give?

Professor 5: I'll be interested in seeing what you do with the information in the long–run. I don't know that I would have said that I thought about what you asked about specifically in the terms you asked. But it is something that I do think about, the idea of what is counseling; even the term wisdom versus knowledge has been part of my program. So a lot of it is not exactly breaking ground, but like I said a couple of times I think I've made some connections that are useful to me. It's fun to talk about it. It's certainly fun to have someone say, "Gee, I want to listen to you." I honestly a lot of times worry that I'm not being particularly wise because when I listen to myself say these things it's like I've thought about it a lot and I have it all together, and that's exactly the time that something happens that connects me that I don't have it all together. So in listening to myself, liking some of the answers that I gave and thinking about having to pull things together, there's a little bit of a fear that I will just reinforce my own hubris. As I listen to myself I sense that in myself. I don't know what you call it, arrogance, or whatever. It like, "Ah, gee, I have it all together." The interview feeds that some. So, by now having said that' I'll either feel good about having said it or feel worse because it's so wise to realize it.

Chapter 9

WISDOM IN A FEMINIST AND PSYCHODRAMA PERSPECTIVE

Introduction of Transcript 6: This interview was done on November 16, 1990. When the Professor 6 was interviewed, she was the professor of counseling psychology and her age was forty–five years old. On that time her career experience of studying of counseling psychology was twenty–one years. She still works as the professor at the Department of Educational and Counseling Psychology, University of Kentucky and right now she is sixty–five years old. She indicated that her theoretical orientation of counseling was a feminist and psychodrama approach.

Author: First, I would like to ask several questions about your personal backgrounds. How old are you?

Professor 6: I am 45.

Author: Why did you choose counseling as your career?

Professor 6: I think I have one answer for when I chose it, and probably another answer that I understand now. I think I have always been drawn to understanding people; making sense out of them and the world; and always been conscious of people's feelings and then was someone who was good to talk to. So I think that was it as a choice. I initially was choosing between student personal and counseling, and decided I didn't like student personal.

Author: I am mainly concerned about what was your motivation to be a counselor.

Professor 6: It sounds vague and general, but I think mainly the interest in people.

Author: There are lots of different theoretical or philosophical counseling approaches. What is your main philosophical counseling approach?

Professor 6: I have two primary ones: I'm a feminist therapist and psychodrama. I have two minor ones: which are Gestalt and Cognitive Behavioral approaches.

Author: If you had to choose one great psychologist, especially in the counseling area, which would you prefer?

Professor 6: ....

Author: I asked mainly about three, I thought the large therapeutic approaches are Freud's psychoanalysis, Carl Rogers' humanistic, also behavioristic approaches, maybe the other two would be Ellis and Perls. Anyway, among the main three, what would you prefer?

Professor 6: Are you restricting my choices?

Author: Yes.

Professor 6: Out of the ones you mentioned, probably Carl Rogers would be the one I would be most drawn to. I don't like Ellis. I like Gestalt therapy but I don't like Perls. Psychoanalysis — I think Freud had enormous problems with women being assertive. I think part of problem is that we have many different reasons why we choose these different psychologists. And I would even name non–psychologists that I would choose.

Author: When did you start studying counseling?

Professor 6: 1969.

Author: Then, you have been working 21 years.

Professor 6: Yes.

Author: Well, then, let's go on to the main interview questions. What is wisdom? Would you define and describe what wisdom is according to personal and counseling experience?

Professor 6: I think that it's a knowing. I think it has intuitive components, as well as intellectual. And my hunch is that the wisest people are the ones who know and trust themselves. Wisdom is finding creative, receptive response to a situation. Wisdom is the ability to see all sides.

Author: Can you give a specific example and think out 'this is kind of wisdom' if you've had an experience?

Professor 6: The problem I'm having is that I'm trying to decide whether I can use the example I have, because it's somebody else's, and I'm trying to figure out a different way to say it. A woman I have a great deal of respect for tells a story about herself of growing up in a fairly dysfunctional family where there was a lot of denying going on about what was happening in the family, and particularly she had a sibling, who was probably schizophrenic, but it doesn't matter; and there was probably a history of other people in the family. And the family denied that there was anything wrong with the way these people thought and acted. And at a young age she often pointed out that "I think something's wrong with so–and–so." And she talked about an experience where she decided to believe herself, and trust her inner–voice despite the fact everyone around her was telling her she was wrong. To me that was an experience of wisdom — that part about learning to trust oneself, to be aware of oneself; but it's not just am inner–process, I think, involves the motion of having good contact with the environment, of being able to take–in information clearly from the outside as well as from one's inner–self. But the key in there seems to.... I believe in trusting yourself.

Author: In the same way, what is not wisdom? Would you explain what wisdom is not from personal and counseling experience?

Professor 6: What is not wisdom? Well I don't know. I guess

I have to do it in pieces. Not wisdom is bringing your life totally as others would have you live it, not listening to self at all. Not wisdom is..., I think wisdom requires a knowledge and appreciation of that which has gone before you, what others thought and created; so not wisdom would be ignorance of history and accomplishment and that kind of thing. I have mixed feelings about that one. I'm sure about that because...., back to wisdom. Wisdom is a balance; not wisdom is imbalance on any dimension I guess. Being too people-oriented, not being people-oriented at all; being too cognitive, not being cognitive at all; those kind of things. It requires a balancing of characteristics. I think what I'm doing is defining for you a healthy person, is what it feels like I 'm doing with wisdom, and I think I may equate those two things. And is a healthy person a wise person? I don't think wisdom has anything to do with age. I don't know how to state that in terms of non-wisdom, but I mean my example was of a five year old or four year old earlier. And I think wisdom spans the whole field.

Author: You mean wisdom is not related to age?

Professor 6: Not really.

Author: What is the difference between a wise person and a good counselor?

Professor 6: None.

Author: No difference.

Professor 6: I don't think so, because I think what's becoming clear to me is that I equate wisdom with health, with mental health, and well, a good counselor needs to be wise. Maybe the wise person may not have counseling techniques. You could be wise and decide not to focus your energy on helping other people express their problems. So the good counselor has to have knowledge about counseling theory and technique. In more cases you have a wise person, and the wise person can channel their wisdom in lots of different areas. I don't think you can have a good counselor who is not wise. You can have a wise person who isn't a counselor. But I don't think you have a good counselor who's not wise.

Author: What kinds of wisdom do you think a counselor should have?

Professor 6: I think I've already said some of them. I think they must know themselves. Secondly they must trust themselves. I think they must have a value system that encompasses a wide range of behaviors. Not only behaviors for themselves, but also acceptance of a wide range of behaviors. I have to trust my values.

Author: Maybe sometimes after you finish a counseling session, you think if I'd had wisdom I wouldn't have gone this way. If you've had those kinds of experiences, would you explain? I think that is why I raised this question. I also think a good counselor should have this kind of wisdom.

Professor 6: You mean to know which path to choose?

Author: Yes, in the counseling session.

Professor 6: Well, that's the intuitive part of wisdom that I talked about earlier. But I also think that wisdom is a knowing that there wasn't only path that might have worked. And I think that's what I also mean about a value system. I think you have to have..., it's not like I'm lacking values. You have to have values that embrace humanity, and in that is ability to see — what I said earlier — a wide range of alternatives that are possible, to see all sides. You know, I said the ability to trust others. I also think in wisdom there's a knowing whom not to trust.

Author: If you need help to solve your problems, what do you think the most important characteristics of the counselor are?

Professor 6: You mean if I were going to a counselor what would I look for?

Author: Yes, the most important characteristics of the counselor?

Professor 6: Empathy. Comfortableness with your own feelings, that they trust themselves and their intuitions, ability to know and express their deep feelings. And open, tentative about offering hypotheses. I would only go to a therapist who was experiential in some way. I went at my theoretical orientation in that way, and that would be psychodrama, Gestalt therapy, psychosynthesis, something in that range because that's how I learned. Someone who's spontaneous, and androgynous; not sexual stereotyping. I don't know what the opposite of mine is, but whatever the opposite of mine — I would want a counselor who has faced some life tribulations and grappled with them and come out on the other side, having a greater knowledge of himself. And I don't want someone who's never had any hard knocks. I don't know how you put that in quality, and main kind of sums up the not part, but I don't know what word you put on. It feeds back into wisdom. I'm not sure you can be wise unless you've had a variety of life experiences, some of them very difficult. And I don't think wisdom comes from an easy-going life.

Author: Which counselor would you choose to help your problems? One is a counselor who tries to teach wisdom for problem-solving. The other is a counselor who tries techniques or skills for problem-solving.

Professor 6: We distinguish the counselor's job in several ways. Sometimes a teacher, sometimes a supporter. But both are teachers, right? You see I don't know what it means to teach wisdom. That's why I'm not sure about what that means I know it means to teach skills for problem-solving. If teaching wisdom means telling me what to, then I wouldn't go there. But I'm not sure that's what you mean.

Author: If you did understand in that way, then I'll change it a little. The counselor who emphasizes wisdom for problem-solving.

Professor 6: Yes, that one. That's because I have lots of problem-solving skills. I don't need skills, I have them.

So I would not be going for counseling there. It's because I already have these, not because I don't value these. I think both are crucial.

Author: This is a very similar question. Do you believe that counselor is basically a behavioral manager, or is a counselor more concerned with the 'ends' of behavior?

Professor 6: What does 'ends' mean?

Author: Ends, purpose of life, not just behaviors.

Professor 6: Existential life–purpose kinds of things.

Author: Yes.

Professor 6: Yes. I pick that counselor definitely helping people find life–meaning and purpose as well as changing behavior.

Author: Do you believe there are general laws which regulate human behavior, such that one can scientifically predict the probable success of a counseling technique?

Professor 6: I don't see the question, I don't like that. But I don't see that what I'm trying to do is to regulate human behavior. I think that given I said to you earlier on the previous question that I am more concerned with purpose, life–meaning and that kind of thing, than regulating anybody's behavior. I believe there are some derived counseling outcomes, that there are general laws that aid in our understanding of those. And that there are specific counseling techniques that you can predict, would be effective with those. There are other counseling techniques which comes from..., which can be helpful or useful. Like the comparing X with Y kind of thing. Sometimes I'm an existential counselor, and sometimes I'm a behavioral therapist, and sometimes I'll try to compare those two approaches. If you are doing it according to science, you probably use the behavioral outcomes. The existential isn't even the basis of how they want to be judged. In term of your study, the existential person would probably want to try and measure in some way, and how do you measure it that the client becomes more wise? That they do define wise purposely; clarify their values and live more purposely. With respect to the treatment of depression, you would expect a person to get less depressed if they have a life purpose. And the behavioral therapist wouldn't go at it through that avenue.

Author: Anyway, a lot of behaviorists still emphasize just a observable behavior and the behavioral principles of neurosis based on those principles those define. Also, even though I have been involved in statistical research, sometimes help people to do statistical analysis, I often wonder whether a statistical output is significant in understanding human behavior.

Professor 6: I know it's not the correct thing to say, but I think that counseling is very hard to research in meaningful way, and how do you measure in a meaningful way what goes on in counseling.

Author: If you were a client, would you get counseling from a counselor like you?

Professor 6: Would I? Yes.

Author: Then, what kinds of benefits would you get from counseling?

Professor 6: I think I help clients learn to listen to their own inner voices, to appreciate their strengths in the way they cope with things, to accept all parts of themselves, to express their feelings and their identity, their sense of who they are. They learn how to be spontaneous. They gain more awareness of themselves. Very few feelings scare me, get me really intense. And if I find a spot like that, like I did a while ago, I went and did some work myself so that I would not..., so that I would be able to work with the client and not be afraid. I take a healthy, non–pathological approach to the client. And I think over time my clients come to do that for themselves, to view most of their ways of coping and behaviors in a positive light. This isn't to say that they don't decide to make some changes. But I think one of the things in therapy is to learn to appreciate how in the past they cope with some difficult situations, and how they may need to add to their repertory of the moment, that that old way of coping was good, but it's limiting them now. But in in there is a deep appreciation of who they are and how they cope.

Author: Usually when I see somebody, I recognize that he or she has strong and weak points about this, this, or that, and so on. Also I see in myself weakness. What about that?

Professor 6: Ugh..., I may de–emphasize the functional aspects of the person too much, not look clearly enough at that. I'm probably not systematic enough in intervening on a behavioral..., you know, when the client says I want to change my behavior today. I think I tend to go for the broader change than the quicker, specific behavior change. I work somewhat at that level, but I don't do it systematically. I think there is a trade-off both ways. I used to think I wasn't very confrontative, and a colleague watched some sessions of mine and said "You're very soft in how you confront, but once you've confronted, you don't let go." I don't know if confrontation.... I know that in non-counseling situations I tend not to confront unless I absolutely have to. So I avoid confrontation until it's right in my face. So I suspect that part of that is there.

Author: Let's go again to a question about wisdom. Where does wisdom come from?

Professor 6: OK. I'm going to take a..., this is not said in an exact way in psychodrama, but I think it is pretty close. In fact, it's the first time I've thought about it. From a psychodrama theory, which believes we're all born spontaneous, and spontaneity means have to ability to effectively cope with novelty from birth — before birth actually. Now I believe that spontaneity and wisdom are very closely tied. So that's led me to..., we were born with the ability to be wise, with an inner wisdom, ability to respond to where we are at that particular moment in time. I know a baby doesn't sit down and write a book, but given the task that; the life–task needed to be coped with at that moment, they have a wisdom. It's the ability to respond if the environment doesn't mess with it, if the environment is facilitative of it. I think wisdom comes from the inside, and it's there from the beginning. I think there's a lot of societal, environmental experience, that distance us from our wisdom and spontaneity, that teach us not to trust our sense of who we are, or whatever. It's not unlike, Carl Rogers' notion of 'positive growth tendency', is that what he calls it, but that the judgement from important people on the outside set up conditions of worth and other things like that, get in the way of staying in touch with our wisdom. So I think probably that the journey for most of us is to go back to our wisdom.

Author: You emphasize right now that wisdom comes from the inside, you try to understand yourself, something like that. It seems like several ways in which you have developed or tried to get wisdom. How have you been developing your wisdom?

Professor 6: I think the counseling experience is where my intent has been to understand myself. I think on a daily basis I try to be aware of myself in what I am doing, and learn from that, and try to..., And I work at things like trying to be aware of projections, try to work at my distortions of perceiving others and taking in information. I have done a fair amount of training in learning how to be more spontaneous, how to recapture I have my spontaneity, and think that is closer to my wisdom. I look for a mentor, role models, people who seem to be wise and how are they living their life, kind of how do they get their kind of thing, how do they in the moment convey their wisdom, how do they tap into it. The woman I talked about, who decided as a young child to trust herself, which the rest of the family was telling her view was wrong, she's in her 70's and every time I'm with her, which isn't often though, I learn more about wisdom and how to be wise. I think I learn something about my own wisdom by being around people who choosing to be around people who are healthy themselves, and who share some common values with me, because it is in that framework that I can trust myself, and by trusting myself learn to get closer to knowing about my wisdom. A lot of training — I've gone to a lot of training and counseling. And I think that's been direct at both acquiring skills but also at becoming a more effective person.

Author: Then, how do you think about the relationship between your counseling experience and wisdom? As you said, as a counselor you've been working for 21 years.

Professor 6: How helping others be wise? I'm not sure what you mean by the relationship.

Author: You have a lot experience. Has your counseling experience helped to get kind of wisdom? Not only helping the client but also understanding yourself.

Professor 6: Well, yes. I think I learn from clients every day that I've seen them. I think that's one the ways I'm wise, is that I listen and I learn from them. I'm especially intrigued by creativity in people, creativity for feeling for themselves, for coping with difficult situations, that kind of thing. And I've had some clients who're taught me a lot about that. It's amazing how creative people are. I think wisdom..., counselors by the virtue of their job maintain a chance of being wise.

Author: What is the best way to teach students in counseling areas to make good counselors?

Professor 6: There are limits on doing this in an academic

setting. I think there's a paradox in trying to prepare counselors in a graduate program — subjective judgments and grades — and that limits what we can do. If I didn't pay any attention to the university or academia, and I just say, "How do I create a good counselor?"

Author: Yes, just generally.

Professor 6: I think they need lots of specific and general knowledge, about psychology, about how people develop, about how people change — counseling theories, personalities, all the technical stuff — all the kind of courses that we try to give. I think they are all important basics. But to that knowledge area it's also important that the counselors know themselves and have come to trust themselves, and have worked through their own problems. So in my model of making the therapist it would be for people to do counseling for a long time. And I encourage them to do that, and I think some of the best counselors I've seen are ones who're been in therapy themselves. The problem is you can't require that in the academic world; you can only encourage it. Another aspect would be to help people clarify their values and their attitudes and to challenge those attitudes that are likely to be harmful or restrictive.

There are some limits there, too, because there are values on values. I think it's important for people who are trained counselors to say, "it's not ok to be a racist", it's not ok to be a sexist", and "it's not ok to stereotype people because of their age or their sexual preference." I think there are some basic values which are debatable in society that are less debatable in the counseling world. That if you are a racist, I don't think you can be a good counselor. There's that kind of thing. I think in training good counselors they have to have a way of watching good counselors as a bridge between the book and then actually sitting down with someone, whose they can do someone harm, and role-modeling. That's one of the things I like about the clinic. Now and then they need the role-modeling as a counseling technique. But I think that people who are teaching need to be open and fairly self-disclosing, and I think that's a pretty radical position. I think that's awful true for counselors. I think there has to be an environment for developing a super counselor, where mistakes are confronted, but the person is not banned. That's one of the problems in academia; it's another problem connected with, that when you actually get to the level of working with real people, it's a bad mistake might make you wonder about whether a person should begin or should not. Let's go back to the personal counseling thing. A good counselor needs to have a very accurate understanding of their interpersonal relating, and helping improve that understanding, or responsibilities that go with the counselor.

Author: If your counselor or psychotherapist were Freud or Skinner, would you get counseling or psychotherapist?

Professor 6: I would not go to Freud.

Author: If you found Freud or Skinner as your counselor in the room, what would you do?

Professor 6: I'm not sure if I understand.

Author: If your psychotherapist were Freud?

Professor 6: And I go into a room and there's Freud?

Author: Yes, or Skinner, do you want to get counseling or therapy?

Professor 6: Let's stick with Freud. Now what do you want to say about, what question am I answering? If he were my counselor, then what?

Author: Would you get counseling or psychotherapy from him?

Professor 6: You mean, would I stay?

Author: Yes.

Professor 6: I would not stay. As soon as I found out it was Freud, I'd say "Bye".

Author: Then, what about Skinner?

Professor 6: No, I wouldn't stay.

Author: Why?

Professor 6: Freud, because I think he devalued women, and didn't have a clue or a knack for understanding women. I know that's too strong, but anyway he hurt us. I don't respect a psychotherapist as he did. When he gave up his theory sexual abuse, sexual problems, he caused a lot of problems just because he got pressure from his male counterparts. He gave women 80 years of injustice, but we're just now moving out of. I'm very angry with him.

Author: Would you get counseling from Carl Rogers?

Professor 6: Rogers. Yes, because he's warm, intuitive

person who trusts himself, has deep respect for the other person. I'm sure he would be sufficient for me to get what I really need out of counseling.

Author: How would you think the relationship between your level of self–understanding and understanding the client's problems?

Professor 6: Absolutely matched. I think whenever I have a block is probably going to end up in a block in understanding the client. So whenever I don't understand myself, it's going to be very difficult for me to understand the client. Real close, there's not probably a 100% correlation, but 80%, something like that.

Author: Have you thought about what is the best way for developing your level of understanding?

Professor 6: Developing my wisdom.

Author: What do you think about the issue the counselor's value–neutral position?

Professor 6: I don't think value–neutral exists. Even if you confide you're confided you're going to not show any of your values, there is no way you cannot show any of your values. And I think having values is a part of being human. If you show me a value–neutral person, I'll show you a person who has no definition. And it would be scary as a counselor. I mean people have got to have a sense of themselves. Maybe that's some part of wisdom. The people who used to say the counselor should try to be value–neutral in the session, I'd say just, weren't aware of where their values were sticking out. Feminist therapy says the counselor has a responsibility to be clear about their value system with the clients in order to give them a choice, and to own their value system.

Author: Do you believe that it is appropriate for the counselor to engage in moral issues during the counseling session?

Professor 6: Depends on the 'engagement'. I mean to help a client explore...?

Author: Involved in the moral issues with the client.

Professor 6: Give me an example.

Author: Maybe not very strong, but sometimes you have a very different point of view from your client's. Not very directly like a debate, but your moral position as a counselor is different from your client's position.

Professor 6: I'll help the client explore their own moral dilemmas about their..., how they feel about, if they're pregnant, how they feel about abortion as an alternative. That's certainly a moral issue. I don't feel like, I hope that what I do there is to help them explore their own reaction on both sides of moral issue, to clarify their own position, rather than impose mine, or debate mine with them. I might debate what I thought with them. Moral issues and value issues are almost indistinguishable, aren't they? It's not very easy to tell them apart. Is it a moral issue to, is it a value issue that men and women should be equal, or is it a moral issue? Certainly many cultures, many people who would say it's not a moral issue. I would say it's a moral issue and involves a value issue.

Author: Would you explain what your position about the issue of a prenuptial agreement is?

Professor 6: I have no idea.

Author: The reason I raised this question is that a lot of sociologists explain the necessity of prenuptial agreement as a current social issue in America according to Time Magazine article which I read. I also want to know how counselors think about and solve a prenuptial agreement.

Professor 6: If only the prenuptial agreements have good protection in them, if they cover strictly things I bring to a marriage, money, land, that kind of thin; I don't think they're fair to say that whatever I make during a marriage, or whatever stays mine. I think marriage is an economic arrangement for one thing, and should be shared resources. I don't even know if I really believe that. It's so tied–up with women's issues. I don't know how to sort it out. It depends on from case to case. So for instance, I have some friends, who got married at age 55 or so; they both came in with a long career, and their own financial resources; each has their own kids from previous marriages. Prenuptial agreements in that marriage was economically equal in many respects, and they came to that marriage on equal footing, and those kinds of conditions, yes, I think it makes sense to protect each of the children from, each of those people to protect their inheritance for whatever. As soon as we get off equal footing, I don't know. Then I think it depends on the situation.

Author: If you had a client who needed help with a prenuptial agreement, how would you help your client?

Professor 6: I'd send them to a lawyer.

Author: You want to send them to a lawyer?

Professor 6: Yeah, I might help them as far as their feelings about it. But I definitely wouldn't help them draw it up.

Author: When you have a value conflict between yourself and a client, then how would you solve that problem?

Professor 6: All my values, I state where I am. I encourage them to do the same. Then we must engage in a conference about whether that value conflict is large enough or important enough that it would get in the way of us effectively working together. If we decide that it's large enough, then I would refer somebody. Another way — I think I do some of this, it's not full-proof — is to screen in the beginning, to know something about the client's values.

Author: When I raised this question, I thought about, as you explained, we are always value system as human beings.

Professor 6: I think it's a matter of degree. How central that value is to that person, and how central that value is to me, plus haw far apart are we. Are we this far apart or are we that far apart? I mean if you've got a value that's very central to that person, and we're very far apart, many clients will say "I'm a very deeply religious person from this religion. I want counseling that will not question that point of the view, where do you stand on that?" And I have to say most of the time..., the answer to that question for me would be you probably need to get a counselor who shares your religious belief, give that that's what you want. They're saying my values are very firm, I don't want them messed, and where do you stand.

Author: Could you explain what the relationship between wisdom and counseling techniques or skills is?

Professor 6: Well, on the counselor side of things, the counselor needs wisdom to choose at any given point in time among a number of skills or techniques one would use. That choice needs to be in some kind of integrated whole. Not "Let's do this empty chair right now, it sounds fun." The person has to be knowledgeable about theory as well as technique. I mean wisdom is there somewhere. I don't know exactly how to define it. It's a knowing the relationship between those two things. Also I think that there's an intuitive part of that process, that one cannot explain totally by theory. On the client side, I think there are many techniques which help the client know something about their own wisdom.

Author: In 1968, Stanley Strong published the interpersonal influence theory in counseling based on Festinger's cognitive dissonance theory. He emphasized there are three important counselor characteristics, that is, expertness, trustfulness, and attractiveness. Since that a lot of research has been done about how clients perceive the counselor's characteristics. According to the recent review about research in especially counseling process, it shows the social influence theory has been the most popular topic. Which do you think is the most important variable among the three variables?

Professor 6: Trustfulness.

Author: What is the second important variable?

Professor 6: From the counselor point of view, not the client?

Author: Not the client. Because you have been working as a counselor, I want to listen to your point of view.

Professor 6: I know. As me as a client, or as me as a counselor?

Author: Yeah, as a counselor, not a client.

Professor 6: Expertness. I have some problems with the narrowness of the definitions of these terms in the literature. So, based on my own definition.

Author: For example, an attractiveness. As you said "I am a feminist", maybe if clients say "I want to choose a counselor with similarity"....

Professor 6: I definitely think that's important. I don't think the kind of expertness of, like, degrees on the wall kind of thing. I think that kind of expertness disappears after a couple of sessions. The kind of expertness that comes from both being on effective person in life and having a great deal of knowledge about the field, is very important.

Author: As the first important variable, you emphasized trustfulness.

Professor 6: I think it's the cornerstone of counseling. I believe that answer to quest with confidentiality or whatever.

Author: What do you think about the relationship between counselor's power in terms of social influence and counselor's wisdom?

Professor 6: I'm trying to think of a word from the literature about different kinds of leaders, or different kinds of role power. There's a kind of role power — which the labels escapes me — that comes from being a very effective person that others are drawn to because of how you conduct yourself. And I believe that kind of power is very important in the counseling relationship. And that's what plays a part in social influence, I also believe the way I define that kind of a role, I believe that most of the time you can say that that person's a wise person.

Author: When you have power, you influence well.

Professor 6: But how? Even the word 'social influence'.... I think I have a lot of social influence with my clients. I also work very hard at having an egalitarian a relationship as possible. And I depend more on — in the egalitarian part of that I'm deliberately trying to reduce my power in the sense of hierarchical power. So it depends on what kind of power we're talking about. There are some theories that want to expand that hierarchical power, or capitalize on it, and there are other theories that want to minimize it. But I think, so there are other kinds of power that are tied to social roles. It's the kind of thing that I think I would have to sit down with a paper. What I am drawn to do at the moment is to jump up and go get a paper that somebody wrote on power, so that I could clarify for myself some of the different kinds of power. I'd want to look at the different kinds of leader roles, and I want pull out some stuff on social influence and compare those definitions, and then I could answer your question. I mean that's tough question, a very complex question without real specific definitions. I'd probably give my own definition, but to do that I'd need to go.

Author: When I asked about counselor's power, I intended this. If you have three high levels — expertness, trustfulness, and attractiveness — then I think you have power as a counselor because you have influence based on the social influence theory.

Professor 6: But you see the contradiction there, I mean yes, I have social influence. But the contradiction for me is that at the same time I have social influence. I am trying to help this client come to trust themselves, and learn about their own choices at an inner level rather than be socially influenced. You know what I'm saying? So I want to be very careful how I use my social influence.

Author: When I raised this question, I thought a counselor needs wisdom, how to try to keep the balance.

Professor 6: Right, the balance is there, there's paradoxes there, and I think maybe the only way of out of that I think is with wisdom. And I hope the majority of the time I'm able to do that. I mean that is use of my social influence in the service of the client learning to wise.

Author: Now I asked all main questions. I want to listen to your comments and feedback about this interview.

Professor 6: Some of the questions are confusing to me, and I don't know if it's one of those kinds of things, using words which have many different meanings. It's not that they are not good questions, it's not, you know, writing a good paper, or article or a book or something about these things, but they're hard to answer in the moment without putting a lot of thought into them and being real precise about definitions. I thought it was an interesting process to define wisdom, and just to ask a person to define wisdom. I learned from that that my definition of wisdom is very tied-up in the trust of myself, and knowing self, it's not like I'm a philosopher, that's for sure. I've never thought of myself as being one of wisdom and spontaneity, I've known some about that relationship, but I don't think I've ever used the word 'wisdom' there before, and I think that after talking with you that's clear to me. That the person I see as most spontaneous is also very wise. What I think is going on by the questions you're asking, the basic question is "What is wisdom?" and "How important is it for a counselor to process and use?" Now I think your question about what the difference is between a wise person and a good counselor. I never thought about that in quite those words, but that was an interesting point.

Chapter **10**

WISDOM IN A PROBLEM-SOLVING PERSPECTIVE

Introduction of Transcript 7: This interview was done on November 27, 1990. When the Professor 7 was interviewed, he was the professor of counseling psychology and his age was forty-two years old. On that time his career experience of studying of counseling psychology was twenty years. He still works as the professor at the Department of Educational and Counseling Psychology, University of Kentucky and he is sixty-two years old. He indicated that his theoretical orientation of counseling was a problem-solving, humanistic with behavioral techniques approach.

Author: First of all, I would like to ask a few questions about your personal backgrounds.

Professor 7: Okay.

Author: Now, how old are you?

Professor 7: 42 years old of age.

Author: Why did you choose counseling as your career?

Professor 7: Well, at the time when I was in college, I was looking for something in psychology area and looking for different types of programs and found the rehabilitation counseling and felt that this would be an appropriate type of applied counseling area and would be an area which could relatively practice and have job opportunity as the Master degree level. At that time I was just looking at the Mater degree types of things. I wanted a career that involved direct contact with clients and would also be a type of opportunity in job and profession which I would be able to interact with other professionals abd community resources. But I selected rehabilitation counseling.

Author: I am wondering what your motivation when you decided studying counseling was.

Professor 7: I wanted to go some kind of field beyond the bachelor degree. I was getting my bachelor degree in psychology. I realized that it would not be sufficient to working in a human service area. There were other alternative areas that you could do with a degree. One alternative would be teaching. I was a little interested in being a public school teacher because I really wanted to confine at the classroom. You can go into sales types of work. You can be an insurance sales person, but I wasn't interested in that. You can go into public relations and advertising areas, but I thought that wasn't what I was pursuing in my mental point of view. I wanted something that would be concrete and would be able to keep on my interest in the psychology major area.

Author: There are lots of different counseling approaches. I want to know what your main philosophical or theoretical orientation in counseling area is.

Professor 7: I feel that the most effective approach, the way counselors typically practice today, would be a short-term intervention, basically the problem-solving approach that combines humanistic and behavioral techniques. That focuses on an individual. That looks at helping individual determine who he/she is in terms of looking at behavior change, looking at paradigm that helps somebody's behavior, but also looks at techniques that assist or consolidate clients to move in a direction of desire of change. So that would be a combination of both behavioral and humanistic approaches based human nature of individual. Basically I believe that it's important to raise self–esteem of people. I think that many of difficulties people count are lack of self–esteem, low self–image, sense of poor self–worth, loneliness. My view is that helps somebody to feel better about himself, spoken by how they feel but get reinforcement by environment or doing things that make them feel better about themselves. That's a kind of approach I use as a theoretical frame.

Author: If you had to choose one approach among a Freudian, a humanistic (Rogerian) and a behavioral approach, which one would you choose?

Professor 7: If I just had to choose one, I really would not choose a Freudian. I would be close to the humanistic approach combined with behavioral techniques.

Author: When did you start studying counseling area?

Professor 7: The first counseling class I took was the class of guidance counseling. I believe that I took that in my senior year in college. I was in psychology major. I took other psychology classes such as experimental, social, general psychologies, motivation and perception. But the counseling class I took was actually in my senior year.

Author: Can you tell what year it was?

Professor 7: I think that it was 1970.

Author: That means you have been working around 20 years in the counseling area.

Professor 7: That's right.

Author: Now, let's go on to the main questions on this interview.

Professor 7: Go ahead.

Author: What is wisdom? Would you define and describe what wisdom is according to your personal and counseling experiences?

Professor 7: I think that wisdom is a constructive variable that someone develops over period time. Wisdom is not something that somebody can read about, study about. I think that wisdom is accumulation of experiences and knowledge, combination of both book reading and learning, studying as well as experiences. People acquire wisdom through working with other students and clients, through professional activities, through constructive research. Wisdom is being able to understand and assess situations and people, being able to understand how people behave and how situations occur, and being able to know how to function with any given situation in order to provide counseling to clients. Wisdom is something that comes from individual having positive self–esteem, being able to understand relationships, being able to understand how human nature functions, and being able to convey that to other people, not to impose that, but to convey that students, colleagues, peers, to maintain relationship. The wise person is somebody who is able to draw upon from his/her experiences and knowledge, apply that at any given situation. Wisdom is something being able to know and understand the situation, being able to rationally deal with it without losing control and without being hot tempered, being able to give unbiased assessment and judgment and how to respond to a situation.

Author: Then, what is not wisdom? Would you describe and

explain what wisdom is not from your personal and counseling experiences?

Professor 7: Well, it is not something that is imposed on somebody. It is not something that is given without being asked. It is not something that is based solely on opinion, is based on experience, is based upon being able to learn to most experiences. It is not something that is acquired over night or quickly. It is not something that you learn from textbook. I don't think it is something that can be taught. It is more than attitude, more than approach. Wisdom can be varied from different people. Different people can have different perspectives. I think that the wise person is somebody who is able to communicate values without imposing values. Someone who has wisdom is able to communicate how he/she can handle a given situation without expecting that someone else would use that solution or answer. It's a difficult question to answer what it is not because I think that certain degree varies from person to person. I think people can be wise in different areas depending upon what their area and expertness is.

Author: You did explain what wisdom is or what is not wisdom. Now, what is the difference between a wise person and a good counselor?

Professor 7: I think that a good counselor is a wise person. I think you can have differences between somebody knowing technical skills of counseling and knowing how to say the right things. That doesn't someone is wise. The ability to have right techniques doesn't make somebody wise. The ability to know when to apply techniques and what techniques to utilize makes somebody wise. So, for example, if you could review counseling tapes, all counselors' answers would be technically correct and appropriate, but may not be wise for that client because they missed the boat for that client. So when I look at a good counselor, I say a good counselor is really a wise counselor. You can have a good counselor who is not wise by being able to say the right thing but not say the right way and the right time.

Author: By what you are saying, I understand your own idea that a good counselor is a wise person, but I don't see exact differences between a wise person and a good counselor.

Professor 7: You don't see a difference. A wise counselor is able to communicate his/her experience and knowledge through types of questions asked, is able to utilize counseling situation to help the client without imposing values, communicating certain set of values. A good counselor who is not wise may just know the right thing say but not have experience and knowledge to know when to say that right thing. I may say that he technically looks right but may not be beneficial for clients.

Author: Then what kinds of wisdom do you think the counselor should have?

Professor 7: I think that learning counseling is on-going process. You never have finished counseling. You always learn process and always change process. The counselor should be knowledgeable about human nature, about theories of personalities, should be knowledgeable about how people change. The wise counselor should know aspects of different cultures, different cultural background and orientation, should be able to not impose values, or not impose expectation on individual, should be willing to listen to carefully what a client says, to encourage client to listen carefully. The wise counselor should facilitate and encourage client to be able to develop his/her own sense of variety. A wise counselor will be one who does that. A wise counselor is one who does not dictate clients, does not tell clients what they should do, but should be able to help clients come to their own conclusion. A wise counselor is one who helps clients achieve their goals, develop their techniques.

Author: Now, please imagine a role–playing situation. If you need help to solve your problems, what do you think the most important characteristics of the counselor are?

Professor 7: I prefer someone who has, the very basic characteristic in any human relation, empathic understanding, someone who listens, who in empathic listener, is able to clarify asked questions, who does not impose values, who tries to have positive regard, who is accepting, who is genuine, who is concrete. That is the basic simple characteristic. Beyond that, someone who demonstrates trustworthiness, demonstrates interest in a relationship, someone who has wisdom. That's what I have described and defined, who is willing to share that wisdom in an appropriate way without imposing his/her solution on me for whatever problem might be, who is understanding of reasons why a person would be unable to solve difficulty in responding certain circumstances. That's what I am looking for.

Author: Which counselor would you choose for solving your

problems? First, the counselor who tries to teach wisdom for problem-solving; second, the counselor who tries to teach techniques or skills for problem-solving.

Professor 7: First one.

Author: Why? Would you explain about that?

Professor 7: I think that the first person is more effective in long run in terms of helping for a person to achieve self-actualization rather than specific techniques. I think that the first counselor would be able to help in terms of being able to find techniques. In my case, I would say that I would have ability to do most of things needed to be done. It might be just responding more effective. For example, I might know how to deal with another student or another faculty member. So my need would be to define to do it more appropriately. The second approach would be for someone who has not that, who does not know how and what to say. So I would go to the first approach.

Author: Do you believe that the counselor is basically a behavioral technician (or manager)? Or is the counselor more concerned with the 'ends' of human behavior?

Professor 7: I think the counselor is more concerned with

the 'ends' of human behavior, not just technician.

Author: Why? Would you explain more about that?

Professor 7: I think, if we are going to be successful in the long run, we have to be more than technician. We have to be people who can help clients be able to make change both at immediate level in terms of problem–solving, short–term intervention, but also long–term level in terms of permanent solution and help the clients not just deal with immediate crisis but apply those techniques and skills when the counselor is not available to them, help clients develop a kind of background to know how to solve future problems. I think that the second counselor is more appropriate.

Author: Do you believe that there are general laws which regulate human behavior, such that one can scientifically predict the probable success of counseling techniques.

Professor 7: I think there are laws we are going to know them. I think in some way maybe in 50 years from now we will know what they are. I don't think we know them right now. I think at one level there are biological determinant behaviors. I don't think we know what those are yet. At another level, I think if we know those biological determinant behaviors, we could have some prediction of some general types of behaviors. But I think at this point our knowledge is very limited. I think the strides that are made of in future are going to be more based upon medical knowledge and medical information, brain mapping, physiological rather than behavioral, in advance medical ground rather than humanistic counseling ground. But that doesn't rule out having one–to–one counseling or group counseling at all. I think we are going to a better job in terms of medication, for example, control certain behaviors and certain types of dysfunction. I think we will have the better medication in future. But the long way off right now.

Author: I still didn't get an exact picture relating to my question. You emphasize medication in the future. By what you are saying, my understanding is that medication based on scientific investigation will try to find general laws to regulate human behavior in the future.

Professor 7: I think that right now medication is very rudimentary and very crude. I think in 50 years from now much more we will be able to apply medication or drugs to deal with specific problems and specific behaviors. The better knowledge of what parts of brain control are different functions, the better knowledge of relationship between person's cultural background of how that performs upbringing and biological determinant behavior. That's all very dangerous subject to get into. But I think that's the direction we are going to get into.

Author: If you were a client, not a counselor, would you get counseling from a counselor like you?

Professor 7: Probably yes.

Author: Then, what kinds of benefits or advantages would you get from counseling?

Professor 7: I would do look for a counselor who would be active, who would not be passive like a Freudian counselor or therapist, would be someone who is problem–solving oriented, someone who basically would communicate with same value, would have same value, similar value I have.

Author: OK then, would you describe just a little bit your strong points you think you have for your client's change?

Professor 7: That's always difficult to describe a person's own strong points. I would say that I would see strong points that someone else might not see in me. I would say that I think, my world of view is positive, would be affect. I would try to get people to change behavior. I usually say, "This is what you want to now. Where do you want to be in 6 months from now? How do you get from what you want now from someone else? What do you want to do? What do you want to achieve?" I take a very kind of active stand, take stand to encourage people, that tries to combine of changing behavior with talking types of therapy and counseling to get people think of what they want to be and act on that, to do things to change that. That's kind of what I look for in myself. But again I think that it's important to have not just behavior therapy, behavior modification, what you set up behavior system without person's interaction and involvement.

Author: You already explained what is wisdom and what is not wisdom. Now I want to ask a question about wisdom. Where do you think wisdom comes from?

Professor 7: It comes, I believe, from person who is able to communicate, probably comes from something inside somebody. I think a lot of people who can wisdom not really have interest in communicating with others. I think a lot of people who don't have wisdom either try to communicate or don't try to communicate. I think it starts by somebody who is interested in working with helping other people. He doesn't have to be a counseling person. He can be a mentor in business who brings someone in training how to do a job. It can be, you know, someone who trains a successor, someone who is interested in doing that kind of thing. Wisdom comes from somebody who is interested in people, interested in helping someone, interested in a large society which they live in, or interested in the better society, the better employees who work for jobs they have or whatever might be. So it's a matter if application of knowledge that somebody has. On the other hand, there are people who don't have interest in communicating those things.

Author: Then, how have you been developing your wisdom?

Professor 7: You are making an assumption I've been developing wisdom. I don't know I have been developing or not. I would say if I have been developing it, it's a matter of what I described earlier, a matter of doing a lot of different reading not just in literature of counseling and psychology but also just trying to read books and newspapers, knowing as much as I can about many things as I can, and trying to learn from experiences that I have. I think that's part of wisdom, learning from experiences. And then when someone calls upon me to help them with problems and make decision, then I will apply what I know and what I learn. Hopefully I'll be able to draw upon all those things that I just described to help person make a decision or select something. That's on-going process.

Author: Maybe I think you already explained a little bit. How do you think about the relationship between your counseling experience during last 20 years and wisdom?

Professor 7: I think that my ability to be a better counselor has been improved all the period of time. I hoped that I am able to learn from things I said, experiences and techniques, books and so on. Hopefully I am able to apply that in a way what is improved each time I worked with somebody. Now again you know, I think beside that on the other hand, the world changed. You have to keep up with different values, attitudes, and expectations people have. So I think that sometimes I ought to have wisdom. When I was 24 years of age, values of people at that time are different from values of people who are 24 years of age today. Being able to understand how those change, not just say for what I did when I was 24, but to say what people now do, how and what has changed. I don't think in the long run that's a lot of time, but you know, it's 18 years ago right now, things have changed. It's important to conveying wisdom not just to apply the solutions that were involved appropriately in the early 1970's but look at what separate things from all I did. Things have changed. A wise person is able to understand that.

Author: Right now I want to be a good student, and also in future I hope I will be a good instructor and a good counselor. Now I want to learn from your point of view. What is the best way to teach students in counseling areas to make a good counselor?

Professor 7: I think one of the best things to do is to be a role model. I think a good way to communicate counseling ability is through supervision of people in counseling. Now I am going beyond basic lecture classes in counseling. I think that people need basic lecture classes, need to read books, need theories, know the techniques, know how a thing's done, and then need to practice that. I think a real task teaching someone comes in in terms of supervision of person and ability to supervise somebody and provide different, wide and open ways of doing things. I think that's what people really want students in counseling to practice counseling. You have to go out and apply it and help client. Counselors have to integrate any variance between what they learn from books and their experience in the field of clients.

Author: When you explained your personal background, you said that your main approach is the problem-solving approach, being combined of behavioral and humanistic approaches. Now, if your counselor or psychotherapist were Freud or a radical behaviorist like Skinner, Perls, or Ellis, would you get counseling from them?

Professor 7: Would I get from many of those? Probably I would come to Albert Ellis if I had to choose one. I think Perls is a little bit too confrontational for me.

Author: What about Freud?

Professor 7: I think a lot of what Freud did was accurate and excellent. But I think his approach is false. I think his approach is too time-consuming. I might be uncertain about one life event. Freud, his working and dealing was hysterical reaction and someone's paralysis in one hand. He really had in that aspect traumatic incidence. I am not certain where behavioral function is. I don't know I agree with that I agree with talking part of it, I am not certain I agree with free association completely. I am not certain I agree with lack of contact between client and counselor or therapist. I am not certain I agree with techniques and theory going back someone's traumatic event and discovering everything, you know, kind of putting and setting back together in the right way. So I don't think I would choose it.

Author: Then, would you get counseling or psychotherapy from someone who emphasizes a totally different approach from yours?

Professor 7: Probably not. If I have no choice, I would. Again I think the key thing here is person communicating counseling skills which I described earlier, positive regard, empathy, genuineness, concreteness. That comes across, I think that can be effective. Beyond that, I think you don't have to be somewhat compatible with styles of counselor's using. If you are not compatible theoretically, I think that counseling isn't effective at all.

Author: How do you think the relationship between your level of self-understanding and understanding your client's problem?

Professor 7: Well, I think that a part of empathy comes from a person experiencing in his/her life, experiencing frustration, experiencing failure, experiencing family problems. I think that being empathic is a part of developing wisdom too. Knowing how to deal with those, handle those things you don't want to make those happen or you don't want to stay with. Well, a lot of things happen, for example, you got a few death of your family, you are going to make a wife, and so on. I think it's important to learn about those, learn about your reaction and other's reaction. If you are young, you kind of think that goes on forever. I think as you get older, you get better to put things from the other's perspective.

Author: What do you think about the issue of counselor's value–neutral position?

Professor 7: I think it's almost impossible to be value–neutral because I think no matter whom the counselor is, they communicate some values when they work with clients. You know, counselor comes in jeans, blue jeans, has sandals on, that communicates some values rather than counselor comes in jackets, ties, that communicates other values. I think you can't be value–neutral. I think you can say, "OK, I am communicating values. I have values, but I am not here for imposing on you. I am here and help you to define your values. So forget how I look, let's concentrate on you. We can talk about different values and different value systems, but we are focusing on you. I am going to be who I am. I expect you accept that. I accept who you are." That's a part of counseling process. I am not gonna be somebody I am not. If I am counseling an Asian client, I am not gonna try to say as I am a real Asian. But it doesn't look in that way who I am. This is who I am, and then ask the client to accept that.

Author: A lot of sociologists and lawyers emphasize prenuptial agreement before marriage. So I have been wondering what counselors think about this issue. Would you explain what your position about the prenuptial agreement is?

Professor 7: I am not certain how I do answer that. My understanding of a prenuptial agreement is that something brings his/her own possessions into marriage, and prenuptial agreement says that this party brings this item, this matter of wealth and the other party brings these all here and when they get divorce or death, they would decide how they divide up. So a lot of times a prenuptial agreement occurs in second marriage. Well, the other family members from first marriage, children might claim to some of properties. I think that's a part of prenuptial agreement. That's what I am understanding it. I don't think that counselor would take a position on that. I think that's one of legal questions from my counseling training point of view.

Author: Now, if you had a client who needed help about a prenuptial agreement, how would you help your client?

Professor 7: I would not help them. That's not a role that a counselor is doing.

Author: OK, now we can think about that in this way. You sent your client to a lawyer because you think that's not your role. After the client talks with a lawyer, the lawyer sent the client to you. Then, how can you help him?

Professor 7: Perhaps the way to do it is talk with clients about what they want to enter a prenuptial agreement or not, what their implications are. But I wouldn't get specifics if what would be contents of that agreement. That's a legal question. I would talk with clients about pros and cons of prenuptial agreement from a legal point of view, how clients decide their willing to go into that. As far as it would be contents on that, I don't believe it's a counseling question.

Author: When do you have value conflicts between yourself and client, would you explain how you solve that problem?

Professor 7: It depends on how serious value conflicts are. A counselor says, "I don't like it, I have prejudice against people with Asian background." The counselor says that to you. That becomes a point of saying "You can't be my counselor. I have to have somebody who accepts something like that." I think there are genuine differences. There will be differences people. But I think it would be a framework of respecting other people. That's a part of counseling process to work those out, to understand those, to understand different value systems. So I would contact and accept people, say, "My values are different from yours. That doesn't mean that we can't work together as client and counselor." I think that's certainly very appropriate to deal with value conflicts because I think how clients learn by going beyond just their values. I think a lot of times people have difficulty functioning because they have difficulty knowing about they deal with other values they don't take. Those values can be a way of behaving, could be an approach of education, could be a lot of different values, appearance, presentation, and so on. I think it's important for counselor to work with clients, to help clients examine different values, different circumstances.

Author: Let's go back again to a question about wisdom. Could you explain what the relationship between and counseling techniques or skills is?

Professor 7: I would see that wisdom comes in an application of those techniques or skills, application of knowing when to do something or not to something, when to raise something or not to raise something, sensitivity to doing different thing for client, sensitivity to knowing how career and some events affect client. it's to me application of wisdom comes in being able to sensitivity to needs of different individuals and being able to know the impact that certain event might have. For example, a counselor never has experience of death of someone close of a family. A client comes in who has. It may be somewhat difficult really to know that impact that they didn't have experience on themselves. Beyond that, a whole meaning of death is different cultures. Life has different meaning and has different impact to the same event to a person who has 20 siblings versus someone who doesn't have, in one system versus another system. So that might be family values communicating in that way. The part of it might be cultural. But I think having a lot of experiences, learning from those without imposing how the counselor handle or respond to it, just to know the different way of handling of it, I think, makes the counselor more sensitive to clients.

Author: In 1968, Stanley Strong published the social influence theory in *the Journal of Counseling Psychology.* Many researchers have investigated the counselor's characteristics relating to the social influence theory since he suggested that. According to the social influence theory in counseling, there are three important counselor's characteristics: expertness, attractiveness, and trustfulness as perceived by the client. Now I am asking a question. Which do you think is the most important characteristic among those three variables?

Professor 7: I think first of all sometimes expertness may not be the best. Sometimes someone, who looks like so an expert, may be frightening someone. They say that person knows everything. They are scared of them. I think trustfulness is generally the most important variable.

Author: Then, what is the second important variable?

Professor 7: I think probably attractiveness would be the second characteristic. I think if you get trustfulness first, then attractiveness can flow from that. You might be initially attractive to someone, but you can't trust them, the relationship will fall apart. Expertness, I think, someone could be too smart sometimes in a sense. You can't ever be too smart, but you become awfully too smart. That can be turn off the people. I think trustfulness is first, I think it follows by attractiveness, then expertness. But I think expertness might be changeable with attractiveness.

Author: How do you think about the relationship between the counselor's power in terms of social influence and the counselor's wisdom?

Professor 7: I think the counselor's power derives, you mean counselor's power is authority?

Author: What I mean is the counselor's power in terms of social influence. Especially, many researchers who are interested in social influence theory say that the counselor's three characteristics (expertness, attractiveness, trustfulness) are very related with the counselor's power because the counselor is always influencing clients directly or indirectly in the counseling situation.

Professor 7: I think that the counselor's power derives from trustfulness. I think the counselor has to be very careful not to abuse that trustfulness, misuse that trustfulness for clients in terms of social influence. I think again that the counselor has to be very careful to cultivate with clients misusing that in the relationship. The counselor has to be very careful to be sensitive to change a client's goals and needs in terms of the application of that. Also in counseling relationship, I think trustfulness comes first, has to move things along, has to be some attractiveness even if counselor and client are different. Some common grounds to have relationship move along and then expertness is able to come through. Trustfulness and attractiveness kind of set the table to allow expertness to come through.

Author: I think you explained about counselor's power in terms of social influence. But my main question is, what is the relationship between the counselor's power in terms of social influence and the counselor's wisdom?

Professor 7: I think the wise counselor is able to utilize power in a way that helps a client achieve what he/she wants to achieve, not abuse or misuse power. The wise counselor determines what the goals are, and then utilize wisdom to help a client achieve that without manipulating in a negative sense what the client does or does not do, without abusing the counselor and client's relationship, without taking advantage of that, without manipulating the client's feeling and behavior. That's what the wise counselor does.

Author: Now I asked all my main questions. Would you any comment and feedback about this interview?

Professor 7: I think those are very thoughtful questions. I don't have any problem with the questions. They are very thoughtful. That's not easy to answer. I have given answers, but they are difficult and deeper like an iceberg. You can get, you know, one answer, but an actual answer is much more depth, much more complex than the given simple answer. I had no problem good and best as I can answer in that. If you go to people and ask the same questions, they give different answers.

Chapter **11**

REFLECTION AFTER THE IN-DEPTH-INTERVIEW

Right now I am reminding of what I performed seven in-depth interviews with my professors with struggling to find the counselor's necessary wisdom as a student and a researcher 20 years ago. I can confidently say that those experiences during my journey of counseling expertise were the most important and invaluable learning. That is because I have learned how to be a wise counselor from those in-depth interviews. Now as a professor in counseling specialty, I would like to strongly assert that all counselors need to have somewhat of wisdom to be effective helpers. To be an effective counselor for helping clients' problem solving and well–being, counselors need not only knowledge and experience but also wisdom based on those. That is, we in counseling specialty need to be wise counselors who are really striving for clients' change with their wisdom derived from practical knowledge and experience. Then, let's go back to the twenty years ago riding on a time machine.

As an interviewer, I thought that my position would be a little bit delicate because my interviewees were all my professors in my department. So I was sort of anxious after I made the appointment with Professor 1. On the other hand, I also felt full of curiosity and excitement, expecting to learn and understand what I wondered about personally. My first interview was so successful it relieved some of my anxiety. As soon as the interview started, my curiosity as a researcher and a student took over, not giving me any time to worry, and made me pay attention to the process of interviewing and the answers of the interviewee.

Professor 1 showed good responses to my questions and we had a meaningful personal discussion after the interview. Particularly, my first interview not only encouraged me but also taught me a lot when I listened to my tape recording again. I recognized that I expressed my opinions several times after Professor 1 answered my questions. It was wonderful feedback. I learned how to control through listening to the interview tape.

Another learning process for me was to really understand the concept of the researcher as an instrument in qualitative research. Even though my research was not a real field study by both participant observation and informal interview, I really felt that every question which raised, my attitude during the interview, relationship with interviewees, and my belief systems influenced the interviews. Especially I have been thinking that as a researcher I was an especially good instrument for my study of the counseling psychologist's wisdom.

I came from a different cultural soil and habit. I have observed and participated in American culture, more broadly Western culture for the last five and half years. For example, when I was in my country, I heard that my friends and a lot of people around me say, "You are so liberated." After my arrival in America, I have always felt that I am very conservative here. I have observed a lot of differences between myself and a lot of people. We don't often recognize our blind spots, like fish not understanding that water is absolutely important for it to survive.

I also recognized that I have changed both my thoughts and behaviors. My American friends' feedback often made me aware of my change. At times I have felt that my left leg was in the Western culture and my right leg was in the Oriental culture. There is a Chinese proverb, "If you not only know yourself but also know your enemy, you always beat your enemy." I often asked myself "How can you integrate Western thought, culture and Eastern thought, culture?" Now I clearly know that I could not integrate both without thoroughly understanding Western thought.

My learning from the interview process and my experience in America during last five and half years were that an effect of cultural differences is very important in the understanding of counseling approaches. It would be not appropriate if many effective counseling theories and techniques or skills in American culture were directly applied to Korean culture without considering cultural differences. My experience in America has made me know and understand through my blind spots which I didn't know I had when I was in my country. My task to make the comprehensive counseling way based on wisdom might be solved if I thoroughly understood the concept of wisdom based on my understanding of counseling both in Oriental and Western culture.

Once I started interviewing professors, my main reading and meditation to understand wisdom related to counseling has been wisdom which is understood in the Eastern culture. Without clearly figuring out my understanding of wisdom, as a researcher I might not have interpreted and integrated a lot of good ideas derived from the interviewees' experiences. I tried to understand wisdom in three ways. First, I tried to interpret what is wisdom in linguistic way. The Chinese word (智慧) for wisdom is meaningful. I found that wisdom figuratively means that a comet (彗) hits the heart (心) of someone who is continually meditating about and seeking wisdom with his accumulated knowledge and experience. Analogically this word means and suggests the way by which Buddha got enlightenment through his struggle. The second was Lao-Tzu' explanation of wisdom. He wrote the phrase, "To understand others is knowledgeable, to understand yourself is to be wise" (Te-Tao Ching, chap. 33). Lao-Tzu's mention also reminded me of Socrates' "Know yourself". As the third, I found one good proverb to explain the wise man. It says that "An intelligent mind acquires knowledge, and the ear of the wise seeks knowledge" (Old Testament, Proverbs 18: 15). This shows well the difference between intelligence and wisdom. It suggests that a wise person is a good listener.

I think that another important thing for the comprehensive counseling model based on wisdom is not only understanding of the concept of wisdom but also understanding of a human being, that is, ourselves. During the interview period, I as a practicum counselor went to one Junior High School, Fayette County, Kentucky, and observed and consulted students in special education classes every Tuesday. Those students didn't read and write English although they can fluently speak English. Only such that event gave me a big impact. One day I felt disappointed observing students' performance and their not paying attention to the teacher. I scribbled and wrote several words in English, in Chinese and in Korean. Especially when I wrote the Chinese word meaning human being (人間), I got a good insight related to an interpretation about "What is human being?" The first character (人) of the Chinese word of human being means a man. The second character (間) means a time period. This character can be divided into two parts. The first part (門) means door. The second part (日) means day. By trying further elemental linguistic analysis of the first part (門), I found that it has two doors, opening door and closing door. And I gave meanings those opening door and closing door in an abstractive interpretation. I presumed that the opening door means a door of birth and the closing door means a door of death. Therefore a meaning of the Chinese of human being can be very abstractively interpreted as he enters in life from the door of birth and lives days and exits into the door of death. What I mean it is that human being as an existential being has to be aware of his only once living time period.

I was particularly excited and amazed that the Chinese word of "human being" includes the meaning of both man or being (人) and time (間). This idea startled me. Heidegger (1926), who contributed to the hermeneutical approach in modern philosophy, wrote his great book, 'Being and Time'. The concept of Dasein, being in there, which Heidegger advertised from his ontological point of view rather than epistemological point of view to understand a human being, seems to be understood by interpreting the Chinese world of human being. What I mean is that we need to understand not only language but also its meaning and culture because Chinese is a pictorial language. We are living our life depending on each other everyday, demonstrating what the Chinese word, "human being" means. As a Zen Buddhist often emphasizes "Life itself is everlasting presence", we need to meaningfully live every moment.

My interviewees have developed their theories and have built their belief systems as professors and counseling psychologists. As a researcher and a student, I needed to understand their ways of teaching and counseling experience. Many counseling psychologists formulated counseling theories through their mirrors, that is, their philosophical beliefs or perspectives, needs, values, points of view concerning human beings, and so on. I also evaluated, accepted, and criticized their theories through my mirror. If some theories grow and flower in my philosophical earth, I think that is desirable to adjust my Oriental philosophical beliefs, needs and values. I believe that my thought and personality have been developed more by the humanistic and existential approaches than by psychodynamic and behavioral approaches from the comparison and investigation between the Oriental philosophies and various counseling theories, and also from the observation of myself.

I think I especially learned a lot during the interviews because the interviewed professors expressed their personal beliefs, experiences and feelings which they have accumulated for 20, 30 or 40 years. I believe that a lot of their comments were what we never learned in classes. The in-depth and long interview could be the better way in learning their points of view.

I also observed the professors were struggling to organize their ideas to answer some questions. I really think that some questions are not easy and are "tough" as one professor expressed. Three interviewees among seven were over sixty years old. I recognized that their approaches were generally humanistic and they expressed directly and indirectly their concern about young counselors' attitudes. For example, one professor was critical of people entering counseling today who are motivated essentially by entrepreneurial and financial goals. They wish to set up a shop and make money, and lots of times meddle in people's lives without knowing what they are doing. He said very cynically that he thinks that "If a person is wise, it is spite of counseling." Also impressive to me was the expression, "Psychologists are playing scientists."

The best way to understand each interviewed professor's emphasis about wisdom related to counseling is to read the whole transcript. When I didn't read in the whole context of discussion, that is, when I took segments to analyze and compare each question, I felt I missed a lot. I got the same kind of feeling that I missed the important parts as I was late to the theater to watch a movie. Of course, I think it is important for a researcher to compare and analyze each question for getting subtle difference after understanding the whole idea of each interviewee. One thing I pondered over was what the best way to show the transcript data for readers was. Particularly, it would be more difficult if I had over 10 in-depth and long interview transcripts. Frankly, I had a painful experience when I cut off each part of the transcript to combine all seven professors' invaluable transcripts.

I also recognized that it was very important to get each interviewee's personal background, especially his/her theoretical or philosophical counseling orientation. When the interviewer received personal background information before asking the principal questions, he could somewhat predict an interviewee's response, which helped organize main questions and further questions based on that information.

Another important aspect of the in–depth interview was for the researcher to structure all questions appropriately. It was not helpful to rapidly change the issues and contents. The relation of all questions and the appropriate order of each question aided in obtaining more information and to explore deep opinions and ideas. In summary, the interviewer needed to get the whole picture before entering into the principal interview questions.

It was a good idea to ask the interviewees to correct the interview transcripts. Of course, such a promise to return a transcript to an interviewee was a burden to the researcher and to interviewee. But according to my transcript experience, it was important to get the exact information and terms particularly because the research was related to exploring difficult issues or theoretical approaches.

Generally speaking, it was not easy to do a qualitative

research compared to a quantitative research even though each approach has its limitations and difficulties in accomplishing a good research. Frankly, I felt it was difficult, and it took a lot of time. But I think that the difficulty and challenge helped me learn.

PART 3

WISDOM OF THE COUNSELOR

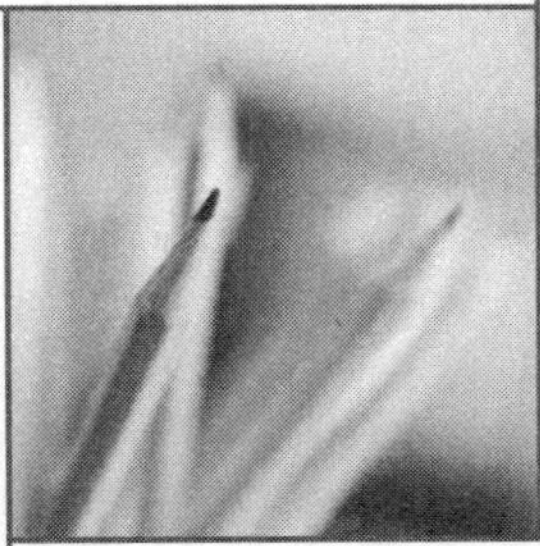

Chapter 12

WISDOM DEFINED BY THE EXPERIENCED COUNSELORS

I strongly believe that every human being can be wise because wisdom itself is, not a object concept, a very subject concept. Therefore, to be wise we need to be wisdom-seekers. I start this chapter with two basic assumptions related to wisdom. one assumption is that wisdom is, not one dimensional, multi-dimensional. Regarding to the acquisition of wisdom based on the first assumption, we can assume that one's specialty effects one's domains of wisdom. Different specialty areas might make different experts emphasize different domains of wisdom. Sternberg (1985) also suggested that there were some differences in implicit theories of wisdom across fields of specialization although components of wisdom showed considerable overlap among different specialties.

Another assumption is that there is difference of degree in wisdom as we say this person is wiser than that person. That is such that we generally say that one's mental horizon is higher than another's mental horizon. We also say that one's degree of wisdom depends upon one's degree of experience. Training and practice in a domain related to fundamental life issues have been found to enhance wisdom-related knowledge (Baltes et al., 1995; Smith et al., 1994; Staudinger et al., 1992). Examining this phenomenon within the context of training and practice in clinical psychology, it was found that clinical psychologists showed performance advantages in comparison to professionals without training in human service-related fields (Jordan, 2005, p. 178).

How do experienced counseling psychologists define? Based on those two assumptions, the present author sought to answer that question with the interview data obtained from the seven professors in counseling psychology. The following was summarized from the seven transcripts. It consists of segments which have several implicit or explicit definitions of wisdom.

Wisdom Defined by Professor 1: Wisdom is to be clear about what is important and what is preferable. What are you really aiming toward? What do you really want? Or what is going to be important as a whole? Wisdom is the answer to such questions. So I would expect counselors trying to be wise, to be aware of what is vitally important or what is not so important for the client and for the counselor in terms of what is good for persons, what is good for people who are going to be involved with the clients.

We are trying to help somebody make decisions by think through the implications of their choices. It's not wise to be too much in a hurry, to push prematurely for closure. People need to make good choices. Wisdom is making good choices, choices about a relatively wide group of people, and about a relatively long-term plan.

The wise person needs to think in broad terms, think in terms of consequences. Wisdom comes from being curious about self and others and interpersonal relationships, and being curious, and well informed, about the broader world. Having lived a long time is not highly correlated with being wise. The counselor is wise when one makes relatively good choices about techniques. Wisdom means letting go of things that don't work, and also having a notion as to something which might be helpful.

The present author sought the essential ingredients of wisdom in counseling. The following statements were gleaned from transcript of the in-depth interview with Professor 1 in counseling psychology. Statements summarize his comments.

Components of wisdom implicit in definition by Professor 1 are as follows.

- Being clear about what is important and what is preferable
- Awareness of what the client views as important
- Having a broad view of life
- Making good choices
- self-awareness
- Effective observer of human relationship
- Confidentiality
- Willingness to help
- Leaving the choice to the client
- Learning by doing
- Experience of a variety of counseling cases
- Emphasizing curiosity more than knowledge
- Representing attitudinal more than intellectual
- Openness to another person's experience
- Recognizing different values
- Referring to somebody when you can't help

- Good choices about techniques or skills
- Not playing the game, being honesty
- Expanding experience
- Learning by experience

Wisdom Defined by Professor 2: Wisdom is a thing that young people do not have, which middle age people do not have, which old people do have. Wisdom is a way that logic is expressed to young people. And the way is important because the way is a style, a method of transmitting logic and the experience from one generation to another. That is the behavioral way of looking at wisdom because it has to do with how those ideas are transmitted. It has nothing to do with the philosophical basis of wisdom. It has to do with the behavioral questions of wisdom.

How do you get? Through two kinds of experiences: reading about it, and doing it. Wisdom is probably not a common knowledge. Wisdom is something to which not everyone has access. If everybody knows it, that is not wisdom. Wisdom is something special. Wisdom struggles with why and why not. A wise person can observe many of the variables which influence a person's behavior, and a wise person can ask many, "what if questions" about those variables. What if we try this, what will happen? A wise person can ask questions that can't be answered.

Wisdom comes from the experience of human observing who is wise. If somebody doesn't observe common experience, knowledge, and behavior and try to make sense out of them, then he isn't very wise. So wisdom is derived from human experience. Wisdom occurs or is developed by trying to learn what one really needs to know about an area or domain. The fact that we even ask the question is the beginning of wisdom. Experience precedes wisdom.

The following statements were gleaned from transcript of the in-depth interview with Professor 2 in counseling psychology. Statements summarize his comments.

Components of wisdom implicit in definition by Professor 2 are as follows.

- Age (Old people have wisdom)
- A way that logic is expressed to young people
- A method (style) of transmitting logic
- Reading and doing
- Not having common knowledge and something special
- Struggling with why and why not
- Judgment for people's good
- Understanding of the relationship between work, love and play
- Booking learning and experience

- Logical, positive way of thinking
- Not having only a bag of skills
- Understanding relationships
- Not knowing how to fix problem right now
- Common experience
- Observing the wise person
- Human experience
- Experience and reading in the given areas
- Focusing both success and failure (Seeing strength and weakness)
- Ability to say "I can do or I can't do"
- Handing the client's problems
- Valued position and value interaction
- Knowing your limits and learning
- Staying away from areas which you don't have experience
- Knowing your values
- Finding somebody who knows more about it than you do
- Not dealing with those things beyond you
- Knowing when to use techniques
- Ability to choose those techniques to help clients
- Ability to make the client fee safe
- Social influence

Wisdom Defined by Professor 3: Wisdom is something that was defined by Aristotle as the pursuit and application of virtue. Aquinas also refers it as a form of a higher skill, what he calls syndersis — the application of principles of life to specific problems with a perspective. Wisdom is essentially the habit of virtue and virtue is related to judgment — making appropriate judgments within the sequence and order of your own life and that of other people.

Wisdom is not technical competence. Wisdom is not knowing how to do this, or that or how to deal with applications because no two circumstances are ever alike. Wisdom is not a state that one can enter into and remain in. It is a constant seeking. One can always become wiser and begin to understand more and more as years pass.

The wise person is indeed like Socrates. The wise man knows how to ask the right questions. He may not know what a final answer is, but he continues being a seeker of the truth. Wisdom is like what we refer to in Christianity as grace. It's a gift of God. It isn't necessary to earn. It isn't merited. People just have it. One has to be a seeker of wisdom. We all seek to know the how the world works together, to understand the nature of good or evil, to understand what is right and what is wrong, what is true, what is false. One doesn't acquire wisdom overnight. One has to continue acquiring wisdom. Wisdom is a process of seeking.

The following statements were gleaned from transcript of the in-depth interview with Professor 3 in counseling psychology. Statements summarize his comments.

Components of wisdom implicit in definition by Professor 3 are as follows.

- Pursuit and application of virtue
- Habit of virtue
- Good judgment
- Not technical competence
- Constant seeking for perfection
- Not having entrepreneurial and financial desire
- Studying philosophy
- Studying religion
- Knowing how to ask the right question
- Being a seeker of the truth
- Having practical wisdom
- Knowing what you can do or not
- Being aware of individual differences
- Knowledge in assessment and diagnosis
- Being proactive
- Learning by models
- Searching for models
- Having a wide range of experience

- Being supportive
- Providing clients with food for thought in order to consider new options
- Making good hypotheses
- Having wide range of knowledge
- Emphasizing the process of continual growth
- Interest in what is good or what is bad, what is true and what is false
- Seeking the good life
- Meditation
- Not determinism
- Accepting and understanding
- Process of seeking

Wisdom Defined by Professor 4: Wisdom implies a certain amount of experience with the world and cognitive knowledge of it. You don't have wisdom if you are ignorant. But that's just the first level. Much more important is an attitude toward life which I would call essentially a religious attitude of acceptance and trust, existential trust, and a notion of integration and balance measure, realizing that the world has all kinds of evil and good in it, and not having unrealistic expectations of the world or demanding ideal solutions.

Wisdom goes beyond simply a cognitive perceptual knowledge to an affective sense of acceptance and trust — existential trust — in the sense that Martin Buber used the term. What is not wisdom is that the specific parts of wisdom are standing alone. Certainly, cognitive knowledge by itself is not wisdom. The sense of existential trust and acceptance of the world is not wisdom if it is devoid of knowledge of the world. To lack wisdom totally is to lack any sense of integration. Wisdom is not something you have or you haven't. It is on a continuum. Maybe everybody has a little bit of wisdom.

Wisdom is sort of a generalized way that people are integrated. Wisdom does not involve merely cognitive knowledge about objects or about people considered as objects. Wisdom has to do with the way human beings relate to one another or the world. A person who has wisdom is a person who lives appropriately in relationships with other people and with the universe. Wisdom implies some degree of intelligence. It comes from the grace of God, and being more specific than that, it comes from being around wise people. If you are never around people with wisdom, you are going to have a hard time having it just come out through your genes. I am not saying it's impossible, but it's going to be much more difficult. Wisdom is not just a matter of cognitive knowledge but it's a matter of experience. Part of wisdom is accepting limitations on your own ability to know everything.

Part of wisdom is learning to confine yourself and limit yourself to something that you can handle and you can do, and if the person seems to need something else, then you send him somewhere else. Wisdom implies a large broad perspective, and so techniques can fit into a broad perspective, but they don't if they seem as here's one here's one, here's one. Techniques without wisdom are almost worse than useless.

Wisdom is essentially the I–Thou relationship. It's impossible to have wisdom without having a great deal of power, just as it's impossible to have power without. Wisdom cannot exist all by itself. It always exists as a sort of integration of these things that we are calling power here, techniques and so forth.

The following statements were gleaned from transcript of the in-depth interview with Professor 4 in counseling psychology. Statements summarize his comments.

Components of wisdom implicit in definition by Professor 4 are as follows.

- Attitude toward life
- Acceptance and trust

- Existential trust
- Not cognitive knowledge
- Intention — difference between the wise person and the good counselor
- Not technician
- Sense of integration
- Health personality
- Generalizing thing (Wholeness)
- Way human beings relate to one another or the world
- Having some information
- Ability to refer somebody
- Accurate empathy
- Unconditional positive regard
- Congruence
- Recognition of my own limitation
- Realizing limitation of counseling
- Positive faith and confidence
- Tolerance
- Some degree of intelligence
- Desire for wisdom
- A matter of experience
- Associating with wise people
- Looking at the world in a long range perspective
- Not behavioral management, not power and control

- Learning by doing
- Learning by being a client
- self–examination
- Understanding your own value
- Ability to put values in practice
- Having a moral perspective
- Learning to confine yourself
- Limiting yourself to something that you can handle and do
- Certain knowledge of techniques
- Techniques with wisdom
- Ability to integrate
- Having a large and broad perspective

Wisdom Defined by Professor 5: Wisdom is knowing what you know and what you don't know and being able to make a distinction between the two. Wisdom is the ability to act appropriately, which sometimes includes not acting; the ability which incorporates knowledge of yourself and knowledge of context and anything else that you could possibly bring in to be able to act appropriately, to act in a constructive way for the good of others, for the good of yourself. The idea of knowing when you don't know implies flexibility. Wisdom is the ability to be flexible, and to realize that what you don't know can hurt you and what you do know changes. It doesn't always apply the way it has in the past.

Not having wisdom is thinking you have wisdom. Wisdom is not a thing, a quantity. It is a process. Not being wise is assuming that what has been wisdom in the past is wisdom now, is applicable now. It is knowing what to keep and what not to keep, or knowing how much of a thing to use at a particular time, or knowing how to use a particular skill, a particular interaction, and being able to be aware of it not being adequate in that particular context, and the knowing somehow, if not how to change it, at least how to admit that it's not right, and that can incorporate asking for help, or sometimes you can be appropriate giving–up and just crying in a corner.

The main piece of wisdom would be to know your limitations. The first thing, sort of an addition of flexibility, is to know just how flexible you can be before you would snap. Wisdom isn't just one category of action or knowledge. If part of wisdom is knowledge, then the knowledge of certain skills that are applicable is a requisite; when to use those skills and when not to use them. Part of wisdom is asking, "Well, this is how much I know, this is how much I don't know; haw far from here to there can I go? How much should I try? Should I go find somebody else who knows more? How much is it worth to me to prove to myself what I know this?

Wisdom comes from everywhere. It comes from life experiences and being open to them, being willing to examine them. You can gain wisdom in the sense of learning that there are some things that it would be just as well not to experience. A necessary but not sufficient condition to live life, to become wise, is that you have to live life, and you have to experience things, you have to be open to experiences, to take them and incorporate them in a Piagetian sense, revive your schemata. But your simply experiencing anything is not going to make you wise.

In order to perpetuate the process of gaining wisdom and expand it, wisdom has to be a process of being able to extract from the experience, extract but incorporate into what is already there. Part of wisdom is a knowing about the extent and limitations of your power on both ends; not only how powerless you can be in certain situations, but how powerful you can be.

The following statements were gleaned from transcript of the in–depth interview with Professor 5 in counseling psychology. Statements summarize his comments.

Components of wisdom implicit in definition by Professor

5 are as follows.

- Spontaneity
- Ability to be flexible
- Ability to make decisions, enjoy life, feel creative
- Knowing what you know and what you don't know
- Realizing what you don't know and you can hurt clients
- Humbleness
- Knowing how to ask the right question
- Willing to go with your own confusion
- Realizing that sometimes there's not an answer or closure
- Having a world perspective
- Ability to cope with
- Tolerating of your mistakes
- Some skills at communicating your wisdom
- Being perceptive
- Knowing your own limitations
- Knowing when to use your skills
- Knowing client's limitations
- Asking the right question
- Struggling with difficult problems
- Willingness to be there when client need help
- Being more role-oriented
- Being honest, genuine with the client

- Letting the client make choices
- Life experience
- Being open to experience
- Being willing to examine experiences
- Incorporating experiences
- Ability to learn from your experiences
- Having a lot of different experiences
- Tolerating the pain
- Being willing to be a client at times
- Having listening skills
- Having confrontation skills
- Knowing how to use skills
- Knowing your limitation of power

Wisdom Defined by Professor 6: Wisdom is a knowing. I think it has intuitive components, as well as intellectual. And my hunch is that the wisest people are ones who know and trust themselves. Wisdom is finding a creative, receptive response to a situation. Wisdom is the ability to see all sides.

A lack of wisdom is to live your life totally as others would have you live it, not listening to self at all. I think wisdom requires a knowledge and appreciation of that which has gone before you, what others have thought and created. So a lack of wisdom would be ignorance of history and accomplishment. Wisdom is a balance; a lack of wisdom is imbalance on any dimension. Being too people-oriented, not being people-oriented at all; being too cognitive, not being cognitive at all; those kinds of things. It requires a balancing of characteristics. I think what I am doing is defining for you healthy person, that is what it feels like I am doing with wisdom, and I think I may equate those two things, a healthy person and a wise person.

I don't think wisdom has anything to do with age. And I think wisdom spans the whole field. I also think that wisdom is a knowing that there wasn't just one path that might have worked. And I think that is what I also mean about a value system. You have to have values that embrace humanity, and in that is ability to see a wide range of alternatives that are possible to see all sides.

I said the ability to trust others. I also think in wisdom there is a knowing whom not to trust. I believe that spontaneity and wisdom are very closely tied. So that's led me to believe we were born with the ability to be wise, with an inner wisdom, ability to respond to where we are at that particular moment in time. I know babies don't sit down and write books, but in accomplishing the tasks that need to be coped with at that moment, they have wisdom.

I think wisdom comes from the inside, and it's there from

the beginning. I think there's a lot of societal, environmental experience, that distances us from our wisdom and spontaneity, and that teaches us not to trust our sense of who we are. It's not unlike Carl Rogers' notion of a "positive growth tendency." He says that the judgment from important people on the outside sets up conditions of worth and other things that get in the way of staying in touch with our wisdom. So I think that the journey for most of us is to go back to our own wisdom.

I have done a fair amount of training in learning how to be more spontaneous, how to recapture my spontaneity, and think that is closer to my wisdom. I look for a mentor, role models, people who seem to be wise and how are they living their life, kind of how did they get their kind of thing, how do they in the moment convey their wisdom, how do they tap into it. I think I learn something about my own wisdom by choosing to be around people who are healthy themselves, and who share some common values with me, because it is in that framework that I can trust myself, and by trusting myself learn to get closer to knowing about my wisdom.

I thought it was an interesting process to define wisdom, and just to ask a person to define wisdom. I learned from that process that my definition of wisdom is very tied up in the trust of myself, and knowing myself. I'm not a philosopher, that's for sure. I've never thought of myself as being wise and spontaneous, I've known some about that relationship, but I don't think I've ever used the word 'wisdom' there before, that the person I see as most spontaneous is also very wise.

The following statements were gleaned from transcript of the in-depth interview with Professor 6 in counseling psychology. Statements summarize his comments.

Components of wisdom implicit in definition by Professor 6 are as follows.

- Intuition
- Being intellectual
- Knowing and trusting the client
- Being creative
- Receptive response to a situation
- Ability to see all sides
- Learning to trust oneself
- Self-awareness
- Ability to take in information clearly from the outside and one's inner self
- Trusting yourself
- Balancing of characteristics
- Spanning the whole world

- Value system that encompasses a wide range of behaviors
- Trusting your own values
- Values that embrace humanity
- Ability to see a wise range of alternatives
- Empathy
- Comfortableness with your own feelings
- Being open, tentative about offering hypotheses
- Being spontaneous
- Not sexual stereotyping
- Having a variety of life experiences
- Experiencing difficulty in life
- Good teacher
- Changing behavior as well as finding life-meaning
- Listening to your own strengths
- Accepting all of one's parts
- Identifying oneself
- Ability to cope with effectively
- Self-understanding
- Acquiring skills
- Looking for mentor
- Having lots of specific and general knowledge
- Having experiences as a client in therapy
- No prejudice of racism

- Role-modeling
- Watching good counselors
- Role-modeling as counseling technique
- Openness and self-disclosing
- Having an accurate understanding
- Responsibility
- Being a warm, intuitive person who trusts himself/herself

Wisdom Defined by Professor 7: I think that wisdom is a constructive variable that someone develops over a period of time. Wisdom is not something that somebody can read about, study about. I think that wisdom is the accumulation of experiences and knowledge, a combination of reading and learning, studying as well as experiences. people acquire wisdom through working with other students and clients, through professional activities, through conducting research.

Wisdom is being able to understand and assess situations and people, being able to understand how people behave and how situations occur, and being able to know how to function with nay given situation in order to provide counseling to clients. Wisdom is something that comes from an individual having positive self-esteem, being able to understand relationships, being able to understand how human nature functions, and being able to convey that to other people, not impose it, but to convey it to students, colleagues, peers, to maintain relationship.

A wise person is somebody who is able to draw from his/her experience and knowledge, and apply that in any given situation. Wisdom is being able to know and understand the situation, being able to rationally deal with it without losing control and without being hot tempered, being able to give an unbiased assessment or judgment and knowing how to respond to a situation.

Wisdom is not something that is imposed on somebody. It is not something that is given out without being asked. It is not something that is based solely on opinion, it is based upon experience, it is based upon being able to learn from most experiences. It is not something that you learn from a textbook. I don't think it is something that can be taught. it is more an attitude, more an approach.

Wisdom can be varied with different people. Different people can have different perspectives. I think that the wise person is somebody who is able to communicate values without imposing values. Someone who has wisdom is able to communicate how he/she can handle a given situation without expecting that someone else would use that solution or answer. I think people can be wise in different areas depending upon what their area and expertness is.

Wisdom comes, I believe, from the person who is able to communicate; it probably comes from something inside somebody. I think a lot of people who could have wisdom do not really have an interest in communicating with others. I think a lot of people who don't have wisdom either try to communicate or don't try to communicate. I think it starts by somebody who is interested in helping other people. He doesn't have to be a counseling person. He can be a mentor in business who trains someone how to do a job. It can be someone who trains a successor, someone who is interested in doing that kind of thing.

Wisdom comes from somebody who is interested in people, interested in helping someone, interested in a larger society in which they live, or is interested in a better society, better employees who work effectively in the jobs they have. So it is a matter of application of knowledge that somebody has. On the other hand, there are other people who don't have an interest in communicating those things. I think that is part of wisdom — learning from experiences.

The following statements were gleaned from transcript of the in-depth interview with Professor 7 in counseling psychology. Statements summarize his comments.

Components of wisdom implicit in definition by Professor

7 are as follows.

- Having a high self–esteem
- Constructive variable that some develop over a period of time
- Accumulation of experience and knowledge
- Combination of both book reading, learning as well as experience
- Professional activities
- Good relationship with colleagues
- Ability to understand and assess people and situations
- Not losing control and being hot tempered
- Good assessment and judgment
- Knowing how to respond to a situation
- More than attitude and approach
- Understanding different perspectives
- Communicating values without imposing values
- Ability to know when to apply techniques and what techniques to utilize
- Saying the right thing at the right time and the right place
- Knowledge of human nature
- Knowledge of specific and general psychology
- Not imposing values and expectations
- Encouraging clients to listen carefully

- Willingness to listen to carefully what a client says
- Empathic understanding
- Being a good listener
- Clarifying asked questions
- Having a positive regard
- Acceptance and genuineness
- Congruency
- Trustworthiness
- Demonstrating interest in a relationship
- Self-actualization rather than specific techniques
- Communicating with same or similar values
- Having a positive view of world
- Learning from experience
- Belief of counseling as on-going process
- Keeping up with different values, attitudes, and expectation people have
- Being a role model
- Giving supervision of people in counseling
- Knowing different, wide and open ways of doing things
- Not time-consuming
- Understanding of value differences
- Sensitivity to doing different things for client

Chapter 13

RELATIONSHIP BETWEEN WISDOM AND COUNSELING

Experienced counseling psychologists emphasized that counselors basically need not only counseling techniques but also wisdom for helping clients. In this chapter, we will see how seven professors explain wisdom in counseling such as relationship between wisdom and counseling techniques, necessity of counselor's wisdom, and wisdom as characteristic of a good counselor. The following comments were summarized from the seven professors' transcripts.

Wisdom in Counseling Posited by Professor 1: A counselor ought to have a broad view of life. The wise person needs to think in broad terms, think in terms of consequences and the good counselor also does that. Being self-aware is a prerequisite for being a good counselor. Some wise people are not particularly interested in helping other people make good decisions. They should not become counselors. For those people who decide to go into counseling, I would want to be wise and therefore I want them to be well read. The narrowly educated person who doesn't read, who isn't aware, who's very ethnocentric, could not be a good counselor.

The counselor should be curious about lots of things. An unexamined life is not worth living. Helpful counselors would be curious about people who had made changes and tried to understand what happened to them and how they talked about them, and what problems arose in their experiences.

We are playing scientists. People learn best by doing. There are choices all the time, good choices as to what techniques ought to be effective or not effective here. I could say counselors are wise when they make relatively good choices about techniques. I don't see wisdom and counseling techniques as being very closely related. I would always come down on the side of wisdom rather than technique. Wisdom is what we all are looking for, trying to increase our wisdom, our understanding of our world and of people, help them find their way in the world.

Wisdom in Counseling Posited by Professor 2: A good counselor may not know anything about wisdom. A good counselor may be extremely effective with techniques. A good counselor can use a cookbook and solve all the problems of the world. A wise person can think, a good counselor can do. It is unusual to find a thinker and doer in one person. The good counselor counselor's characteristics related to wisdom are three things: work, love and play. They should have knowledge about and understanding of the relationships between the things that make up work, love and play.

Wisdom is being able to observe the elements, the stuff that makes up something. The kind of counselor that I want has wisdom. The kind of counselor I don't want is a good counselor, but what I do want is a wise counselor. A bag of tricks will not provide a permanent solution because I believe that the wisdom is seeking relationships that might have a permanent effect. What I prefer is a wise counselor. The guess that I have is that a wise counselor would be able to increase my own personal breadth of wisdom. My guess further is that the bag of tricks of a counselor would not add anything to wisdom. There are a million people in the world who wouldn't want a wise counselor. They don't want that stuff. They want to know how to fix it right now. That's the place for technique-oriented people. A wise counselor, one who has had experience and knowledge will say, "Hey, each of those techniques is just a part of a larger picture." My good counselor has a little bit of wisdom, and a little bit of wisdom is like an infection; ut spreads and spreads and spreads. How I make somebody a good counselor is by having them focus upon what they can do well and what they can do badly, because I believe that what any person must see is both their successes and their failures. What I would do in teaching somebody to become a wise counselor is to have them tell me about their successes and tell me about what they can't do.

The client doesn't benefit from the therapist not having a higher level of understanding about each of the various client problem areas. A counselor who cannot take care of the client well is not going to help the client. So the counselor needs to learn to become wise, to see the strengths and weaknesses in order to deal with them or not deal with them. A counselor who has a value-free position is not wise, and rather he/she is a technique-oriented person.

Wisdom in Counseling Posited by Professor 3: A program which technique-oriented misses the whole vision of what it is to be a good person, a rational person and a logical person and above all to be a wise person. I think that for the most part people entering into counseling today are motivated essentially by entrepreneurial and financial needs. They wish to make money and set up a shop, lots of times they really meddle in people's lives without knowing what to do. So I think if a person is wise, it is in spite of counseling.

Wisdom is something that is helpful if that is part of the character of a person. But if it is not part of the character, then counseling can be a very hollow and shallow experience both for the counselor and for the client. A person may be a good counselor but not necessarily wise. I don't think that being a good counselor is necessarily identical with beginning on the path of wisdom.

A good counselor ought to have elements of wisdom, ought to be concerned about other people. The counselor should have real practical wisdom: the practical knowledge to know when not to do something and to know when to do something and above all to know what is the difference between the two: to know when it is possible to help and when it is only possible to be supportive. So I think that in so far as the counselor knows what he/she can do and what he/she cannot do, that this the a kind of practical wisdom.

Usually people who come for counseling want some immediate help. So I think that one should focus on the techniques and skills, after that if counseling goes on for some time, then perhaps wisdom can be a part of the process. It is very difficult to teach wisdom, techniques of wisdom. One learns more by models. Just as one doesn't acquire wisdom overnight, one doesn't acquire good counseling skills overnight. It is a process of growing. If you have a certain amount of wisdom, you can gear yourself to the understanding of the client.

A lot of counseling takes place in a very simple manner, sometimes just from people talking over a cup of coffee. Wisdom is a process of seeking and counseling is a kind of technique, a kind of competency you develop. I see no intrinsic relationship between counseling techniques or skills and the development of wisdom. I see a possibility that people who engage in efforts to help other people in the process bring some wisdom in their own lives.

Wisdom in Counseling Posited by Professor 4: The difference between a wise person and a good counselor would be an intention. A person who calls himself a counselor intends, in his relationship, to counsel the other person. A wise person does not necessarily intend to do anything within that particular relationship and will sort of do what the relationship calls for.

I think that a counselor who lacks wisdom is not a very good counselor. He is a technician, and there are a lot of technicians running around. A person who is wise is not necessarily a counselor. Many wise people have never in any formal or official sense done any counseling, although I think that when other people come to them for help or advice, they are in a kind of counseling relationship. I certainly would not want somebody who deals with techniques alone, but on the other hand, I don't think it is possible to work with wisdom alone. I guess I want somebody who can integrate the two. One without the other is pretty useless. If you have wisdom, then you know the importance of techniques.

What I feel is that everybody knows about the existence of techniques. Very few people are aware of the existence and importance of wisdom. I would like to have a counseling training program that emphasizes wisdom. I have never used the word wisdom a great deal in referring to counseling, but the terms I have been using are pretty equivalent of wisdom. I would like to see our counseling program emphasize that.

If the counselor has wisdom, then one of the things he wants to do is be wisely knowledgeable and techniques. You cannot know about every kind of technique, but part of wisdom is accepting limitations on your own ability to know everything. Wisdom always include a certain knowledge of techniques and a knowledge of your limits of what you know. Counseling techniques do not necessarily involve wisdom at all, but I would say that techniques, well used, require wisdom. That is if all you have got is a grab bag of techniques, you are going to pull this one out this kind of client. People don't like to be treated with techniques, even clients don't like techniques. They like to feel that they are dealing with a real human being. We can't get away from techniques. But if you are limited to just techniques, if that's all, then you are in real trouble.

I think a lot of students in our counseling program bring in a fair amount of wisdom with them. If a student comes and doesn't have any wisdom, any ability to integrate, to see the big picture, and uses this technique and that one and that one, which is what we teach, we think there is something wrong with that student. There is something wrong with him, but the problem is we haven't emphasized the wisdom or the integration at all.

Wisdom in Counseling Posited by Professor 5: The difference between a wise person and a good counselor is that they overlap on a Venn diagram basis. The best counselors are wise people who know how to convey their wisdom and/or use it appropriately to help someone else. But you can be a wise person in a lot of ways and not know how to help someone else.

The main piece of wisdom which the counselor should have would like to know his limitations. That doesn't mean that he can't try. I would as a matter of fact think a good counselor would continue to try to expand, so that he/she would be less limited. Counselors need to know their limitations, sort of a corollary that they need to know their clients' limitations.

I would definitely choose the counselor who emphasizes wisdom for problem-solving. If I had somebody who only knows how to teach skills or techniques, if the situation required more than that, I wouldn't get what I need. I would choose the counselor who had the most flexibility. Someone who has wisdom could learn counseling skills. As far as wisdom, particularly in regard to counseling, I think part of the way to learn is that you will not wisdom per se, just learning skills, but in order to open yourself up to taking the risk that is essential to gaining wisdom, you have to have some skills initially, and you have to have enough confidence in those skills to operate in a risky situation. The indiscriminate use of skills without gaining the wisdom of how to use them, at best, is going to relatively ineffective; at worst, damaging.

Wisdom in Counseling Posited by Professor 6: There is no difference between the wise person and the good counselor. Because I think what's becoming clear to me is that I equate wisdom with health, with mental health, and well, a good counselor needs to be wise. Maybe the wise person may not have counseling techniques. You could be wise and decide not to focus your energy on helping other people express their problems. So the good counselor has to have knowledge about counseling theory and technique. In more cases you can have a wise person, and the wise person can channel his/her wisdom in lots of different areas. I don't think you can have a good counselor who not wise. You can have a wise person who isn't a counselor. But I don't think you can have a good counselor who's not wise.

To be a wise counselor, first of all, I think they must know themselves. Secondly they must trust themselves. I think they must have a value system that encompasses a wide range of behaviors. Not only behaviors for themselves, but also acceptance of a wide range of behaviors. I have to trust my values. The most important characteristics of a counselor are empathy, comfortableness with your own feelings. I would want a counselor who has faced some life tribulations and grappled with them and come out on the other side, having a greater knowledge of himself. And I don't want someone who's never had any hard knocks. It feeds back into wisdom. I'm not sure you can be wise unless you've had a variety of life experiences, some of them very difficult. And I don't think wisdom comes from an easy–going life.

A psychodramatic theory suggests we're all born spontaneous, and spontaneity means to have the ability to effectively cope with novelty from birth — before birth actually. Now I believe that spontaneity and wisdom are very closely tied. I think the counseling experience is where my intent has been to understand myself. I think on a daily basis I try to be aware of myself in what I am doing, and learn from that, and try to. And I work at things, like trying to be aware of projections, try to work at my distortions of perceiving others and taking in information.

I think I learn from clients every day that I see them. I think maybe that's one of the ways I'm wise, in that I listen and I learn from them. I'm especially intrigued by creativity in people, creativity for feeling for themselves, for coping with difficult situations, that kind of thing. And I've had some clients who taught me a lot about that. It's amazing how creative people are. I think counselors by the virtue of their job receive the possibility of becoming wise.

Whenever I don't understand myself, it's going to be very difficult for me to understand the client. The best way for developing your level of understanding is developing your wisdom. On the counselor side of things, the counselor needs wisdom to choose at any given point in time among a number of skills or techniques one could use. That choice needs to be in some kind of integrated whole. Not "let's do this empty chair right now, it sounds fun." The person has to be knowledgeable about theory as well as technique. I mean wisdom is there somewhere. I don't know exactly how to define it. Wisdom is a knowing of the relationship between theory and technique. Also I think that there's an intuitive part of that process, and that one can't explain totally by theory. On the client side, I think there are many techniques which help the client know something about their own wisdom.

There's a kind of role power that comes from being a very effective, that others are drawn to because of how you conduct yourself. And I believe that that kind of power is very important in the counseling relationship. And that's what plays a part in social influence. I also believe the way I define that kind of role, that most of the time you can say that person is a wise person. I mean that is utilization of my social influence in the service of the client learning to be wise.

Wisdom in Counseling Posited by Professor 7: I think that a good counselor is a wise person. I think you can have difference between somebody knowing technical skills of counseling and knowing how to say the right things. That doesn't mean someone is wise. The ability to have right techniques doesn't make somebody wise. The ability to know when to apply techniques and what techniques to utilize makes somebody wise. So, for example, if you could review counseling tapes, all counselors' answers might be technically correct and appropriate, but may not be wise for that client because they missed the boat for that client. So when I look at a good counselor, I say a good counselor who is not wise by being able to say the right thing but not say it the right way and at the right way.

The wise counselor is able to communicate his/her experiences and knowledge through types of questions asked, is able to utilize a counseling situation to help the client without imposing values or communicating a certain set of values. A good counselor who is not wise may just know the right thing to say but not have experience and knowledge to know when to say that right thing. I may say that he technically looks right but may not be beneficial for clients.

I think that learning counseling is an on–going process. You never finish learning. You always learn process and always change process. The counselor should be knowledgeable about human nature, about theories of personalities, should be knowledgeable about how people change. The wise counselor should know aspects of different cultures, different cultural backgrounds and orientation, should be able to not impose values, or not impose expectation on an individual, should be willing to listen carefully to what a client says, to encourage clients to listen carefully. The wise counselor should facilitate encourage clients to be able to develop his/her own sense of variety. A wise counselor will be one who does that. A wise counselor is one who does not dictate to clients, does not tell clients what they should do, but should be able to help clients come to their own conclusions. A wise counselor is one who helps clients achieve their goals, develop their techniques.

I think that my ability to be a better counselor has improved through all the period of time that I have been counseling. I hope that I am able to learn from things I said, experiences and techniques, books and so on. Hopefully I am able to apply that in a way that has improved each time I worked with somebody. I think besides that the world has changed. You have to keep up with different values, attitudes, and expectations people have. So I think that sometimes I ought to have wisdom. It's important in conveying wisdom not just to apply the solutions that were involved appropriately in the early 1970's, but to look at what separates things now from what I did. Things have changed. A wise person is able to understand that.

To be a good counselor, one of the best things to do is to be a role model. I think a good way to communicate counseling ability is through supervision of people in counseling. Now I am going beyond basic lecture classes in counseling. I think that people need basic lecture classes, need to read books, need theories, know the techniques, know how things done, then need to practice that. I think the real task of teaching someone comes in terms of the ability to supervise somebody and provide different, wide and open ways of doing things. I think that's what people really want students in counseling to practice. You have to go out and apply it and help the client. Counselors have to integrate any variance between what they learn from books and their experience in the field with clients.

I think that a part of empathy comes from a person's experiences in his/her life: experiencing frustration, failure, and family problems. I think that being empathic is a part of developing wisdom too. Knowing how to deal with those problems, handle them, you don't want to make worse problems happen or you don't want to stay with. Well, a lot of things happen: for example, you have a few deaths in your family, you are going to take a wife, and so on. I think it's important to learn about those, learn about your reactions and others' reactions. If you are young, you kind of think that life goes on forever. I think as you get older, you get better at seeing things from the other's perspective.

I would see that wisdom comes in an application of those techniques or skills, of knowing when to do something or not to do something, when to raise something or not raise something, sensitivity to doing different things for the client, sensitivity to knowing how career and some events affect clients. To me, application of wisdom comes in being able to be sensitive to the needs of different individuals and being able to know the impact that a certain event might have. For example, if a counselor never has the experience of death of someone close such as a family member, and a client comes in who has, it may be somewhat difficult really to know the impact of that. Beyond that, a whole meaning of death is different in different cultures. Life has different meaning and has different impact to the same event to a person who has 20 siblings versus someone who doesn't have, in one system versus another system.

I think a wise counselor does not utilize power in an authoritarian way. A wise counselor is able to utilize power in a way that helps a client achieve what he/she wants to achieve, not abuse or misuse power. A wise counselor determines what the goals are and then utilizes wisdom to help a client achieve that without manipulating in a negative sense what the client does or does not do, without abusing the counselor–client relationship, without taking advantage of that, without manipulating the client's feeling and behavior. That's what a wise counselor does.

Chapter 14

COUNSELOR'S WISDOM EMPHASIZED BY POTENTIAL CLIENTS

Every human being has a kind of problem and sometimes he gets a help from someone to solve his little or big problem. If he has any kind of big problem that he has difficulty to solve for himself, he needs help from an expert. I dare to say that the corpse has no problem. So we can say that all individuals are potential clients. And all potential clients have some expectations about their counselors when they seek counseling to solve problems. What kinds of characteristics of the counselor do clients implicitly think of being important as an effective counselor? In this chapter I will try to show somewhat of the above question's answer related to the counselor's wisdom emphasized by potential clients.

To find the counselor's wisdom posited by potential clients, college students were asked to provide their views about characteristics and components of wisdom that counselors should have. A survey using open–ended questions was administered to two undergraduate classes. The data was analyzed by content analysis. The performed research's purpose, methods and procedures, and found results are as follows.

Purpose

The study was done to explore college students' (who might be potential clients) concepts of wisdom in counseling psychologists. The study was able done to investigate definitions of wisdom in counseling in a group of nonprofessionals. The plan was to examine their views in comparison with those of the seven interviewed professors obtained from the in–depth interview. This information was then used in designing the items in the Counseling Psychologists' Wisdom Scale.

Method and Procedure

Two undergraduate classes from the main campus of the University of Kentucky, one was a developmental psychology class, the other a logic class. The present author explained the purpose of this survey to the instructors of those two classes. The subject sample consisted of a total of forty college students (Logic nine, Developmental Psychology 31). The age range of the subjects was 18-44 (average age was 25.4). In gender, the number of male subjects was 15 and the number of female subjects was 25. Particularly, the number of subjects having experience as a client in counseling relationship was twenty–two (56.4%).

The present author developed a survey questionnaire to obtain personal background and three open–ended questions directly related to the counseling psychologist's wisdom and characteristics. These questions were composed of relating to questions in the in–depth interview. The main three questions used as research instrument are as follows.

Question 1: If you need help to solve your problems, what do you think are the most important characteristics of the counselor?

Question 2: What kinds of wisdom do you think the counselor should have?

Question 3: What is the difference between the wise person and the good counselor?

The present author used content analysis to classify the responses from the forty subjects to find the counselor's wisdom.

Counselor's Wisdom Posited by Potential Clients

The following descriptive statements are developed from the open–ended survey responses of the forty undergraduate students. The frequencies in parentheses of each characteristic and component were considered important criteria in the classifications. The found results are summarized under each open–ended question that had been presented to the subjects.

Question 1: If you need help to solve your problems, what do you think are the most important characteristics of the counselor?

The following content components provide a summary of the college students' expectations of the counseling psychologist's characteristics given in response to Question 1. The total number of responses of fifty content components was 177. The numbers in parentheses show frequencies of responses.

- Empathy (15)
- Recognizing importance of listening skills (a good listener) (11)
- Listening skills (10)
- Communication skills (8)
- Counseling experiences (8)
- Openness and receptiveness (8)
- Expertise (7)
- Caring (7)
- Understanding (7)
- Objectivity (7)
- Availability (5)
- Patience (5)
- Ability to solve problems (5)
- Confidentiality (4)
- Sincerity (4)
- Good judgment (4)
- A sense of humor (4)

- Professional training (4)
- Understanding of value differences (4)
- Personality (4)
- A willingness to help (3)
- Appropriate cost (3)
- Knowledge (3)
- Trustworthiness (2)
- Understanding of client's uniqueness (2)
- Positive self–esteem (2)
- Integration (2)
- Aptitudes (2)
- Intelligence (2)
- Friendliness (2)
- Honesty (2)
- Education (2)
- Sensitivity (2)
- A lot of skills (2)
- Positive attitude about life (2)

Besides the above content components as important characteristics of the counselor, fifteen content components having only one frequency were: Intuition of insight, Same gender, Respected, Self–actualization, Not imposing values, Self–help techniques, Common sense, Knowing how to ask the right question, Genuineness, Understand the problem,

Experience as a client, Knowledge of assessment and diagnosis, Credibility, Humble (not arrogant), and Age.

As being appeared in subjects' responses by Question 2, the nine most important characteristics of counselors that potential clients expected were: Empathy, Being a good listener, Listening skills, Communication skills, Counseling experiences, Openness and receptiveness, Expertise, Caring, and Understanding.

Directly to find the counselor's wisdom, Questions 2 was asked to subjects as follows:

Question 2: What kinds of wisdom do you think the counselor should have?

The following content components provide a summary of the undergraduates' expectations of the counseling psychologist's wisdom given in response to Question 2. The total number of responses of fifty-three content components was 132. The numbers in parentheses show frequencies of responses.

- Knowledge of their specialty (11)
- Experience in life (8)
- Education (7)
- Objectivity and lack of prejudice (6)
- Communication skills (6)

- Insight or intuition (5)
- Professional training (4)
- Common knowledge (4)
- Counseling experiences (4)
- Understanding of different perspectives (4)
- Reading broadly (4)
- Empathy (3)
- Open–mindedness (3)
- Friendliness and gentleness (3)
- Understanding of human nature (3)
- Understanding of cultural differences (3)
- Common sense (3)
- Stability (2)
- Understanding of different age groups (2)
- Expertise in problem areas (2)
- Patience (2)
- Relationships (2)
- A lot of techniques or skills (2)
- Positive self–esteem (2)
- A sense of humor (2)
- Sensitivity (2)
- Good judgment (2)
- Ability to handle problems (2)
- Personality (2)

- Understanding of human uniqueness (2)
- Self–actualization (2)

Besides the above content components as the counselor's wisdom, twenty–one content components having only one frequency were: A sense of practical reality, Good listening skills, Recognizing importance of listening skills (a good listener), Understanding of cognitive process, Self–understanding, Professional activities, Ability to see all sides, Knowledge of physical medicine, Caring, Not to impose moral values, Availability, Motivation, Knowledge of assessment and diagnosis, Synthesizing various approaches, Appropriate cost, Certification or licensure, A willing to help, Ethical responsibility, Thinking logically, Understanding of human suffering/pain, and Sincerity.

According to the found result by Question 2, the important components of counselors' wisdom that potential clients emphasized were as follows: Knowledge of their specialty, Experience in life, Education, Objectivity and lack of prejudice, Communication skills,? Insight or intuition, Professional training, Common knowledge, Counseling experiences, Understanding of different perspectives, and Reading broadly.

By question 3, the present author classified subjects' responses into characteristics of the wise person and the good counselor as follows.

Question 3: What is the difference between the wise person and the good counselor?

A. The wise person:

- Is someone who is very knowledgeable.
- May not have the qualities I listed in question 1.
- Would just be a good 'resource center' and lack the warm, personal side a good counselor should have.
- May express his views at the wrong times and not socially listen to the patient.
- Has more insight to what is going to happen as a result of something else.
- Knows everything about the subject but is unable to help at times.
- Can be wise in one area not related to problem area for client
- Is one who I feel is book smart and has good knowledge of their field but may lack in experience with people.
- May have a lot of knowledge about many things but may not be able to express it clearly.
- May be well–trained and know be the right things to say at the right time.

- Understand why a person may needs help.
- Will probably mind their own business.
- Has common sense and knowledge of his profession (or education) and be able to relate this to individuals.
- May only need a few words to get his point across where it can really hit home, in the heart, as well as mind
- Has many great attributes.
- Wisdom comes genuinely through experience and without it you're really nothing but maybe at best an objective opinion.
- Knows when and how to help the person in an unbiased fashion in order to bring out the best in them.
- Has knowledge.
- May have significant knowledge about psychology.
- Has much knowledge and can use it for his personal use.
- Is a person who can discern and emphasize with others.
- Knows the importance of things.
- Has the know how.

B. The good counselor:

- Should be a person very concerned with the person involved well-being.

- Has same attributes of a wise person and counselor's characteristics.
- Can take his knowledge of his field and effectively and sufficiently use it to help others without being domineering or intimidating.
- Should be effective.
- His intentions may be noble but his knowledge may be lacking in the specific field of the problem.
- Should be a good friend who will listen and help to the best of his ability to help you to overcome your problems.
- Really knows what to say and how to say it.
- Will not condemn someone and should be gentle and understanding.
- Guides you along rather than set you on a path.
- Knows enough about the subject to help the person seeking counseling and discover the problems and figure out a possible solution.
- Is one who has probably experienced some of problems himself.
- Is well trained and has knowledge of manuals and resources which a wise person does not.
- Should have enough information about various subjects to be able to give the "right and comforting answer" to someone in need of help or advice.

- Is not only well–trained but is down–to–earth, sincere and genuinely interested in helping others.
- Puts his thoughts in motion to help his client , friend, student, etc.
- Will try to provoke healthy thinking in other individuals.
- Does not necessarily have to have common sense but does have a good education and practical experience.
- May be able to say the right things and present his view abstractly.
- Must be able to listen without passing judgment (good or bad) and to express to an individual his/her concern and desire to help one in need.
- Would be a good listener who contributes their past experiences into helping the person; Has knowledge and ability to truly care about their client and relate to their client; Knows how to utilize psychological knowledge in helping patients.
- Maybe does not have knowledge as much as the wise man can use his knowledge but can use his knowledge to help others through problems.
- Can use and communicate knowledge.
- Must know how to listen with an understanding of the client's viewpoint and background.
- Has good communicative and listening skills.

- Tells you what is best in your position.
- Should be able to express wisdom while treating others with understanding and compassion.
- Knows what one should or shouldn't take whether it's important or not.
- Executes the wisdom with style, careful of not manipulating client.

A major finding result by Question 3 showed that potential subjects generally emphasized that counselors need to be wise in order to be good or effective. Their responses showed that the wise person and the good counselor are overlapping concepts. That is, subjects who emphasized no difference between the wise person and the good counselor explained that a good counselor has wisdom as a wise person. In defining the good counselor, potential clients implicitly thought that he would have or display more attitudes of caring, intention, effectiveness, and specific knowledge in helping clients than the wise person.

Chapter 15

BECOMING A WISE COUNSELOR

Each person has a unique wisdom. People use their own wisdom to guide their lives. Conventional wisdom is often referred to as if it were accepted by everyone. Everyone conjures up his/her own metaphor of the mind for his/her needs. In the same way, counseling psychologists may develop and define their wisdom based on their personal background and theoretical orientation.

As societies develop, occupations or careers become differentiated and specified. Modern psychology was differentiated from philosophy in that it emphasized the scientific method and research of human behavior rather than the metaphysical method in the study of the human mind. Counseling psychology in particular is one of area of psychology which can enable people to change and adjust. Particularly counseling psychologists as applied psychologists teach, guide, and help clients to achieve their well–being by making them change their minds and behaviors. In performing their job for helping client, they mainly depend on verbal communication similar to a Socratic method which philosophers have used. That is, Socrates' dictum, "The unexamined life is not worth living." seems pertinent to most counselors who are responsible for helping clients make changes by examining their internal and external life problems and behaviors.

To be an effective helper, counselors need to become wise counselors as seven experienced counseling psychologists indicated by their in–depth interviews. Based on reviewing researches on the characteristics of effective counselors, Welfel and Patterson (2005, pp. 13-18) suggested ten important qualities possessed by them as follows.

- Effective counselors are skillful at reaching out.
- Effective counselors inspire feelings of trust, credibility, and confidence from people they help.
- Effective counselors communicate caring and respect for the persons they are trying to help.

- Effective counselors are able to reach in as well as to reach out.
- Effective counselors manage conflict between client and counselor effectively.
- Effective counselors attempt to understand the behavior of the people they try to help without imposing value judgments.
- Effective counselors recognize clients' self-defeating behaviors and help them develop more personally rewarding behavior patterns.
- Effective counselors have expertise in some area that will be of special value to the client.
- Effective counselors are able to reason systematically and to think in terms of systems.
- Effective counselors are culturally competent; they are able to understand the social, cultural, and political context in which they and all other people operate.

You as a reader will find mostly overlapping between the above characteristics of effective counselors and wisdom components of wise counselors in this chapter.

Counselor's Wisdom Emphasized by Experienced Counselors

All seven interviewed professors were experienced counseling psychologists who have accumulated their knowledges and experiences over twenty years as a scientist–practitioner. As a student and a researcher, I strongly believe that counselors can learn by paying attention to what they wanted to give counselors in training from their experience of expertise in counseling specialty in the in–depth interviews.

The interviewed professors directly and indirectly indicated that counselors need to have wisdom to solve clients' problems. They emphasized that counselors need to be a wise counselors with wisdom rather than good counselors without wisdom to be effective counselors. So counselors need to become wise counselors who can spread clients their wisdom for solving their problems.

Wisdom may not be simply defined in two or three sentences. As interviewed professors in counseling psychology tried to define wisdom, their definitions suggested not just one type of knowledge or specific experience, but something derived from consideration of multiple factors at given different times and situations. It seems clear that experience and knowledge precede wisdom. That is, interviewed professors defined wisdom based on their unique personal experience and their knowledge and understanding of social and natural phenomena.

Probably the first important finding from in-depth interviews with professors in counseling specialty was that counseling psychologists appeared to define wisdom based on their unique personal experience. In this way, wisdom is very person-centered. It focused on what is important and meaningful in a person's life. For example, two interviewed professors explained how wisdom related to their religious beliefs, while other interviewees never referred to God. In other words, everybody understands and interprets life through his own unique lens based on his knowledge and experience, thus individual knowledge and experience precede wisdom.

A second important finding was that counseling psychologists' definitions of wisdom reflected their philosophical and theoretical orientation in counseling. The words and contents which interviewed professors used to define wisdom were related to their belief systems and theoretical orientations. For example, one interview who preferred Alfred Adler's individual psychology emphasized the ability of the individual to make good choices as wisdom as Adler emphasizes reorientation of life style by good choices and creative self of human nature. He also said that the counselor wise when one makes relatively good choices about techniques. Another interviewed professor who preferred the cognitive behavioral therapy perspective defined wisdom with more practical and behavioral contents: work, love, and play. A third interviewee, who preferred the phenomenological approach broadly applied, emphasized a constant process of seeking rather than technical competence as wisdom. A fourth interviewee, who combined Martin Buber's views with an humanistic existentialism approach, explained wisdom in terms of I–Thou relationships and existential trust and acceptance. A fifth interviewed professor who preferred a psychodrama perspective emphasized flexibility as a part of wisdom. A sixth interviewee who preferred a feminist therapy combined with a psychodrama approach used spontaneity as a part of her concept of wisdom from her psychodramatic point of view. The last interviewed professor emphasized self–esteem in an application of techniques or skills from his humanistic approach which was applied in combination with behavioral techniques.

A third major finding from the in–depth interviews was

that the seven interviewed professors defined wisdom related to their speciality, counseling psychology. Wisdom in counseling was related to sensitivity toward and ability to influence human relationship, human growth, desirable adjustment, and helping clients to make changes. They mainly emphasized a healthy personality as a major component of wisdom. Sternberg (1985) asserted that implicit theories of wisdom show considerable overlap across field of specialization, yet nevertheless, there were differences. According to Sternberg's study, specialists in four different areas defined wisdom differently. For example, art professors emphasized insight, knowing how to balance logic and instinct, how to transform ideas creatively into concepts, and sensitivity. These aspects of wisdom would seem quite relevant in the mature appreciation and evaluation of ant. On the other hand, business professors emphasized maturity of judgment, understanding of the limitations of one's actions and recommendations, knowing what one does and does not know, possession of a long-term perspective, knowing when not to act as well as one should act, acceptance of reality, good decision making, the ability to distinguish substance from style, and appreciation of the ideologies of others. These aspects of wisdom would seem particularly relevant in making and evaluating business decisions. Philosophy professors' view on wisdom would seem relevant to the construction and evaluation of philosophical arguments. Finally, physicists' view on wisdom would seem to be helpful in attaining a deep understanding of the nature. of physics and its place both in science and in the world. In terms of Sternberg's explanation of the dependence of one's views of wisdom on one's specialty, it appeared that interviewed professors in counseling specialty tended to define wisdom relevant to helping clients make changes, to human growth, to problem-solving, and to a definition congruent with their roles as counseling psychologists.

A forth major invaluable finding was that all seven interviewed professors emphasized the importance of wisdom regarding acquiring and using techniques and skills in counseling. For example, one interviewed professor explained that the wise counseling psychologist makes good choices about techniques. Another interviewee criticized acquiring skills without wisdom. He preferred a wise counselor who emphasizes wisdom rather than a good counselor emphasizes a bag of tricks. A third interviewed professor defined as not a technical competence but a constant seeking. He explained that a technique-oriented program misses the whole vision of what it is to be a good, rational and logical person. A fourth interviewee emphasized that techniques, well used, require wisdom. He explained that if a counseling psychologist is limited to just techniques, he/she would be in real trouble. A fifth interviewee explained that the indiscriminate use of skills without gaining wisdom, at best, is going to be ineffective; at worst, damaging. A sixth interviewee defined that wisdom is knowing the relationship between theory and technique. The last interviewee explained that wisdom comes in an application of techniques and skills.

Wisdom for Becoming a Wise Counselor

By the in–depth interviews with seven professors in counseling psychology, the present author found 234 ingredients of wisdom in counseling. And by the open–ended questionnaire survey with forty potential clients, he also found 309 elements related to counselor's important characteristics and wisdom. Finally by a content analysis of the collected 543 ingredients of counselor's wisdom, he found 70 components of the counselor's wisdom and developed the Counselor's Wisdom Scale consisted of 70 items. By a further data analysis with increase subjects, it was found that one item is unappropriate (No, 1998).

Therefore, 364 counselors (202 American counselors, 162 Korean counselors) emphasized the following 69 components as important contents of counselor's wisdom:

The wise counselor is, has or displays:

- good relationships with a variety of people.
- knowledge of assessment and diagnosis.
- a likable personality.
- an understanding of human uniqueness.
- professional training.
- "common" sense.
- empathy.
- expertise.
- a good listener.
- a good observer of human relationships.
- positive self-esteem.
- communication skills.
- ethical responsibility.
- an understanding of cultural differences.
- self-understanding.
- good judgment.
- intelligent.
- objectivity and lack of prejudice.
- stable.
- a willingness to help.

- an understanding of different perspectives.
- intuition or insight.
- a sense of humor.
- patience.
- considerable life–experience.
- someone who keeps confidentiality.
- a sense of reality.
- honest.
- credible.
- available.
- open.
- sensitive.
- a good observer.
- a good supervisor.
- someone who knows when and how to use techniques.
- curious.
- flexible.
- the pursuit and application of virtue.
- certification or licensure.
- a broad base of information.
- someone who reads broadly.
- an understanding of human suffering/pain.
- knowledge of philosophy.
- had good teachers.

- creative.
- spontaneous.
- a good relationship with colleagues.
- sincere.
- thinking logically.
- command of many skills or techniques.
- an understanding of his/her limitations.
- someone who refers to other professionals for help.
- a positive attitude toward life.
- trustworthy.
- intellectual skills.
- an integration of knowledge and experience.
- a broad view of life.
- experience as a client.
- caring.
- humble.
- someone who knows how to ask the right question.
- an understanding of the client's limitations.
- (is) a role model.
- able to see all sides.
- an understanding of sexual and racial differences.
- someone who is involved in self-actualization.
- someone who is involved in professional activities.
- someone who attempts not to impose values.

According to No's (1998) research, a total of 364 counselors (202 American counselors, 162 Korean counselors) participated and evaluated the above components of the Counselor's Wisdom Scale. They evaluated the following 24 components to be very important. According to the ranks of means (the number of parenthesis is an order of importance), the most important 24 components of counselor's wisdom are as follows.

- The wise counselor is a good listener. (1)
- The wise counselor is someone who keeps confidentiality. (2)
- The wise counselor displays empathy. (3)
- The wise counselor has and displays ethical responsibility. (4)
- The wise counselor displays trustworthy. (5)
- The wise counselor is a good observer of human relationships. (6)
- The wise counselor has and displays communication skills. (7)
- The wise counselor has and displays an understanding of human uniqueness. (8)
- The wise counselor has and displays self–understanding (9)
- The wise counselor is credible (10)

- The wise counselor has and displays an understanding his/her limitations. (11)
- The wise counselor is a good observer (12)
- The wise counselor is honest (13)
- The wise counselor has and displays a positive attitude toward life. (14)
- The wise counselor has professional training. (15)
- The wise counselor has and displays good judgment. (16)
- The wise counselor has and displays objectivity and lack of prejudice. (17)
- The wise counselor is stable (18)
- The wise counselor has an integration of knowledge and experience. (19)
- The wise counselor has and displays intuition or insight. (20)
- The wise counselor is sincere (21)
- The wise counselor has and displays a willingness to help. (22)
- The wise counselor has an understanding of different perspectives. (23)
- The wise counselor has positive self–esteem. (24)

The following Table 1 shows ten components of the counselor's wisdom that American counselors and Korean counselors considered as being very important. As the rank order of counselor's components of wisdom in Table 1 differently appears, they had more or less different perception about degree of importance and contents of the counselor's wisdom components.

As being shown in Table 1, it was found that both American and Korean counselors emphasize six components of wisdom; someone who keeps confidentiality, a good

<Table 1> The most important ten wisdom components emphasized by American counselors and Korean counselors

	American counselors(N=202)	Korean Counselors(N=162)
Rank	Components of wisdom	Components of wisdom
1	someone who keeps confidentiality	a good listener
2	a good listener	empathy
3	ethical responsibility	trustworthy
4	communication skills	self-understanding
5	a good observer of human relationships	professional training
6	empathy	a positive attitude toward
7	trustworthy	someone who keeps confidentiality
8	an understanding his/her limitations	understanding of human uniqueness
9	a good observer	ethical responsibility
10	good judgment	credible
10	understanding of human uniqueness	

listener, ethical responsibility, empathy, trustworthy, and an understanding of human uniqueness as very important wisdom components for becoming a wise counselor.

Suggestions for Becoming a Wise Counselor

Everybody wants a happy life and seeks for wisdom of life for his/her happiness and well-being. Counselors provide their professional services for clients to be able to achieve their well-being. For effective helping, counselors need to understand their roles as helpers in order to achieve ultimate purposes of counseling. Counseling is the helping process that a counselor with professional training and a client with necessity of helping as the co-subjects of counseling activity together make efforts in order to improve the client's well-being by achieving his problem prevention, development and growth, and problem solution by extending his self-awareness (No, 2005, p. 19). Therefore, counselors need to become wise counselors who can provide effective helping for clients' well-being.

They say that a wise man solves problems or questions from others' points of view. Counselors need to learn understanding themselves and the world from different points of view. So beginning counselors need to learn wisdom in counseling specialty from listening what experienced counselors and potential clients emphasize in order to become wise counselors. Based on the found results about wisdom of the counseling psychologist, I would like to suggest several important characteristics necessary for becoming a wise counselor.

A wise counselor is a good listener.

Experienced counselors often say that just the counselor's good listening makes clients solve their problems. Fritz Perls, the founder of Gestalt therapy, said that the opposite of listening is fighting because a listener understands others from good listening, while a fighter doesn't understand or fight with others from not listening. To become wise counselors, beginning counselors have to keep in mind that listening is the most important component of a wise counselor. A wise counselor believes and emphasizes that the counselor's good listening precedes most of counseling skills for effective helping.

A wise counselor has and displays ethical responsibility and is particularly someone who keeps confidentiality.

Ethical responsibility including confidentiality is one of

key components of counseling related to identity of counseling specialty. Counselors are basically experts who work for clients' benefits. That is, counselors' major role is not for just desirable change but for change that a client wants. Ethically counselors' imposing their values on clients is not appropriate even though their intentions are for clients' benefits. Counselors are with their clients and are for them by being involved in counseling relationship for clients' own benefits. Therefore counselors' ethical responsibility precede their applications of counseling techniques or skills for clients' change.

Confidentiality, which is central to developing a trusting and productive client–counselor relationship, is both a legal and an ethical issue. Although most counselors agree on the essential value of confidentiality, they realize that it cannot be considered as an absolute (Corey, 2005, p. 41). An original root of confidentiality in counseling has been often referred to Christians' or Catholics' confessions to their priests. If a client who is involved in counseling relationship thinks that his counselor would reveal his private secrets expressed in counseling sessions, he might not seek for counseling or not reveal his very important secrets to his counselor. A wise counselor considers that confidentiality is a major cornerstone of counseling specialty.

A wise counselor displays empathy or empathic understanding.

Empathy is the counselor's ability to reflect the client's subjectively experiencing and interpreting affects, behaviors, and cognitions related to his life events. Accurate empathy emphasized as an important attitude of the counselor by Carl Rogers is the cornerstone of the person–centered approach. Carl Rogers defined empathy by using concepts of both "as if" and "internal frame of reference" as follows; empathy means that "Never without losing an assumption of *as if* a counselor were a client, the counselor reflects to the client the feelings and meanings of his experiencing grasped by the client's *internal frame of reference.*" Empathic understanding implies that the counselor will sense clients' feelings as if they were his/her own without becoming lost in those feelings. Counselor's empathy results in clients' self–understanding and clarification of their beliefs and world–views (Corey, 2005, p. 173). Alfred Adler, the founder of Individual Psychology, explained that social interest as a value expressed through empathy means "To see with the eyes of another, to hear with the ears of another, and to feel with the heart of another" (Ansbacher & Ansbacher, 1956, p. 135). Empathy is an understanding about a client's subjective experiencing derived from good listening, while sympathy is compassion about a client's objective facts derived from just observing. A wise counselor strongly believes that empathy is the most powerful determinant of client's self–understanding and progress.

A wise counselor has or displays trustworthiness, credibility, and honesty.

Clients' perception about counselors' trustworthiness, credibility, and honesty influences not only on whether they are maintaining in counseling relationship or not but also on clients' revealing private secrets to their counselors. Strong (1968) suggested that trustworthiness is one of counselors' important characteristics that clients perceive based on his social influence theory. Trustworthiness communicates to clients that the counselor can be relied on to behave in ethical ways, possess the knowledge and skills needed to provide effective treatment, protect the client from harm and humiliation during treatment, show respect for the client, and advocate for what is best for the client (Seligman, 2006, p. 23).

Effective counselors are also credible and honest. In counseling relationship, clients continually evaluate and perceive counselors' credibility and honesty by observing their verbal and nonverbal expressions. A credible counselor's expression is perceived as believable and honest, free of hidden agendas or ulterior motives. He is viewed as honest, straight–forward, and nonmanipulative, again supporting the general belief that he can be trusted (Welfel & Patterson, 2005, p. 14).

The honest person doesn't play the hypocrite. The counselor is an expert providing a client with helping with honesty. The counselor cannot reveal his genuine attitude without honesty. An effective counselor understands that honesty without caring is cruel. Honesty is present in caring as something positive. The counselor is honest in trying to see truly. To help the client, the counselor must see the client as he is and not as he would like it to be or feel it must be (Mayeroff, 1990, p. 25).

Carl Rogers emphasized three counselor's necessary and sufficient conditions; genuineness or congruence, unconditional positive regard, and empathic understanding as not counseling techniques but attitudes. To be effective counselors, counselors need to understand and change their attitudes related to human nature as both a person and an expert. A wise counselor believes that trustworthiness, credibility, and honesty are the counselor's important attitudes for becoming an effective counselor.

A wise counselor is a good observer and is particularly a good observer of human relationships.

Most of clients' problems seem to be derived from human relationships. Therefore to be an effective helper, the counselor needs to be a good observer of human relationships. We can say that good observation is the cornerstone determinant for change. George Kelly, who emphasized person as scientist, claimed that "every man is, in his own particular way, a scientist" (Kelly, 1955, p. 5). Observation is the basic attribute of scientist. As a person needs a keen observing for becoming a good scientist, the counselor needs to be a good observer of human relationships for becoming an effective counselor. Albert Bandura, being reputed as the most influencing psychologist, emphasized the importance of a person's self–efficacy based on his observational or vicarious learning. People's beliefs about their personal efficacy constitute a major aspect of their knowledge. Self–efficacy beliefs are constructed from four principal sources of information: enactive mastery experiences, vicarious experiences, verbal persuasion, and physiological and affective states (Bandura, 1997, p. 79). A wise counselor strongly intends to be a good observer of human relationships for becoming an effective counselor with high self–efficacy.

A wise counselor has and displays communication skills.

They often say that counseling is the specialty providing clients with the best lip service because counselors perform their roles to make their clients change in a desirable direction for clients' benefits by their lip services. The reason that counseling psychology is called not only as science but also as art might be because counselors develop communication skills by scientific researches and apply developed communication skills for clients' benefits by their wisdom at the right way. An effective counselor produces desirable outcomes for clients' benefits by using their verbal and nonverbal responses at the right time. Therefore, a wise counselor emphasizes that counselors should improve abilities to display their communication skills for becoming effective helpers.

A wise counselor has and displays self-understanding, particularly an understanding his/her limitations, and an understanding of human uniqueness.

Socrates said that "the unexamined life is not worth living." Experienced counselors often mention, "Counselor, know yourself." To become a wise counselor, the counselor continually needs to examine himself for self-understanding and understanding of his limitations because he cannot appropriately perform his helping activities without thoroughly knowing himself. Effective counselors make their best endeavors to expand their mental horizons of knowledge and experience in counseling by their self-understanding including their limitations and understanding of human uniqueness. The effective counselor is aware of his strengths and weaknesses and is also aware of being able to harm his clients if he doesn't understand his limitations. Therefore, a wise counselor believes that counselors have to make earnest endeavors for expansions of self-awareness and understanding of human uniqueness for becoming effective helpers.

A wise counselor has and displays a positive attitude toward life.

We assume that most of clients' problems are derived from their negative attitudes toward life. We also presume that founders of major counseling theories basically emphasized their clients' change from negative attitudes toward life to positive attitudes toward life. Sigmund Freud might believe that his patients can recover abilities to work and love by his psychoanalysis. Carl Jung emphasized that our life is a journey of self-actualization or individuation. He said that "my life is a story of the self-realization of the unconscious"

(Jung, 1961. p. 3). Alfred Adler emphasized that everyone writes his novel about journey of life by his major concepts, fictional finalism and creative self. He believed that an individual is a unique being for overcoming inferiority and striving for superiority. He also believed that everyone can recover confidence and responsibility by encouragement. He showed his positive attitudes toward life by his understanding human nature as being for striving for superiority (self–actualization). He mentioned that "to be a human being means oneself to feel inferior."

Carl Rogers believed that a person has an self–actualizing tendency and he can achieve his self–actualization by wisdom of organism and valuing process. He also said, "experience, for me, is the highest authority." His positive attitudes toward life are showed by his proposition, "the organism has one basic tendency and striving — to actualize, maintain, and enhance the experiencing organism" (Rogers, 1951. p. 487). Jacob Moreno believed that a person can recover his spontaneity and flexibility by his psychodrama. Victor Frankl asserted that a person is searching for his meaning of life by Logotherapy derived from his personal experience. William Glasser believed that a person can achieve his success–identity and what he really wants by his wise choice (thinking) and carrying out (doing). Albert Ellis and Aron Beck emphasized that a person can lead a happy life by his rational belief system and positive automatic thought.

Counselors basically have positive and optimistic orientation toward life. They believe that a person's positive attitude toward life has a close relationship with his self–esteem. If a counselor has negative attitudes toward life, he has to remember not being able to give an appropriate help to clients and furthermore needs to change his negative attitudes positively. In many counseling cases, counselors' roles are to help clients change from their negative attitudes to positive attitudes toward life. A wise counselor emphasizes that counselors have to be able to display their positive attitudes toward life for clients' benefits for becoming effective counselors.

References

Abe, M. (1985). *Zen and western thought.* Honolulu: University of Hawaii Press.

Ansbacher, H. L., & Ansbacher, R. R. (Eds.) (1956). *The individual psychology of Alfred Adler.* New York: Harper Torchbooks.

Aristotle (1984). Nicomachean Ethics. In J. Barnes (Ed.), *The complete works of Aristotle.* Princeton, N.J.: Princeton University Press.

Arlin, P. K. (1990). Wisdom: The art of problem solving. In R. J. Sternberg (Ed.), *Wisdom.* New York: Cambridge University.

Auerbach, A. H., & Johnson, M. (1977). Research on the therapist's level of experience. In A. S. Guerman, & A. M. Razin (Eds.). *Effective psychotherapy: A handbook of research.* New York: Pergamon.

Baltes, P. B., & Smith, J. (1990). Toward a psychology of wisdom and its ontogenesis. In R. J. Sternberg (Ed.), *Wisdom.* New York: Cambridge University.

Baltes, P. B., Staudinger, U. M., Maercker, A., & Smith, J. (1995). People nominated as wise: A comparative study of wisdom-related knowledge. *Psychology and Aging*, 10, 155-166.

Bandura, A. (1997). *Self-efficacy: The exercise of control.* New York: W. H. Freeman and Company.

Barak, A., & LaCross, M. B. (1975). Multidimensional perception of counselor behavior. *Journal of Counseling Psychology*, Vol. 22, No. 6, 471-476.

Barrett, W. (1979). *The illusion of technique.* New York: Anchor Books.

Baum, L. F. (1976). *The Wizard of Oz.* New York: Ballantine Books.

Bernstein, R. J. (1988). *Beyond objectivism and relativism: Science, hermeneutics, and praxis.* Philadelphia: University of Pennsylvania Press.

Brent, S. B., & Watson, D. (1980). *Aging and wisdom: individual and collective aspects.* Paper presented at the meetings of the Gerontological Society of America, San Francisco.

Burgess, A. (1962). *A clockwork orange.* New York: Ballantine Books.

Catania, A. C., & Harnad, S. (Eds.) (1988). *Theselection of behavior: The operant behaviorism of B. F. Skinner: Comments and consequences.* NewYork: Cambridge University Press.

Clayton, V. (1982). Wisdom and intelligence: The nature and function of knowledge in the later years, *International Journal of Aging and Human Development,* Vol. 15(4), 315-321.

Clayton, V. P., & Birren, J. E. (1980). The development of wisdom across the life span: A reexamination of an ancient topic. In P. B. Baltes & O. G. Brim (Eds.), *Life-span development and behavior.* New York: Academic Press.

Cooper, A. M. (1987). A historical review of psychoanalytic paradigms. In A. Rothstein (Ed.), *Models of the mind: Their relationships to clinical work,* pp. 5-20. Madison: International Universities Press.

Corey, G. (2005). *Theory and practice of counseling and psychotherapy* (7th ed.). Belmont, CA: Brooks/Cole.

Corey, M. S., & Corey, G. (1989). *Becoming a helper.* Pacific Grove: Brooks/Cole Publishing Company.

Csikszentmihalyi, M. (1994). *The evolving self: A psychology for the third millennium.* New York: HarperPerennial.

Csikszentmihalyi, M. (1997). *Finding flow: The psychology of engagement with everyday life.* New York: BasicBooks.

Erikson, J. M. (1991). *Wisdom and senses: The way of creativity.* New York: W. W. Norton & Company.

Fassinger, R. E. (1987). Use of structural equation modeling in counseling psychology research. *Journal of Counseling*

Psychology, Vol. 34, No. 4, 425-436.

Frankl, V. E. (1985). *The unheard cry for meaning: Psychotherapy and humanism.* New York: Washing Square Press.

Gadamer, H. G. (1989). *Truth and method.* (rev. ed.). (Weinsheimer, J., & Masshall, d. G., Trans.). New York: The Crossroad Publishing Co.

Havens, R. A. (1989). *The wisdom of Milton H. Erikson: human behavior and psychotherapy.* New York: Paragon House Publishers.

Heather, N. (1976). *Radical perspectives in psychology.* London: Methun & Co.

Heidegger, M. (1962). *Being and time.* (J. Macquarrie & E. Robinson, Trans.). New York: Harper & Row Publishers.

Henricks, R. G. (Trans.). (1989). *Lao-Tzu Te-Tao Ching.* New York: Ballantine Books.

Heppner, P. P, & Dixon, D. N. (1981). A review of the interpersonal influence process in counseling. *Personal and Guidance Journal*, 59, 542-550.

Heppner, P. P., & Heesacker, M. (1983). Perceived counselor characteristics, client expectations, and client satisfaction with counseling. *Journal of Counseling Psychology*, Vol. 30, No. 1, 31-39.

Holliday, S. G., & Chandler, M. J. (1986). *Wisdom: explorations in adult competence.* Basel, Switzerland: Karger.

Jordan, J. (2005). The quest for wisdom in adulthood: A

psychological perspective. In R. J. Sternberg and J. Jordan (Eds.), *A handbook of wisdom: Psychological perspective* (pp. 160-188). New York: Cambridge University Press.

Jung, C. G. (1961). *Memories, dreams, reflections.* New York: Vintage Books.

Kahn, M. (1991). *Between therapist and client: The new relationship.* New York: W. H. Freeman and Company.

Kelly, G. (1955). *The psychology of personal constructs: A theory of personality.* New York: Norton.

Kinkade, K. (1973). *A Walden Two experiment: The first five years of Twin Oaks community.* New York: William Morrow & Company.

Kitchner, K. S., & Brenner, H. O. (1990). Wisdom and reflective judgement: Knowing in the face of uncertainty. In R. J. Sternberg (Ed.), *Wisdom.* New York: Cambridge University.

Kramer, D. A. (1990). Conceptualizing wisdom: The primacy of affection-cognition relations. In R. J. Sternberg (Ed.), *Wisdom.* New York: Cambridge University.

LaCross, M. B. (1980). Perceived counselor social influence and counseling outcomes: Validity of the counselor rating form. *Journal of Counseling Psychology,* Vol. 27, No. 4,320-327.

Lang, G., Molen, H. V. D., Trower, P., & Look, R. (1990). *Personal conversations: Roles and skills for counsellors.* London: Routledge.

MacIver, R. M. (1955). *The pursuit of happiness: A philosophy for modern living*. New York: Simon and Schuster.

Marias, J. (1967). *History of philosophy*. NewYork: Dover Publications.

Maslow, A. H. (1976). *The farther reaches of human nature*. New York: Penguin Books.

Maxwell, N. (1984). *From knowledge to wisdom: A revolution in the aims and methods of science*. Oxford: basil Blackwell, p. 2.

Mayoff, M. (1990). *On caring*. New York: HarperPerennial.

McCracken, G. (1988). *The long interview*. NewburyPark, CA: SAGE Publications.

Midgley, M. (1991). *Wisdom, information, and wonder: What is knowledge for*. London: Routedge.

No, A. Y. (1993). *Wisdom as defined and perceived by counseling psychologists*. University of Kentucky, Unpublished doctoral dissertation.

No, A. Y. (1998). A Comparison of wisdom perceived by Korean and American counseling psychologists. *Journal of College Counseling*, Vol. 9, No. 2, 217-243

No, A. Y. (2005). *Theory and practice of counseling psychology*. Seoul: Hakjisa.

Pascual-Leone, J. (1990. An essay on wisdom: Toward organismic processes that make it possible. In R. J. Sternberg (Ed.), *Wisdom: itsnature, origins, and development* (pp.244-278). NewYork: Cambridge University.

Perls, F. S. (1971). *Gestalt therapy verbatim*. New York: Bantam

Books, Inc.

Perls, F. S. (1978). Gestalt therapy and human potentialities. In F. D. Stephenson (Ed.). *Gestalt therapy primer.* New York: Jason Aronson.

Plato (1987). The republic. In E. Hamilton & H. Cairns (Eds.), *The collected dialogues of Plato including the letters.* Princeton, N.J.: Princeton University Press.

Polkinghorne, D. (1983). *Methodology for the human sciences: Systems of inquiry.* Albany, NewYork: State University of New York press.

Rogers, C. R. (1951). *Client-centered therapy.* Boston: Houghton Mifflin Company.

Rogers, C. R. (1971). Toward a modern approach to values: The valuing process in the mature person. In C. R. Rogers & B. Stevens (Ed.). *Person to person: The problem of being human.* New York: Pocket Book, 4-21.

Rogers, C. R., & Skinner, B. F. (1972). Some issues concerning the control of human behavior: A symposium. In M. Karlins & L. Andrews (Eds.), *Man controlled: readings in the psychology of behavior control.* New York: The Free Press, 239-263.

Roth, P. (1991). Interpretation as explanation. In D. R. Hiley, J. F. Bohman, & R. Shisterman (Eds.), *The interpretive turn: philosophy, science, culture.* Ithaca: Cornell University Press, 179-196.

Sallis, J. (1986). *Being and logos: The way of platonic dialogue.*

Atlantic Highlands, N.J.: Humanities Press International, Inc.

Seligman, L. (2006). *Theories of counseling and psychotherapy: Systems, strategies, and skills* (2nd ed.). Upper Saddle River, N.J.: Pearson Education.

Seligman, L., Reichenberg, L. W. (2010). *Theories of counseling and psychotherapy: Systems, strategies, and skills* (3rd ed.). Upper Saddle River, N.J.: Pearson Education.

Skinner, B. F. (1971). *Beyond freedom and dignity.* New York: Bantam/Vintage Books.

Smith, J., Staudinger, U. M., & Baltes, P. B. (1994). Occupational settings facilitating wisdom-related knowledge: the sample case of clinical psychologists. *Journal of Consulting and Clinical Psychology,* Vol. 62, No. 5, 989-999.

Staudinger, U. M., Smith, J., & Baltes, P. B. (1992). Wisdom-related knowledge in a life review task: Age differences and the role of professional specialization. *Psychology and Aging,* 7(2), 271-281.

Sternberg, R. J. (1985). Implicit theories of intelligence, creativity, and wisdom. *Journal of Personality And Social Psychology,* Vol. 49, No. 3, 607-627.

Sternberg, R. J. (Ed.) (1990). *Wisdom: Its nature, origins and development.* New York: Cambridge University Press.

Sternberg, R. J., & Jordan, J. (Eds.) (2005). *A handbook of wisdom: Psychological perspective.* New York: Cambridge University Press.

Strickland, B. (1971). The philosophy-theory-practice continuum: A point of view. In C. E. Beck (Ed.), *Philosophical guidelines for counseling.* Dubuque: WM. C. Brown Company.

Strong, S. R. (1968). Counseling: an interpersonal influence process. *Journal of Counseling Psychology,* Vol. 15, No. 3, 215-224.

Strong, S. R., & Matross, R. P. (1973). Change processes in counseling and psychotherapy. *Journal of Counseling Psychology,* Vol. 20, No. 1, 25-37.

Taranto, M. A. (1989). Facets of wisdom: A theoretical synthesis, *International Journal of Aging and Human Development,* Vol. 29(1), 1-21.

Thoreau, H. D. (1968). *The world great classics: Walden.* Connecticut: Grolier Enterprises Corp.

Vander Zaden, J. W. (1985). *Human development* (3rd ed.). New York: Alfred A. Knopf, Inc.

Wallwork, E. (1991). *Psychoanalysis and ethics.* New Heaven and London: Yale University Press.

Wampold, B. E., & White, T. B. (1985). Research themes in counseling psychology: A cluster analysis of citation in the process and outcomes section of the Journal of Counseling Psychology, *Journal of Counseling Psychology,* Vol. 32, No. 1, 123-126.

Welfel, E. R., & Patterson, L. E. (2005). *The counseling process: A multitheoretical integrative approach* (6th. ed.). Belmont, CA:

Thomson Books/Cole.

Whitehead, A. N. (1974). *Science and philosophy*. New York: Philosophical Library, Inc., 174-183.

Index

Name

Content

About the Author

An Young No is Professor of Department of Psychology, Chonnam National University. He received his M.A. in counseling psychology from Seoul National University, 1983 and his Ph.D. in counseling psychology from the University of Kentucky, 1993. He is a certified counseling psychologist of Korean Counseling Psychology Association, a certified counseling supervisor of Korean Counseling Association, and a certified trainer of Active Parenting. He is a trustee of Korean Counseling Psychological Association, Korean School Counseling Association, and Korean Child/Adolescent Counseling Association. He is an editor of Korean Journal of Counseling and Psychotherapy, and the Korea Journal of Counseling. He is a president of Korean Adlerian Counseling Association.

His main concern and interest area is to explore basic assets, attitudes, wisdom that an effective counseling psychologist must have, and to construct and develop education, training, and supervision programs for counselors. His counseling approach is broadly humanistic approach and he uses diverse techniques of Adlerian counseing, Person-Centered Therapy, Reality Therapy, Gestalt Therapy, and Existential Counseling according to clients' age and presenting problems. He basically believes that all counseling approaches are paradoxical and counselors use paradoxical techniques.

Recently he is interested in developing a group counseling program appling paradoxical techniques based on Gestalt Therapy and Zen. And he is involving in developing a self-encouragement group counseling program based on Individual Psychology. He is also involving in studying for understanding human being' behavior by body-mind interaction. His e-mail address is aynoh@jnu.ac.kr

<Authored Books>

A. Y., No., & H. J. Song. (2006). Principle and Skills of counseling. Seoul: Hakjisa.

A. Y., No. (2005). Theory and practice of counseling psychology. Seoul: Hakjisa.

A. Y., No., & Y. S., Kang. (2003). Personality psychology for human growth. Seoul: Hakjisa.

A. Y., No. (2002). Counseling psychology explored with 101 subjects. Seoul: Hakjisa.

A. Y., No. (1998). Journey of life with counselor: Introduction of counseling theories. Seoul: Joong-ang Aptitude Publisher.

A. Y., No. (1996). Supervision of adolescence counseling. Seoul: Adolescence Counseling Center.

A sound mind in a sound body.
An unsound mind in a sound body.
A sound mind in an unsound body.
An unsound mind in an unsound body.
A sound body in a sound mind.
An unsound body in a sound mind.
A sound body in an unsound mind.
An unsound body in an unsound mind.

Becoming A Wise Counselor

–현명한 상담자 되기–

2011년 3월 25일 1판 1쇄 인쇄
2011년 3월 30일 1판 1쇄 발행

지은이 • 노안영
펴낸이 • 김진환
펴낸곳 • (주) 학지사
121-837 서울시 마포구 서교동 352-29 마인드월드빌딩 5층
대표전화 • 02-330-5114 팩스 • 02-324-2345
등록번호 • 제313-2006-000265호

홈페이지 • http://www.hakjisa.co.kr
커뮤니티 • http://cafe.naver.com/hakjisa

ISBN 978-89-6330-639-1 93180

정가 15,000원